I

Hipper
Than
Our
Kids

Hipper Than Our Kids

- ■ -

A Rock & Roll Journal of the Baby Boom Generation

■

BRUCE POLLOCK

Schirmer Books
An Imprint of Macmillan Publishing Company
New York

Maxwell Macmillan Canada
Toronto

Maxwell Macmillan International
New York   Oxford   Singapore   Sydney

Schirmer Books
An Imprint of Macmillan Publishing
  Company
866 Third Avenue
New York, NY 10022

Maxwell Macmillan Canada,
  Inc.
1200 Eglinton Avenue East
Suite 200
Don Mills, Ontario M3C 3N1

Macmillan Publishing Company is part of the Maxwell Communication Group of Companies.

Library of Congress Catalog Card Number: 92–39752

Printed in the United States of America

printing number
1   2   3   4   5   6   7   8   9   10

Library of Congress Cataloging–in–Publication Data

Pollock, Bruce.
    Hipper than our kids : a rock & roll journal of the baby boom
generation / Bruce Pollock.
        p.   cm.
    Includes index.
    ISBN 0–02–872063–6
    1. Rock music—United States—History and criticism. 2. Baby boom
generation—United States.   I. Title.
ML3534.P625 1993
781.66'09—dc20   92-39752
                                                          CIP
                                                          MN

The paper used in this publication meets the minimum requirements of American National Standard for Information Sciences—Permanence of Paper for Printed Library Materials. ANSI Z39.48–1984. ⊗™

To Rebecca Tracy

Acknowledgments

To John Wagman . . . who led to Rita, who led to Robert, who led to Jonathan, who led to . . .

Contents

Contents

Hipper
Than
Our
Kids

Introduction

We Gave You Rock & Roll

(1955–   )

As the columnist and country songwriter, Lewis Grizzard, once almost said: "Rock & roll is dead . . . and I'm not feeling too good myself."

Another equally great pundit might just as well have added: "I've seen the future of rock & roll . . . and it's all in the past."

To which, I think Burl Ives, or else Jiminy Cricket, responded: "Rock & roll is dead . . . and I don't care!"

As for myself, to paraphrase Marc Anthony, I come here not to bury rock & roll, nor, like Imogene Coca, to excessively praise Caesar, nor, like Lee Iaccoca, to sell anyone a bill of goods, but merely to trace the music's passage, as well as our own, from youth to middle age, through our most significant songs, in the process revealing not only the fondest hopes and deepest dreams of a generation, but also some of the forgotten and surprising, often unintentionally ludicrous, hidden messages embedded in the end–grooves of our lives.

Actually, when it comes to paraphrasing (or sampling) bromides, I much prefer the line from the sneaker com-

1

mercial that goes: "To believe that what is true in your inmost heart for you is true for all men; that is genius." Which is to say that as a charter member of the above generation, speaking for all of us now at, just past, or approaching the age of the fabled rock & roll single— itself no more now than a quaint and dimly–remembered artifact of a quaint and dimly–remembered culture—I believe in my inmost heart that if we were not the ones who actually invented rock & roll, we were certainly the ones who bought it, adopted it, adapted it, embraced it—did everything short of wearing it out, like an old sneaker. So, while there may have been "rock & roll" existing before us, going under a variety of other names, being danced to by older teenagers and adults, mostly in parts of town we'd never dared set foot in, it was only after Elvis Presley's arguably better half got bleeped from "The Ed Sullivan Show" on nationwide TV in 1956, that a sub–teen genera- tion in pajamas was shell–shocked straight into puberty overnight.

Undeniably the largest audience ever to arrive at once to the Brooklyn Fox to make a public spectacle of itself, there were none among us who were then cynical enough to see this historic moment in a cosmic nutshell: the power of TV to influence a bunch of horny kids, the effects of censor- ship in action, rebellious youth versus know–nothing adults in the living room battleground of a Sunday night; and more: a white man taking all the credit, visibility, and riches from his black counterparts; the white man himself becoming a victim of forces beyond his control—his manager, the American dream in a handbasket— betraying our trust by turning plastic almost instantane- ously. In fact, by 1957, we needed Elvis and as many more as could be mass–produced, to slake our enormous hunger.

Informed by Mort Sahl, Captain Video, Lenny Bruce,

Pinky Lee, Jean Shepherd, Clarabelle the Clown, Jack Kerouac, "My Little Margie," Marlon Brando, Captain Kangaroo, James Dean, Les Paul, Leo Fender, and "The Make Believe Ballroom" as much as the McCarthy hearings, Ike, the "Checkers" speech, Guy Lombardo, Hank Snow, and *The Man in the Grey Flannel Suit*, we carved out of the available sources a unique all–purpose amalgam that would stand until the millennium and probably beyond, managing at the same time to extend our own pubescent period well into middle age! As participant/observers in our chosen deviant subculture, we danced on "The Lloyd Cole Show" in our olive green junior high school graduation sports jackets, pioneered the fine art of lip–synching (years before Milli Vanilli transformed it into a "career move"), and in general were perceived to have come of age together as a definable unit on the cover of Life Magazine—taking to "The Twist," the colleges, the streets, the altar, almost as one. Part of a demographic monstrosity old enough to mourn our first (and only) president, we persevered through tears, one night in 1964 sitting so close to the stage at the Gaslight Cafe in Greenwich Village that we got hit with the spray as Bob Dylan spat out "Mr. Tambourine Man," "She Belongs to Me," "Gates of Eden," and "It's All Right Ma, I'm Only Bleeding." We sat up nights deciphering his lyrics, and others, finding faces in the trees on album covers, and hidden meanings in the grooves of certain songs that suggested Paul Is Dead, Buddy Holly Is Alive, and Who Killed the Kennedys—leading almost inevitably to the creation of our signal artform—Rock Criticism.

That these anal predilections sometimes led us far astray, is attested to by no less a sage than Roger McGuinn, founder of the Byrds: "People imagined all these things going on," he once told me. "Oh, this guy's a great spokesman, a great statesman, a great artist. I think it was definitely an overestimation of the people involved. The fact is, it was just punks trying to play music, usually."

Yet it was precisely because we took our precocious punks so seriously, more seriously than they deserved to be, perhaps, obviously more seriously than they took themselves, that there could have been a Woodstock, a Woodstock Nation, and a Woodstock Nation commemorative map and calendar (still sold to tourists at the Woodstock General Store).

While it is a fact that the last remaining stragglers of the baby boom generation were born the year after the Kennedy assassination, the year the Beatles unseated Elvis from the throne, because I see the formative political and cultural (as well as rock & roll) experiences and perceptions of the group born between 1945 and 1952 as so profoundly different from the post–Elvis portion of the generation (although the influence of what we set in motion remained pervasive), my commentary applies primarily to kids in their forties, kids of the Top 40—and all of our fortyish or pushing–forty or forty–sympathizing kindred spirits—a loopy, off–center, out–of–touch–with–the–mainstream, small–but–vocal–minority for whom the most representative modern artist was not Andy Warhol, but Herman Rorschach, whose ink blots provided each of us our own individual way of beating the odds, the draft, and the system, much as rock & roll did in the beginning.

If most of us—and rock & roll—wound up happy recruits (more or less) in that selfsame system sooner or later (sooner than we hoped, later than our parents thought possible, and vice–versa), it is not necessarily true that rock & roll is to blame or that this is in any way a crucial moral failure; the opposite may be just as close to the truth. In any case, taking into account the accounts of its demise, roughly every couple of years dating back to 1955, the year after it was officially delivered by rough-neck hillbillies and rowdy blacks, apparently stillborn, into the hands of its mortal enemy, Tin Pan Alley, we can see that this is the natural order of pop culture: the systematic dilution for the masses of the pioneering work of the Underground, making idols of the few and ignoring the many foot soldiers who broke the hallowed ground. In this context, in rock & roll, as in life, change and misinterpretation is inevitable, but, as in all statistical spectator sports, just another part of the fun.

Was Elvis laughing or drugged when he sold the under-class black experience to polite white society with his flaming hips? Did Jimi Hendrix essentially do the same with a flaming guitar? Who really wrote "Blowing in the Wind" Were the Ronettes bigger teases than the Shangri–Las? Could the Beatles have beaten up the Rolling Stones? Could Donna Summer fake an orgasm better than Madonna—or is Robert Plant still the all–time champ? Does Kiss have more in common with Alice Cooper than the New Kids on the Block have with the Beastie Boys? And who pulled the strings for Milli Vanilli? These, I submit, are the sort of heated Hot Stove League queries that mean far more in and out of context than whether rock & roll is alive now or dead or, like most of us, walking wounded.

In order to illustrate rock & roll's part in the manic, mirthful, and quixotic musical comedy of the baby boom, I have compiled in the following chapters, through an ingeniously self–serving analysis of the biggest hits since 1955 (along with selected critical and personal favorites), a kind of universal mixed tape, taking songs both one at a time and in groups of up to twelve, chronologically, month by month, a year at a time, over a series of distinct periods, each defined by a mysterious combination of whim and autobiography. When seen in such historical perspective, these works, and those they inspired, and those that conspired against them, form a kind of soundtrack album to an unmade movie in the mind's inner ear, revealing the unspoken, sometimes insidious movements, messages, and images of nearly forty years of rock & roll.

If at times this investigation into rock & roll's aging process begins to suspiciously resemble a mid–life crisis itself, it is only because keeping current is so demanding a game. This endless night–crawling in the outbacks of the Underground in search of the next new thing—Elvis, Dylan, the Velvet Underground, the Dolls, the Stooges— can be enervating for the beleaguered father on the graveyard shift—unless you're employed in the music business, and then it's a young A&R man's game— discovering before anyone else another new way to market threatening and exotic sounds to the mainstream—the Sex Pistols, the Clash, the Replacements, the Minutemen, Metallica, Public Enemy—either for the easy cash or perhaps in the attempt to link through music the universal visions inherent in distinctly separate and unequal American extremes.

In truth, for the most part, we have long since left this kind of advance scouting to the teenagers and sub–teens just coming into initial artistic, creative, and sexual awareness, for whom rock & roll's message is still the same subversive, intuitive, street–bred coded language it's always been, a subterranean rite of passage—the choice between listening to Elvis, Pat Boone, or the Harptones; Dylan, Elvis, or Robert Johnson; the Beatles or Dylan; the Rolling Stones or Muddy Waters; the Four Seasons or Phil Ochs; the Supremes or Jimi Hendrix; Ozzy Osbourne, Donna Summer, or David Bowie; Guns N' Roses, Ice–T, the Cure, or Madonna, a crucial developmental bench- mark, virtually the dividing line between the hip and the square, the rebel and the traditionalist, the visionary and the truly hopeless. As musically literate as we of this founding generation may be, those of us in the midst of our own mid–life crises now, for whom it is harder to fathom how a life could be saved by the magic of rock & roll anymore, especially after the landslide of 1972, the failure of FM radio, the religious conversion of Dylan, the death of Lennon, and the seduction of Springsteen, have generally shown a preference for sitting back and accepting or rejecting these findings in accordance with our own agendas and desires, rather than instigating any further tonal or tidal movements—although, if my opinion be known, most of my generational cronies have surely evidenced a dwindling tolerance for any kind of musical and emotional change for at least ten years.

But, speaking from the vantage point of someone who has spent more than twenty years on the rock & roll beat, who attended the same summer session at San Francisco State that Marty Balin of the Jefferson Airplane did the year before; who has been stood up by Ricky Nelson in Pitman, New Jersey, in the last year of his life, and embraced by Bruce Springsteen at a Howard Johnson's on I–95 at one in the morning, just days before his face appeared simultaneously on the covers of *Time* and *Newsweek*—I understand as well as anyone the generational imperative that makes us want to hang on to our sagging, aging rock & roll, still wearing dungarees and leather jackets and placing bets on the trotters at the same candystore where we bought our eggcreams for six cents a glass, still believing We Are the World, still hoping We Won't Get Fooled Again. Even after 1987, when so many of us, turning forty, fell down like Chevy Chase and couldn't get up, almost resulting in a whippersnapper revolution led by Debbie Gibson, Tiffany, and Rick Astley, we recovered our balance and our momentum as well as our position of eminence, by culminating a nearly twenty year effort to elect Bonnie Raitt Queen of the Hop.

As we have already learned from witnessing the turgid spectacle of Led Zeppelin dancing atop Paul Butterfield's grave, as a generation we were not only hipper than our parents—in fact, hipper than anyone older than us—but have turned out to be hipper than anyone younger than us as well, including our own children. Whether this perception is entirely accurate or only a product of too many of us believing our clippings for far too long, the alternative of handing so precious a legacy as rock & roll over to a pagan horde of slam dancing nitwits is far too dire to truly consider their opinion of the situation. Instead, we offer them a politically and musically reactionary status quo, a Top 40 dominated by the black music of sex and dancing, an off–off radio underground of violent and threatening sounds, and a League of Decency casting in the bushes for witches, Paul Simon our Eddie Fisher, Cher our Debbie Reynolds. In other words, pretty much what our parents handed us back in 1955.

To them, to you, to rock & roll, I conclude with this birthday message: May you live long, and have lots of hits.

One

Out of the Bad Neighborhoods
(1955–1958)

It was called a Stromberg Carlson and it was the top of the line, a TV–radio–phonograph combination, housed in a solid mahogany cabinet, with ornate wood carvings on the cabinet doors; not just a TV, but furniture; not just furniture, a work of art, one of the first on the block, circa 1950. For my father, the 4F, the black marketeer, it was the ultimate possession, the ultimate obsession; for his son, the Mouseketeer, it became home to Howdy Doody, Captain Video, Martin and Lewis, and, on radio, Mel Allen and Vin Scully and spring training games from Tampa or Vero Beach, and "The Make Believe Ballroom," with Martin Bloch. It was here one Sunday night in 1956, just after "Lassie," on "The Ed Sullivan Show," that Elvis Presley burst into the living room, was heard all over AM radio the next day, and then whirled endlessly on the phonograph and in family arguments at forty–five revolutions per minute every day thereafter. In that one box, with those three distinctly different mediums, you had all the elements you needed for a generation shortly to redefine rock & roll in its own image.

Moving into this nascent television/radio/phonograph age, the average postwar baby boom citykid, pre–Elvis, was very much in the sway of his family's clean and pristine dream of a midcentury–American whitebread pop music normalcy. Though Mom and Dad possibly even lived through their own wild youth of juke joint jazz and big band swing, their Billie Holiday period, maybe a delta blues or bluegrass fixation hidden away in the closets with the raccoon coats, by the mid–1950s they had fallen in with a soothing array of sexy Italian dentists named Perry Como, Julius LaRosa, Frankie Laine, Vic Damone, Frank Sinatra, and Dean Martin. On the distaff side of the ledger, a moony radio slave could swoon to the chaste and crinolined tones of girls just like the girl who married dear old Dad, among them Dinah Shore, Jo Stafford, Patti Page, Joni James, Rosemary Clooney, Theresa Brewer, and, my personal one and only, the pom–pom prim and virginal, Debbie Reynolds, who was being pursued in the funny papers by the bar–mitzvah boy, Eddie Fisher, who would finally make an honest woman of her in 1955.

Over these pristine airwaves, in 1954–1955, the raciest babe going might have been "The Naughty Lady of Shady Lane," by the Ames Brothers. Otherwise, Nick Noble sang "The Bible Tells Me So," Frank Sinatra proselytized for "Love and Marriage," and Bing Crosby gave us the official version of "White Christmas." On the six–inch TV screen, bandleader Mitch Miller was a crusty eminence in his Skitch Henderson beard, Steve Allen, prolific and glib as ever, presided over his own show, and Walt Disney presented "The Adventures of Davy Crockett," which spawned 27 verses of "The Ballad of Davy Crockett," with cover versions by Bill Hayes, Tennessee Ernie Ford, Fess Parker, and at least two hundred and forty–seven high school and college marching bands.

Few in our sheltered milieu were privy, at this point, to

the subversive sounds that were already percolating up from the underground slums and hovels and outbacks of the bad neighborhoods, across the borders of propriety, urged by a force much greater than the salacious beat and wicked licks and leering lyrics—pubescent lust personified, alive, wild, irrepressible. And even those who might have gleaned a salty taste of "Sixty Minute Man" by the Dominoes, "Work with Me Annie" or "Sexy Ways" by the Midnighters, "Lawdy Miss Clawdy" by Lloyd Price, "Hound Dog" by Willa Mae Thornton, "Sh–Boom" by the Chords, or "Gee" by the Crows, would hardly have had the prescience, hurriedly speeding the dial toward the mellow sounds that were more befitting our circumstances, to hear it as inevitable and irresistible, wending an insidious hormonal course from the body to the brain and back again. But "Shake, Rattle and Roll" by Joe Turner, "I'm Your Hoochie Coochie Man" by Muddy Waters, "Annie Had a Baby" by the Midnighters, and "Earth Angel" by the Penguins were being danced to somewhere in the static, somewhere in the night, way beyond the tracks of our limited experience, by kids just a bit older and seemingly much wiser, who lived in a place in the imagination most of us had never been to and had never previously wished to see—a place called Cleveland.

It was in and around this mythic Cleveland that a white disc jockey named Alan Freed would stumble onto the proposition, as he played "race" records to black teenagers at black dancehalls in black neighborhoods, that this latest wrinkle in the history of black music called rhythm and blues could perhaps, like jazz, excite and incite a significant white counterpart, once removed from their Depression–era parents and their lovelorn ballads, waiting for something they could call their own—even if they had to sneak into the bad neighborhoods in the dead of night to steal it.

Still, in 1954, when deejay Freed moved his act to 1010 WINS in New York City, and started playing this music he called "rock and roll," to an expanded constituency, the baby boom market had not as yet produced enough white teenagers to shake, rattle, or roll the public's complacency. Bill Haley and his spitcurl, doing "Go Man Go" and "Rock–a–Beatin' Boogie," was surely no motivation to speed the process. Even Bill's infamous "Rock Around the Clock" bombed when it was first released in 1954. A year later, the numbers were big enough to make it number one, but only because of its use in the movie *The Blackboard Jungle*, thus officially and viscerally recognizing rock & roll as a specific predilection of a deviant subculture of juvenile delinquents—an identification it was never to lose, or justify.

To most well–adjusted baby boom jokers, teetering on teenage in a coonskin cap and a Perry Como cardigan sweater, the image of the hoods and greasers running rampant through the movie to a rhythm and blues beat was as ominious as it was to our parents. But, like the unspoken, intuitive nature of all true soul music, what the men didn't know, the little girls understood in their bones. And if Sam Phillips, another white man, based in Memphis, was looking for a white singer who could translate the dangerous appeal of this outcast music of minorities who had nothing to lose to the masses, via the thrilling clang of a guitar, who do you suppose his intended audience was?

Sifting through demos in his Memphis Recording Service studios, Sam was only a heartbeat away from immortality, and only perhaps a step ahead of the competition in other rural side pockets of civilization, from Tennessee to Texas, where like–minded musicians were coming under the thrall of bluesmen named Howling Wolf, Bo Diddley, Arthur Crudup, Muddy Waters, Otis Rush, and Jimmy Reed. Dozens of insouciant, sideburned hipsters, outlaws, and leather clad junior roughnecks and rednecks, like Gene Vincent, Eddie Cochran, Johnny Burnette and his cousin, Dorsey, Scotty Moore, James Burton, Roy Orbison, Jerry Lee Lewis, and the truck driver, Elvis Presley— who'd all probably seen Brando in *The Wild Ones*, Dean in *Rebel without a Cause*, and had been brave enough or deranged enough to venture into those roadhouses and chicken shacks and honky tonks after dark to ferret out these sounds being played by Amos Milburn and Chuck Berry and Etta James and James Brown and Joe Turner— were now prepared to copy them for their timid brethren in penny loafers: Pat Boone, Tab Hunter, Ricky Nelson, and the rest of us in our coonskin caps.

Starting out in 1954, Elvis's first Sun recordings would come to represent the roiling polyglot of substances that would form the timeless rock & roll stew of his next couple of years: a smidgen of gospel (a hymn for his mother), a dollop of the delta ("That's All Right, Mama"), a dash of pop ("I Don't Care If the Sun Don't Shine"), some country cornpone seasoning ("I Forgot to Remember to Forget"), some uptempo Chicago sauce, in his own natural rockabilly juices ("Mystery Train," "Good Rockin' To-night," "Baby Let's Play House"), salted with a broth of the transmogrified rhythm and blues of the white song-writing team of Jerry Leiber and Mike Stoller, turned black by Big Mama Thornton ("Hound Dog"). It was this cross–cultural, bi–racial, schizophrenic mash—along with a severe case of what was not yet known as "loose hips"—that made Elvis a pyrotechnic presence on the Hank Snow tour until he got thrown off, the ultimate incendiary melting pot of American music for a brief, shining year or so, until Steve Sholes at RCA Records bought his contract from Sam Phillips for $35,000 (Elvis pocketed five) and, arguably, his soul, for a pink Cadillac.

RCA made TV sets; they owned a network. They even

made the 45″ record changers! Could anything have been more inevitable than that they should take the lead in making the sound of rock & roll flesh through the magic of a Stromberg–Carlson, for the pubescent middle class baby boom audience of Howdy Doody and Pinky Lee? In January, 1956, Elvis was a guest on Tommy and Jimmy Dorsey's "Stage Show." In April, he was embraced by Uncle Miltie. In July, he appeared on "The Steve Allen Show" in a Nudie suit, singing "Hound Dog," to a bassett hound. In September, Ed Sullivan nabbed him for three songs, and 80 percent of the country under sixteen saw it.

The following morning, in junior high schools everywhere, "What's an Elvis Presley?" was the current events question on everybody's lips, mentioned in the same kind of adolescent sneer that would adorn Elvis's own lips for the rest of his performing life. For, in truth, few but the perpetually leftback members of terminal detention, who shaved three times a week, and fell asleep in their overcoats in the back of the class, had any inkling of the awesome power of his cowlick. It was only when certain girls started swooning and swaying to the rhythm of his pelvis, that special one, for instance, who looked exactly like Debbie Reynolds, second row, third seat, whom you'd been secretly in love with for the last six weeks, that a wild notion first arose in a generation of repressed goody goodies, that a girl's carefully refined demure appearance could have almost nothing to do with her nocturnal desires and designs. All you needed to do was make a little noise. I mean, after all, even Debbie Reynolds did it . . . with Eddie Fisher no less! Understandably, some could not absorb this revelation and were left in the dust early, almost certain to become fans of show tunes, hopelessly addicted to the visions of security personified by Frank Sinatra, who delivered stinging diatribes against Elvis and his "jungle music," which would not only rot your mind and stunt your growth, but probably go down on your permanent record and prevent you from ever serving your country or taking over your father's appliance business.

For a class of kids, clad in the conservative strait jacket of the 1950s, a prognosis like this held an even more intoxicating promise than the actual music itself!

In 1956, starting with "Heartbreak Hotel," Elvis put 17 songs on the charts that, collectively, spent 25 weeks at number one, and 16 in a row, during which time he was whisked to Las Vegas (where he bombed), and signed up by Hollywood (where he quickly became larger than television—larger than life—in hack movies like *Love Me Tender* and *Lovin' You*), humiliated by Steve Allen and emasculated by Ed Sullivan. While it's undeniable that Elvis (with the help of RCA) utterly changed the American musical guard—much to the dismay of Mitch Miller and Frank Sinatra, to say nothing of Steve Allen and Tommy and Jimmy Dorsey—because he was a non–writer, and as much fan dancer as musician, he was unable to grow beyond his original and radical mixing of the races—he seemed powerless to do anything but occupy a class of his own, self–contained, externally–controlled, drawing from the bank account of his seemingly eternal image, fixed in that amazing year of 1956. Ultimately, whether Elvis sold out or bought in, exploited black music or was its greatest promotor, played it straight or for laughs, or merely revealed himself to be the perfect Republican Richard Nixon would tap a decade and a half later to act as his symbolic narcotics agent, his benevolent overexposure on television successfully decimated his rebel image long before Uncle Sam lopped off the remains of his sideburns and chucked him to Germany in 1958. In sequined flares that would embarrass a merchant marine, and clad in baubles the weight of ten normal men, Elvis the icon would never again regain the innocent danger of his youthful transgressions. Instead, with a repertoire consisting mostly of movie filler like "Queenie Wahini's Papaya," neo–arias like "It's Now or Never," and inspirational drivel like "My Way," Elvis's summary tranformation into the missing link between Dean Martin and Wayne Newton would become a glittering warning to all who dared follow of the bounteous retribution available in America to squash any semblance of original thought. In other words, if so rabid a rebel as Elvis could succumb so quietly (Little Richard? Quick, put him in a movie), what chance did a mere mortal like Roy Orbison have?

Would Roy have been a more uncorruptible spearcarrier? We'll never know. Star–crossed, horn–rimmed, homely as his Texas friend Buddy Holly, who wound up stealing Roy's thunder in death, as Elvis had in life, Orbison was possibly the most inspirational and earthy figure of the entire rockabilly generation—which included several notoriously twisted characters—a writer of considerable depth, a singer of operatic intensity, lover of the doomed Claudette, owner of fragile heart. But Roy's "Oooby Dooby" was virtually lost in all the wild and heart–rending cries of 1956, among them "The Train Kept a–Rollin'" by the Johnny Burnette Trio, "Be–Bop–A–Lula" by Gene Vincent and his Blue Caps, "Blue Suede Shoes" by Carl Perkins, and "Bluejean Bop" by Eddie Cochran.

Along with Sputnik and the Edsel, 1957 brought the Rhythm Orchids (Buddy Knox and Sonny James, with separate number one hits), Buddy Holly, the Crickets, Buddy Holly and the Crickets, the Everly Brothers, and Jerry Lee Lewis into a prominence that—their spiritual leader having been effectively neutered—turned out to be a last hurrah for this historic intermarriage called rockabilly. Although, with names like Elvis, Sonny, Buddy, and Jerry Lee, these pompadoured biker types, ex–navy men, and hillybilly degenerates who would marry their thirteen–year–old cousins, were regarded by many of us citified snobs as far too morally and intellectually dubious to completely identify with, there was still something attractive about their guttural nonchalance that provoked in even the most repressed of us a yearning for the kind of ornery defiance they represented. Other urban types, who had had it with all manner of white exploiters, weren't so emotionally ambivalent.

"I never have hated the man," the rhythm and blues progenitor Bo Diddley once muttered in response to my query about the rise of Elvis Presley. "I just wish he'd have gotten his own act and left mine alone."

Much the same sentiments could have been applied by older black musicians to Al Jolson and Paul Whiteman and hundreds of others; Tin Pan Alley's time–honored tradition of filching and watering down black music whenever it found itself in need of a creative fix, stretched back through the entire musical century. In the 1950s, Elvis and his rockabilly cronies at least brought something new of their own to the mix, a kind of wild white–trash anger and sorrowful abandon that had been pretty much suppressed by other generations of teenagers and musicians, to meet the challenge of the black material head on. Representing the older order of creative borrowing, the Crew Cuts, the McGuire Sisters, Pat Boone, the Fontane Sisters, and Georgia Gibbs, certainly lifted some gems from R&B's finest: Fats Domino ("Ain't That a Shame"), Little Richard ("Tutti Frutti"), the Moonglows ("Sincerely"), the Charms ("At My Front Door"), Lavern Baker ("Tweedle Dee"), Johnny Ace ("Pledging My Love"), and Etta James ("Dance with Me Henry").

Yet, even while some pale versions triumphed on the charts and on the radio, there were more and more white teenagers—fans of Alan Freed, and connoisseurs of late night stations from the wilds of New Jersey, and beyond, where the deejays talked in rhymes and the products advertised between the records were not to be found in the local Whelan's—discovering the black originals, like the dirty parts of *Peyton Place,* and succumbing to the itchy excitement of the real thing, like "Please, Please, Please" by James Brown, "Earth Angel" by the Penguins, "In the Still of the Night" by the Five Satins, "Story Untold" by the Nutmegs, "I Can't Quit You Baby" by Otis Rush, and "Smokestack Lightning" by Howling Wolf.

"I think I was sitting with Carole Klein [King] in Andrea's Pizza Parlor on Coney Island Avenue when 'Earth Angel,' came out of the jukebox," the Brooklyn–born, Juilliard–bound, Neil Sedaka recalled. "I said, 'Oh, this is marvelous!' And that's who I started writing for, groups like the Nutmegs, the Harptones, and the Penguins."

As it had for Oscar Hammerstein and Irving Berlin and Sammy Cahn and Stephen Sondheim before them, access for the more refined New York Jewish branch of musicians to the hurly burly of popular music came through songwriting. Sedaka wrote with his downstairs neighbor, Howie Greenfield, and tried to sell his tunes to Don Kirshner at the Brill Building, actual and metaphorical hub of Tin Pan Alley, located on 48th Street and Broadway. Among Neil's competition was his Brooklyn cohort, Carole King, who teamed up with another brainy kid from the outer boroughs, Paul Simon from Queens.

"Carole would play piano and drums and sing. I would sing and play guitar and bass," Paul explained to me in a 1983 interview. "The game was to make a demo at demo prices and then try to sell it to a record company. Maybe you'd wind up investing three hundred dollars for musicians and studio time, but if you did something really good, you could get as much as a thousand for it. I never wanted to be in groups; I was only after that seven hundred dollar profit."

Paul almost got a whole lot more than that, with 1957's "Hey Schoolgirl" by Tom and Jerry, Tom being his pal since the fourth grade, Arthur Garfunkel. But Jewish family life in the city being what it was in those days—and still is—calmer heads prevailed, sending the buddies instead grumpily toward academia. Yet what could explain Paul's later forays into Brill under the name of Tico ("Motorcycle" by Tico and the Triumphs) and Jerry Landis ("The Lone Teen Ranger"), unless it was a sort of crazed attempt to win Carole King back after she left him for another classmate at Queens College, Gerry Goffin, to form a songwriting collaboration that led not only to their eventual (short–lived) marriage, but, and even more importantly, to a contract for a staff position with Don Kirshner's soon to be legendary Aldon Music in 1958, where Sedaka and Greenfield, and Barry Mann and Cynthia Weil, among others, worked in adjoining cubicles on a dynasty that would rival the one the Yankees had going in the Bronx (and, perhaps not coincidentally, peak in the same year of 1964)?

Pathetic indeed were the attempts of the elder dentists to keep up with this youth explosion of 1956–1957: Perry Como's "Hot Diggity," Eddie Fisher lusting after a "Dungaree Doll," obviously a close friend of Perry's "Jukebox Baby." Frank Sinatra "Learning the Blues," Kay Starr propagating the absurd notion of a "Rock & Roll Waltz," Gale Storm (Margie in "My Little Margie") offering a "Teenage Prayer," and Patti Page, in 1957, crooning "My First Formal Gown," were obviously meant to win back all those good teenagers you never hear about, waltzing to proms and marrying the boy next door, maybe vacationing in New York City, and dancing back to the hotel singing

"Standing on the Corner" and "Joey, Joey, Joey," from *The Most Happy Fella*, or "I Could Have Danced All Night," "I've Grown Accustomed to Her Face," "Get Me to the Church on Time," and "On the Street Where You Live," from *My Fair Lady* or even "Mack the Knife," from *The Threepenny Opera*.

But how could these make–believe laments compete with the fervor and the splendor and the passion and the hunger of "Why Do Fools Fall in Love" by Frankie Lymon and the Teenagers, "Let the Good Times Roll" by Shirley and Lee, "Eddie My Love" by the Teen Queens, "Fever" by Little Willie John, "Church Bells May Ring" by the Willows, "Speedo" by the Cadillacs, and "A Casual Look" by the Six Teens, and all the other tunes, both black and white, that unexplainably popped up in port cities after the bars closed down and urban centers under the moon of love, and across the wide swath of the howling heartland, from the nickel and dime recording studios of fly–by–night criminals and smooth operators who absconded with the masters and the copyrights and the cash? If what Alan Freed had gotten the credit for calling rock & roll was not exactly the primordial Elvis howl it could have been, or the evil rhythm and blues moan it should have been, it was at least, and at last, by 1957, for all extents and purposes, something else, with Chuck Berry, the Coasters, the Rays, and the Dubs mingling with Ricky Nelson, Buddy Holly, Jerry Lee Lewis, Elvis, and Eddie Cochran on the charts, representing a true merger of the country, pop, and R&B influences that would define the best intentions of rock & roll, for a baby boom crowd finally charging into puberty, all at once, like a class of horny 7th graders on the last day of school.

To be sure, however, for the average junior high school kid, the advent of rock & roll was hardly a panacea. While the brave new earthy world offered by R&B—where songs like "Shake, Rattle and Roll" began in bed, and "Work with Me Annie," "Long Tall Sally," "Speedoo," "Seven Days," and "Jim Dandy" ended up there—suggested that cutting–edge thirteen–year–old greasers were regularly winging out to Lover's Leap, each week with a different member of the Poni–tails tied to the hood of their Schwinn, closer to reality were the school dances every Friday night, where the boys stood on one side of the gym, stiff in their new suits, and the girls kicked off their shoes and danced with each other. Despite the increasing presence of rock & roll, at this tender age, boys who didn't know how to dance usually banded together to sneer at those who did—just as on the street corner the guys tossing a ball around would tease one of their own who passed by all dressed up, with a girl, obviously on a date. The non–dancers in these neighborhoods referred to the dancers as queers. Queers were also guys who wore suits to school, got the highest grades, and knew how to talk to girls and teachers without squirming. (As the years went by, however, and one by one the corner boys defected, each having been secretly taking cha–cha lessons for the last six months, often the queers were the ones left playing stoopball on the night of the junior prom).

Somehow, girls instinctively and instantaneously absorbed every new dance variation as soon as it was immortalized on "American Bandstand"—the Lindy, the Slop, the Stroll—while boys still preferred to hang around the bandstand and pretend to be friends with the drummer— even though, personally, you probably had about as much in common with him as you had with the hoods who played salugee with your baseball cap every time you ventured past Third Street into the only candystore in the neighborhood that had a jukebox. To most boys, the art of dancing seemed the product of another culture, polite society, a civilizing force we could not and would not allow ourselves to accept. Secretly, however, we envied those who mastered it, knowing that they had gained honored admittance into teenage coolness, while the footloose, the ungainly, the out–of–step, were doomed to dance alone in perpetual adolescence. Those popular boys who knew how to dance would surely move just as easily (or perhaps had already moved) into the other martial art of maturity: the advanced art of intercourse.

Hopelessly footlocked and tongue tied, if you were lucky enough to have a date on a Saturday night in junior high, the best you could hope for was a little heavy necking back home in the family's finished basement. But even with the Elvis shimmy, the Chuck Berry duckwalk, an R&B legacy gleaned from those staticky stations at the end of the dial, and a southern drawl gleaned from Elvis, that first move was always a moment filled with terror, as boy and girl sat leg to leg on the couch in the darkness and your Perry Como roots invariably popped forth like a pimple on the nose of fate. It is undoubtedly a revealing measure of this generation's ingrained conservative attitude toward sex in the 1950s, that by far our most trusted ally in crossing the divide between sexual innocence and experience was not Elvis, or Eddie Cochran, or any other neo–James Dean rockabilly biker, but rather the calculated mush of Johnny Mathis!

It is beyond fathoming and yet unarguable, that no one could aid a fumbling lover better than Johnny. If you'd been really clever and purchased a Johnny Mathis album (two week's allowance) perhaps seventeen minutes of uninterrupted bliss were in the offing—"It's Not for Me to Say," "Chances Are," "Wonderful! Wonderful!," "Misty" —certainly sufficient background music, theoretically, for the enterprising young couple to indulge their desire for instant gratification, or, if they lived in my neighborhood, for him to unhook her brassiere. While rumors about the nature of Johnny's sexual orientation would not emerge until several years later, the irony of a gay black from San Francisco being sexual mentor to so many mushy whites trying to be black has got to be more than just an accidental epiphany. As is the fact that the album *Johnny Mathis' Greatest Hits* was on the *Billboard* charts for 490 weeks and is to this day one of the all–time LP champs.

But perhaps it does explain why it was at this precise precipitous juncture of 1958, that rock & roll first began to reveal itself as possibly just another phase in the blue moon of American pop, with a processed horde of Brylcream crooners in the mold of the post–TV, finger–snapping Elvis, in a shirt and tie, like Bobby Vee and Frankie Avalon and Bobby Rydell, their Las Vegas pretentions barely concealed, lip–synching greeting card anthems in front of the "American Bandstand" dancers of the first disco era. Suddenly, it seemed, a doorway had opened for professionals to get into the act, Showbiz types, longtime residents of Tin Pan Alley, who learned it from a Fake Book like a wedding band, and projected to the cheap seats while the bride cut the cake. Confused as a kid with a brand new dollar bill in the sway of a fast–talking downtown salesman, who in the generation of thirteen year olds was hip enough to understand the difference between the real stuff and the fake, and clear–eyed and stoic enough to give their hearts only to the former and remain immune to the latter?

In fact, anyone under the hormonal influence of rock & roll during this time period probably has among his favorite songs quite a few that would hardly bear the scrutiny of the passing years, to say nothing of what has been writ in the great critical scroll at which most current pop musicologists bow down, forgetting for the moment that this critical scroll was itself undoubtedly compiled when most current pop musicologists were completing their masters theses in Advanced Rock & Roll in the 1970s. Bereft of such scholarship, a bike rider's idea of R&B at the time may well have been "Yakety Yak" by the Coasters, "The Book of Love" by the Monotones, and "Western Movies" by the Olympics, instead of Chuck Willis's "I'm Gonna Hang up My Rock and Roll Shoes." You could have disdained Elvis's vibrato entirely in favor of Conway Twitty's histrionics on "It's Only Make Believe." And who was there to quantify the difference between "Poor Little Fool" and "Bird Dog," "Short Shorts" and "Splish Splash," "Just a Dream" and "All I Have to Do Is Dream"? With everything happening so fast, it came down most often to the ear of the beholder. So if, for instance, there was in your life an apple–cheeked Debbie Reynolds clone you'd been coveting from afar since the sixth grade, named Jo Ann, it would be entirely possible, appropriate, inevitable even, now that Eddie had left her for Liz, that your favorite song of 1958 would turn out to be neither some moldy Hank Ballard B–side nor a frantic rockabilly raveup, but "Jo Ann" by the Playmates—Donny, Morey, and Chic—which did, in fact, sport one of the more durable and evocative alto sax solos of the 1950s, and the model, it would appear, for the sax solo in "Born Too Late" by the Ponytails, released six months after "Jo Ann," another maudlin classic.

"Oh yeah, I remember the guy, Weintraub or something," chuckled Morey Cohen, fat, balding, pushing fifty, in a suit and tie, when I tracked him down at his real estate office in suburban New Jersey in 1980, still in the grip of that searing sobbing solo. "Every so often I bump into him at Local 802 and he tells me he was playing out of tune on that record and he was ashamed of it. So I tell him, 'That's all right, we sold about a quarter of a million records.' For a while there was a battle on between our record and the original," Cohen then informed me. "What were their names? Oh yes, the Twintones. We did a cover of their tune and ours took off. Never heard of the Twintones after that."

My all–time favorite song, a lousy cover? My all–time favorite sax solo out of tune? If I hadn't already sold all my Playmates singles when I was sixteen—even, inexplicably, "Jo Ann"—I'd have burned them on the spot. Yet, there is a message here that went beyond my petty shattered illusions (next I was sure I'd find out that my second all–time favorite song, "The Hungry Dogs of New Mexico" by Happy and Artie Traum, was sung by a couple of adenoidal New Jersey yodelers, instead of authentic lonesome desert rats)—and had nothing to do with the Playmates. It had nothing to do with the actual Jo Ann either, who, when I went back to inspect my 7th–grade class portrait, sometime shortly after my meeting with Morey Cohen, turned out to be this buck–toothed and pudgy and possibly cross–eyed, frizzy–haired brunette in a middie blouse and bobbysox. Instead, it had everything to do with the magic of rock & roll, especially as delivered in its most compact form, the individual song, whether single or, later on, album cut, and usually heard on the radio, in the dead of night, unknown and unnamed, divorced from its singer, its writer, its image, its technique, its origination, as unearthly and weepy and disembodied as the voice of Nolan Strong whispering the eerie monologue in "The Wind," or, in fact, as the Twintones, these two white guys from Hicksville, Long Island, twins maybe, who created the ineffable "Jo Ann," based on their sister, one burst of passion and universal meaning, and that was it: rock & roll walk–ons, extras, no union cards to fall back on, just one pinch–hit bunt single in the World Series and then back to the minors, the carwash, oblivion. It was about how these songs had the enduring and singular power to utterly transform the soul, envelop the mind, and change the world from the inside out.

"New York was a joke to us," Nashville's Phil Everly sneered, as if in response to my agonized tale. "It was a joke to all of rock. Buddy Holly, Buddy Knox, Jimmy Bowen, Eddie Cochran. You name them, they were all country born and bred. Tin Pan Alley was jive and we knew it."

Although this sounded suspiciously like the sort of tough, backwoods elitism most citykids always had to live in mortal fear of, from boarding school to barracks, in truth, our puny, sheltered, mushy, whitebread, Johnny Mathis–inspired, Debbie Reynolds or Annette Funicello–obsessed sexuality was no match for these tobacco–chewing, no–neck, country studs. Who, for instance, in those early days of Alan Freed and Irvin Feld cross–country tours in covered wagons could Paul Simon have beaten up? Neil Sedaka, sure; Art Garfunkel, unquestionably, but after that, even Lillian Briggs would have probably cold–conked him with her trombone. More ominously in the long run, it was an example of rock & roll's tendency to divide even more than bring together: rural kids versus urban kids, parents versus children, crewcuts versus ducktails, white bucks versus motorcycle boots, television versus radio—Alan Freed versus Dick Clark—rockabilly versus rhythm and blues versus Brill Building pop.

And yet, Leiber and Stoller came back home to New York, ready to parlay their ascent from the rhythm and blues underground of Los Angeles into full scale rock & roll success, having already written "Riot in Cell Block #9," "Jailhouse Rock," "A Black Leather Jacket and Motorcycle Boots," "Kansas City," and "Hound Dog." Arguably the hippest songwriting tandem of the entire 1950s era, their presence here alone should have dispelled all notions of New York inferiority. For toughness, how about Dion DiMucci, leader of Dion & the Belmonts, and reputed member of the infamous Fordham Baldies, emerging in 1958 with "I Wonder Why," and scaring parents of young girls as well as their prospective dates out their minds at the same time?

On the other hand, you can't deny that, starting in 1957 and moving into 1958, the sweet sound of five–part harmony was indeed becoming the sound of the City, from Mount Vernon ("Tonite, Tonite," by the Mello–Kings) to Brooklyn ("One Summer Night" by the Danleers) to Staten Island ("Little Star" by the Elegants) to the Bronx ("Maybe" by the Chantels) back to Brooklyn ("Tears on My Pillow" by Little Anthony and the Imperials). Were these songs and groups as tough as rockabilly, as elemental as R&B? Or were they, as some claimed, another step in the softening process that led Little Anthony to note that "Bob Dylan said we were the last group in the rock & roll era. Actually, the era ended two years after us, in 1960."

Although Bob may have had a hidden agenda (and several layers of meaning, or no meaning at all) behind his epitaph for the era, there is certainly plenty of evidence to suggest that guys like Bo Diddley and Little Richard (who ascended to the pulpit in 1957, after nearly having had his way with Jayne Mansfield in *The Girl Can't Help It*), Hank Ballard and Clyde McPhatter, as well as most of the original R&B groups long since returned to harmonizing back at the foundry during lunch hour, would have been more than happy to see it go, along with their dreams of ever getting their hands on their royalty checks—with 1957's "Over the Mountain, Across the Sea" by Johnny and Joe, "Long, Lonely Nights" by Lee Andrews and the Hearts, and "A Thousand Miles Away" by the Heartbeats as appropriate swansongs.

However, it was a black guy named Chuck Berry, who simply by the strength of his will, saved rock & roll from those who would fulfill the earliest predictions of its imminent demise, with his lowslung guitar and patented duckwalk, and especially with his unrepentant paeans to this hybrid form he'd mastered with "Maybellene," back in 1955, acquiring a white audience to go with his black following, through massively accurate tunes like "Roll Over Beethoven," "Rock & Roll Music," "Sweet Little Sixteen," "Sweet Little Rock & Roller," and culminating, finally, in the jubilant and inspirational "Johnny B. Goode." Much like Leiber and Stoller back in 1953–1954, it was in the combination of white guys writing for a black audience and gaining a white one, and black guys writing for a white audience and keeping their black one, that rock & roll forever made its mark. Song for song, who could match these two forces, as the ultimate chroniclers of our baby boom teens, from quintessentially funky anthems like Leiber and Stoller's "Yakety Yak," to Chuck's trilogy of "Almost Grown," "School Day" and "No Particular Place to Go," you'd be hard pressed to find a more compelling brief for adolescent angst (unless, of course, you were a Brooklyn Dodgers or New York Giants fan). Better still was their gift for humor, in such tunes as "Charlie Brown," "Hound Dog," "Searchin'" and "Along Came Jones" (Leiber and Stoller), which were more than matched by the sly wit of "No Money Down," "Too Much Monkey Business" and "Brown Eyed Handsome Man" (Chuck Berry).

Interestingly, there was another black Berry surely listening to Chuck, as well as to Leiber and Stoller, in 1957 and 1958, and taking notes as he wrote "Reet Petite" and "To Be Loved," for Clyde McPhatter's replacement in the Dominoes, Jackie Wilson. When the Silhouettes hit number one in 1958, with "Get a Job," it was Berry Gordy's protege, Smokey Robinson, who came up with the positive reply of "Got a Job," for his own group, the Miracles, launching for Smokey and Berry Gordy, not only a job, but an empire called Motown Records.

Inevitably, as 1958 progressed, the average Jo Ann–
obsessed, R&B intrigued, Top 40 addict of the mystical
deejay jabber of Alan Freed (now heard over WABC) and
Peter Tripp, Jocko Henderson, and the Good Guys, lying
there in the light of his Stromberg–Carlson AM radio,
began to imagine himself becoming as fearless as the
music, united in grease with the hoods and hicks and
blacks and Italians who first made it. (By the end of 1958,
in fact, the smell of Max Factor's Crewcut, a white guy's
pomade, had fast become one of the essential aromas of the
fifties, the prom night equivalent of hotdogs at the ballpark
or popcorn at the movies). If a four–eyed squirt like Buddy
Holly could snarl, "That'll Be the Day," and a precocious
shrimp like Paul Anka could lust after his brother's
babysitter, "Diana," and wind up becoming one of the
twelve richest bachelors under 5' 2" in America, whether
it was the work of the devil on a holiday or a staff
songwriter on a deadline, the effect was nearly the same; in
its haphazard, hackneyed, and miraculous way, rock & roll
was distilling the essence of the outcast, underclass, repressed and possessed state that was our fifties adolescence to a T—you couldn't even get into the bowling alley
at night unless you were sixteen!—giving us something
popular music had never before given to privileged white
kids: an ally, a forum, and a voice that undoubtedly
prevented another generation from going silent. Surely, if
rock & roll could exist not only against the wishes of the
ruling class but against their best efforts to eviscerate it,
then maybe there was a way out of this box adults had
constructed around the safe, square middle class. If we
were special enough to deserve all this attention, a couple
thousand songs written about us in all of three years, then
certainly the power to control events had to be in our
hands after all!

It was not the first time a particularly powerful succes-

sion of songs would lead us into such a magically mis-
guided feeling. Even in 1958, if you were listening carefully, you could hear the sound of death rattling in the wind:
in Eddie Cochran's "Summertime Blues," in "Claudette"
by the Everly Brothers, written by Roy Orbison, about his
soon–to–be–late–wife, in Chuck Willis's "What Am I
Living For," in "Endless Sleep" by Jody Reynolds, and in
"Rave On," by Buddy Holly—who was about to meet his
own Yoko Ono in the person of Marie Elena, who would
cause him to split from his group and his producer, if not
get on a plane in Clear Lake, Iowa. Late that year, in the
notoriously puritan town of Boston, the forces of organized
repression struck, not for the last time, and a generational
battle came to a head. When it was over, at the stake would
be the head of rock & roll's most fitting fall guy, Alan
Freed.

Freed, like Feld and Clark, routinely touring the country
with his ongoing rock & roll caravan, presenting ten to
fifteen acts in ten to fifteen minute segments, accompanied
by a 25–piece band, with two drummers, brought the
show to Boston one night, where he was greeted by a
rowdy crowd. Freed himself had to quell some mischief in
the balcony. The next morning, the troupe emerged from
their Greyhound in Montreal to find themselves in the
headlines: *Boston Riot—Rock & Roll Show Kills.*

"The insinuation was that it had happened during the
performance, or because of the performance, because of
the Alan Freed show itself," recalled a crestfallen Jo Ann
Campbell more than twenty years later. As one of Freed's
regular performers for several years, the original "Blonde
Bombshell" was on the bus during that fateful trip. "But it
happened long after we left, on the streets of Boston,
around the area, but not during our show, and not because
of it. And then the news just spread from city to city. For
the next three weeks we didn't know if there was going to

be a show or not when we got to a town, because the promoters were frantic. Finally the tour had to be cancelled with two weeks to go. And that is when Alan Freed started running into all of his problems. He began to get a reputation as having a riot–causing show."

Within a year, a Senate subcommittee would take up the chalice of the Moral Majority of the time, hauling Freed in to face charges of accepting payola. When he refused to sign an affidavit claiming his innocence, he was fired from his post at WABC, convicted of two counts of bribery, fined $300 and given a six month suspended sentence. Effectively, he was out of the business.

"There were so many deejays who were envious of him, who loved what began to happen to him," contended Jo Ann. "I admire Alan Freed, because of all the disc jockeys, and believe me, all the major ones were taking it; only Alan told the truth. Some people got out if it very gracefully, although they were just as guilty as Alan. They were able to keep their positions, while Alan Freed lost everything."

Ironically, it was just as the government dropped the other shoe on Freed in 1964, hitting him where he lived, with a bill for back taxes on his payola take, leaving him stone broke when he died of a liver ailment in 1965, that rock & roll was in the process of evolving past the plucky singles he championed, into a new Golden Age that had seemingly little to do with him, Elvis, rockabilly, or R&B, but which could not have existed without them.

Featuring John Lennon and Paul McCartney, during the early sixties, the Beatles were polishing their Brill Building aspirations, crossing Little Richard with the Everly Brothers, in the caves of Hamburg, waiting, like Elvis had, for the guard to change. And a thirteen–going–on–thirty–five year–old, Little Miss Dynamite, the country belter Brenda Lee, voted top female singer in Europe, from 1960–1964, was there.

"When I worked with them they were going under the name of the Golden Beatles," she recalled. "They had most of their songs even then. I tried to get them a contract with Decca Records, but Decca didn't want to know about them."

The world had a few more revolutions to go through before everyone would know about them, an Urban Folk Scare to survive, the seeds of which were barely hinted at in 1958's "Tom Dooley," by the Kingston Trio, a president to elect and dispatch; just a few more innocent years for us to wonder and dawdle under the moon of love, fortified by "Rock & Roll Is Here to Stay" by Danny and the Juniors, "Try the Impossible" by Lee Andrews & the Hearts, Buddy Holly's bravado ("Maybe Baby"), Jerry Lee Lewis's stamina ("Breathless"), and Jim Backus' awe–inspiring laughing jag in "Delicious." If we were basically confused ("I Wonder Why" by Dion and the Belmonts), frustrated ("Summertime Blues" by Eddie Cochran), beleaguered ("Yakety Yak" by the Coasters), lost ("Little Star" by the Elegants), routinely disillusioned ("Just a Dream" by Jimmy Clanton) and betrayed ("You Cheated" by the Shields), we were also capable of glimpsing bliss ("I Met Him on a Sunday" by the Shirelles), knowing heaven ("One Summer Night" by the Danleers), expressing ebullience ("Willie and the Hand Jive" by The Johnny Otis Show), expressing reverence ("To Know Him Is to Love Him" by the Teddy Bears), or just having ourselves a hell of a good time ("Summertime Summertime" by the Jamies)—even if we didn't know who wrote "The Book of Love" by the Monotones, and only understood six of "The Ten Commandments of Love" by Harvey and the Moonglows.

More than that, though we couldn't see it then, and had no commentators in place other than the above–named intuitive street singers to tell us, we'd successfully adopted and co–opted a musical form that would follow us through

the years, sometimes becoming bigger than us, the whole
greater than the sum of its songs, but always reflecting the
unique position of the generation in the dreamlife of the
universe, elastic enough to bend and stretch with our
whims, following us down incomparable stylistic and emotional sidestreets and detours, yet staying near enough to
where it started to define and defend our best and worst
instincts, even when our TVs went from 6 inches to 24,
from black and white to living color, and our middling
junior high school Top 40 concerns collided head on with
the outside world and exploded into a million pieces—at
which point, we would look to the Beatles as much to quell
us as to revive us.

Two

United In
Group Harmony
(1959–1962)

It was at a meeting one night in the mid–1970s of the United in Group Harmony Association, at the Mercury A.C. in East Rutherford, New Jersey, that I first saw in the flesh the legendary Times Square Slim, aka Irving Rose, founder and proprietor of Times Square Records, a four by nothing dump of an oldies emporium that was located down a flight of stairs in the Times Square New York subway station, whose radio show, where he featured the same obscure and treasured artifacts of rhythm and blues as could be purchased only at his store, came crackling out of the static of my shiny red transistor somewhere between 1010 WINS and 1040 WMGM–AM, over WBNX in the Bronx, every other Saturday night in 1959.

There was a standing O as Slim was led out, bent, wracked with emphysema, his voice as nasal as Brooklyn after the rain, instantly recalling to me the tenor and terror of my fourteenth year, a decade and a half back, where Slim was still residing, reliving the glory days of R&B.

"In those years, you knew one thing," he croaked to much applause. "A kid is not going to rape anybody with a

34

record in his hand. Instead of going out and mugging and raping, in those years, every streetcorner had a group of five guys singing a cappella. It's too bad we can't revert back to that . . . ."

If you were to judge it strictly in the roseate hindsight of rock & roll, the harmonious sounds of the forthcoming do–wop era, for baby boom teenagers, both white and black, both male and female—to say nothing of the optimistic tenor of the entire period from 1959 to 1962— seemed to be epitomized nowhere better than in New York City, where it reigned like the Yankees, Maris, Mantle, Berra, and Hector Lopez at the height of their mystique. It was a sound and a feeling as rough, majestic, and spontane- ous as a city that ran all night on nervous energy; every hour a rush hour, every street a misadventure, with sixty–story skyscrapers and asphalt rooftops and stoops from three to seven steps high, Coney Island boardwalks and elevated subway lines, the foam on a perfect egg cream, the salt on a salted pretzel; High School, USA: do–wop guys on the corner and cheerleaders stalking the avenue in packs of twelve.

Absorbing the classics of the black neighborhoods of 1955 and 1956, like "Earth Angel," "Deserie," and "Gloria" into their own ethos of sleeveless t–shirts and cigarette parked behind the ear, mouths working overtime, indigenous white do–wop groups didn't so much have rhythm, as they had passion. In their new used Corvettes, winging out every Saturday night to Neck Road, they immortalized beloved steadies named "Blanche," "Dar- ling Lorraine," "Barbara Ann," up to and including the famed "Runaround Sue" and "Sherry." It was a blissfully harmonious, self–contained world these high school lowlives and makeout men described, wild and endless as the Bronx itself, typified by no one so much as Dion DiMucci, of Dion and the Belmonts, a former Fordham

Baldie, who was perhaps even friends with The Umbrella Man! Dion could walk through Harlem at any hour of the day or night, yodeling, harmonizing, bouncing a rubber ball. No wonder he made the girls all dewy eyed and gooey. No wonder every greaser in spitting distance of Brooklyn and the Bronx took up his wounded macho attitude.

Here then, is a New York City white do–wop honor roll, as Times Square Slim himself would have been proud to announce: Dion & the Belmonts (from the Bronx) with Dion DiMucci singing lead ("A Teenager in Love," 1959), the Capris (from Ozone Park) with Nick Santo singing lead ("There's a Moon out Tonight," 1961), the Chimes (from Brooklyn) with Len Cocco singing lead ("Once in a While," 1960), the Classics (from Brooklyn) with Emil Stuccio singing lead ("Til Then," 1963), the Crests (also from Brooklyn) with the legendary Johnny Maestro singing lead ("The Angels Listened In," 1959), the Demensions (from the Bronx) with Phil Del Giudice singing lead ("Over the Rainbow," 1960), the Earls (also the Bronx) with Larry Chance singing lead ("Remember Then," 1962), the Echoes (again from Brooklyn) with Tommy Duffy singing lead ("Baby Blue," 1961), the Elegants (from Brooklyn, of course) with the incomparable Vito Picone singing lead ("Little Star," 1958), the Excellents (who sang about Brooklyn but hailed from the Bronx) with John Kuse singing lead ("Coney Island Baby," 1962), the Impalas (from the heart of Brooklyn) with a black lead singer, Joe Speedo Frazier ("Sorry, I Ran All the Way Home," 1959), Jay & the Americans (from New York City) with Marty Sanders singing lead ("She Cried" and, with David Black singing lead, before he changed his name to Jay, "Only in America"), the Mello–Kings (from nearby Mount Vernon) with Bob Scholl singing lead ("Tonite Tonite," 1957, "Valerie," 1958), the Mystics (from Brooklyn) with Phil Cracolici singing lead ("Hushabye," 1959), Nino & the Ebbtides (from the Bronx) with Nino Aiello singing lead ("Those Oldies But Goodies," 1961), the Passions (from Brooklyn) with Jimmy Gallagher singing lead ("Just to Be with You," 1959), the Quotations (from Brooklyn) with Larry Kaye singing lead ("Imagination," 1961), the Regents (from the Bronx) with Guy Villari singing lead ("Barbara Ann," 1961), and Vito & the Salutations (from Brooklyn) with Vito Balsamo singing lead ("Gloria," 1962). The Duprees, with Joe Canzano singing lead, were from Jersey City ("You Belong to Me," 1962), and the Four Seasons, with Frankie Valli (Castelluccio) singing lead, were from Newark ("Sherry," 1962), but they rate honorary membership, for accents alone.

Could a black guy sing do–wop? Believe me, this is a question that troubled the sleep of rhythm and blues artists from Shep and the Limelites (Queens) to the Jesters (New York City) to the Jive Five (Brooklyn) to the Cleftones (Queens) to the Monotones (Newark, New Jersey) not one single minute, as they reveled in this New York street heyday in the heart of a teenage Saturday night under the moon of love every bit as much as their blue–eyed brothers on the other side of the El.

Could a group of girls sing do–wop? This was an entirely different question, one which many great musical minds of the time were contemplating around 1960, from Luther Dixon to Phil Spector. Admittedly, the ranks of rock and roll girl singers, solo and in groups, had been pretty slim through the 1950s, from the virginal ponytails of Debbie Reynolds and the Bobettes, to the ponytailed virginity of the Poni Tails, Jo–Ann Campbell, and Patience and Prudence. Connie Francis was like your grownup spinster aunt. Brenda Lee was like taking your little sister to the prom. Even Annette Funicello ("Pineapple Princess," "Tall Paul"), who was the closest thing we had through junior high to a sex symbol, was experiencing a post–pubescent awkward stage, no longer the only girl in the class who had breasts. Over–protected by her mentor, Walt Disney, who stuffed her into a bunch of beach movies extolling a kind of outmoded pom–pom purity, she was no match for the new realities of East Coast cycle sluts in their high school sweaters, with mile–high beehives and blue eyeshadow several inches thick, black skirts several inches above the knee, black mesh stockings, and an aura of unceasing mystery, and unquenchable, unknown—and undoubtedly kinky—desires.

As usual, when it came to acts of physical or sexual or musical prowess, from basketball to heavy petting to jazz, the first stirrings of revolution took place in the black neighborhoods, kind of as an out–of–town tryout for middle America. By the late 1950s, you had the Shirelles (from Passaic, New Jersey) and the Chantels (from the Bronx) operating under that lovingly pejorative rubric of The Girl–Group Sound. The Marvelettes somehow invaded the turf from Detroit, competing with the Chiffons (from the Bronx), the Crystals (from Brooklyn), and the Ronettes (from Queens). But a real girl–group era would not take on national life until the middle class whites of the baby boom could get behind it, with images the average Marilyn Monroe or Natalie Wood–obsessed schlub in the bathroom leafing through *Playboy* could relate to. This kind of powerful identification was not to be found in the efforts of ersatz California girl–groups like Kathy Young and the Innocents, from Los Angeles ("A Thousand Stars"), Rosie and the Originals, from San Diego ("Angel Baby") or the Paris Sisters, from San Francisco ("I Love How You Love Me"); denied neighborhoods, stoops, and rooftops high enough to tune in CKLW from Toronto on a good night, no wonder the boys and girls over there were about to relinquish all chances for equality to be consumed by a salty froth of male bonding called Surf Music. On the other hand, our own Cathy Jean and the Roommates, from New York City ("Please Love Me Forever") was about as viable and visible a role model as Marcy Blaine, from Brooklyn, whose spoiled, whiny, dependent "Bobby's Girl," bespoke a female generation still mired in the possessive, materialistic, retrogressive, unliberated, boyfriend–centric modes of the past. Maybe that's why Phil Spector thought he could exploit Darlene Love, using her as the lead voice of the Crystals on "He's a Rebel," but never giving her the credit. Maybe that's why he fell in love with and married Ronnie Bennett of the Ronettes—or at least the picture of himself she gave him—soon after "Be My Baby" became a hit in 1963.

Hard as it was for the average New Yorker to accept, there actually was rock & roll going on throughout the remaining forty–six states as well—plus newly ordained Alaska ("North to Alaska," by Johnny Horton, in 1960) and Hawaii ("Suzie Darlin'" by Robin Luke, from 1958) —as black music reached peaks of ecstacy with the Marcels in Pittsburgh ("Blue Moon"), Gene Chandler in Chicago ("Duke of Earl"), Lloyd Price in New Orleans ("Personality"), and Jesse Belvin's group, the Shields, coming out of Los Angeles ("You Cheated"). In Detroit, Berry Gordy Jr. was retiring from a ring career with one eye on the chemistry of the Brill Building, scouring his own neighborhood streets for his new Motown record label. One of his first successes was with Nolan Strong's cousin Barrett Strong, who put them on the map with "Money (That's What I Want)" in 1960. Smokey Robinson and the Miracles went to number two in 1961 with "Shop Around," the same year the Marvelettes went to number one with "Please Mr. Postman" and Mary Wells got as far as number 45 with "Bye Bye Baby." In 1962, she had two songs in the top ten ("You Beat Me to the Punch" and "The

One Who Really Loves You," both written by Smokey Robinson). The Supremes got out of high school in 1962, and came aboard with "Your Heart Belongs to Me," which peaked at number 95. Little Steveland Morris got out of public school and came by with his harmonica. Marvin Gaye went to number 46 with "Stubborn Kind of Fellow." The Contours hit the top ten with a Berry Gordy song, "Do You Love Me?" The Falcons had been around since 1959 ("So Fine"), with Eddie Floyd in the group, as well as Joe Stubbs (whose brother, Levi, sang with the Four Tops, who had also been around a while, and who would soon be signed by Gordy, too).

The whole period, in fact, achieved such an integration on the charts and in the minds of group harmony adherents, Elvisaholics, Little Richard addicts, and Fats Dominoites, that to be a rock & roll fan during this time was to acknowledge no racial dividing line for tunes of all colors. White Brill Building guys were writing for black groups; Otis Blackwell, a black guy, was writing for Elvis ("Return to Sender") as well as Clyde McPhatter sound—alike, Dee Clark ("Hey Little Girl") and had written for Jerry Lee Lewis ("Great Balls of Fire," "Breathless"); black groups were imitating white groups imitating black groups—and vice–versa. For those who may see this parity as somehow diluting or damaging to the cause of true black music—the ultimate white co–optation of the black sound far more devastating than Pat Boone or Elvis Presley in their prime—remember, it was during this time when you could hear singles by Jimmy Reed ("Big Boss Man" and "Bright Lights Big City"), B.B. King ("Young Boy Blues"), Freddy King ("Hideaway") and John Lee Hooker ("Boom Boom") on the radio, that white kids who wouldn't have had the nerve to buy a bagel in the slums of Bedford–Stuyvesant were marching in Mississippi for Civil Rights. In 1962, R&B legend Ray Charles brought "I Can't

Stop Loving You," a country song by the white Don Gibson, to the top of the national pops. For another black–country–pop triple play like that you'd have to go all the way back to . . . Elvis Presley. The tune went on to become the number one song of the year, which was either progress, or a severe case of reverse discrimination.

Bo Diddley was on the air in 1959 with the funniest song ever (accidentally) recorded, "Say Man," edging out by the slimmest of margins, Jim Backus's laughing jag–inducing "Delicious," of 1958. Frankie Lymon's career was on the wane, but we had soundalike Jimmy Jones with "Good Timing" and Jimmy Charles with "A Million to One." The Drifters, originally formed by Clyde McPhatter in 1953, entered a new era in 1959, pioneering the use of strings in R&B on "There Goes My Baby," with Ben E. King singing lead. Their comings and goings since then are surely worth a classic comic book all their own. King moved on to a solo career in 1960 with "Spanish Harlem," written by Leiber and Stoller, produced by Phil Spector. Clyde McPhatter wasn't complaining, though, when he had hits with "A Lover's Question" and "Little Bitty Pretty One." In addition to Clyde, great crooners were in abundance, descendants, somewhere down the line, of the original King, Nat King Cole, among them Jackie Wilson ("Doggin' Around", "Night"), Curtis Mayfield and the Impressions ("Gypsy Woman") and the silky soul of Sam Cooke ("Only Sixteen," "Chain Gang," "Cupid"). But, the mainstay sound of the era was still do–wop, from the Flamingos' "Lovers Never Say Goodbye" of 1959, Johnny and Joe's "Over the Mountain, Across the Sea" in 1960, "Daddy's Home" by Shep and the Limelites, in 1961, and "What's Your Name" by Don and Juan, and "Duke of Earl" by Gene Chandler in 1962.

Yet, as heavenly as the do–wop sound is to contemplate in retrospect, its downfall was as predictable as it is painful to remember, when every lip–synching, lip–reading, do–wop hitter, scourges of their neighborhoods, whose main goal in life seemed to be in promoting an extended boy's club adolescence of dirty jokes and dirty fingernails, first chance they got exhibited the same propensity as Elvis for the outsized kind of fame only selling–out in America can offer its young and gullible. Sure, Elvis came home from the service in 1960 a movie star who happened to sing. And every other rocker had already had a bit part in *Don't Knock the Rock*. But I'm talking about Dion and the Belmonts singing Rodgers and Hart's "Where or When"! From the 1937 play, *Babes in Arms*! Sung in the movie by Judy Garland! In the polyester history of lounge lizardry, has there ever been a more sickening turn of events? Then they compounded the tragedy, releasing "When You Wish upon a Star." The Demensions countered with "Over the Rainbow." The Skyliners, who only a year before had defined the essence of ethereal soul with "Since I Don't Have You," confirmed their instantaneous decline in "Pennies from Heaven." Bobby Darin gave us "(Won't You Come Home) Bill Bailey." Bobby Rydell moved one step closer to Atlantic City with "That Old Black Magic." Ricky Nelson, but a short trip from Las Vegas anyway, sang "Yes Sir That's My Baby." Tommy Sands, the Ponytails, and the Five Satins all covered "I'll Be Seeing You." The white do–wop sound seemed particularly vulnerable to the evergreens, with the Duprees taking the dubious honors with "My Own True Love" and "You Belong to Me." It was as if, like Elvis and his penchant for crooning hymns to his mom, Gladys, all these street creatures, turning twenty–one, were suddenly conned into becoming adults, donning suits, and singing arias. Elvis went to the upper reaches with "It's Now or Never," adapted from "O Sole Mio," Jackie Wilson gave us "Night," translated from the original Icelandic, Paul Anka rendered "All of a Sudden My Heart

Sings," translated from the French "Ma Mie." Even Roy
Orbison's brilliant "Crying," cast Roy as a latter day
Pagliacci, howling at the cheap seats.

The Marcels attempted to turn the tables a bit, with
their rollicking do–wop transformation of "Blue Moon."
But Aretha Franklin turned them right back, with her soul
rendition of "Rockabye Your Baby (with a Dixie Melody),"
that was outsold on the charts by the Jerry Lewis version.
Following in the footsteps of their departed mentor, Dion,
the Belmonts bemoaned their fleeting adolescence with
Duke Ellington's "Don't Get Around Much Anymore," as
fitting an epitaph as you could want, for a segment of the
generation that had run out of righteous steam.

If the wondrous sounds of group harmony were done in
by the slow death of assimilation, rockabilly's last best
hope succumbed to a more ignominious fate, on February 3,
1959, commonly known as The Day The Music Died—
when a light plane carrying Buddy Holly went down in a
field in Clear Lake, Iowa, with Ritchie Valens and J.P. (The
Big Bopper) Richardson also aboard. Why that particular
tragedy should have emerged as the symbolic pinpoint
when the dreams and the energy of rock & roll's mythic
white forebears lay irrevocably buried in the slime, is a
subject that has befogged begoggled musicologists, debat-
ing amongst each other astride folding chairs on local cable
access shows after midnight for at least twenty years. You
might just as easily have cited the date that Steve Sholes
signed Elvis Presley to that long–term RCA deal instead of
Bo Diddley, or Alan Freed moved to New York, or Gordon
McClendon invented Top Forty, or Dick Clark popularized
the Hop, or Steve Sholes signed Neil Sedaka to another
RCA deal instead of Hank Ballard, or February 6, 1960,
when Jesse Belvin died in a car crash, or April 17, 1960,
when Eddie Cochran died in a car crash. However, since
rock & roll went largely uncommented upon in the media,

aside from patronizing sneers of derision from anyone older than fourteen, and cable TV was as distant a dream as FM radio at the time, it is left to popular revisionism to suggest that Holly and Holly alone was the only southern–bred bandleader possessed of a neo Hank Williams adenoidal twang, capable of writing tunes of such eternal simplicity and rock & roll veracity that his horn–rimmed visage, had he lived, might have one day replaced Steve Allen in our universal estimation (thus making the eventual creation of Elvis Costello unnecessary). Possibly. Then again, knowing what we know now, he could well have formed a duo with his wife, the bookkeeper, and gone on to host a short–lived summer replacement variety show of dubious repute.

What is slightly more interesting to consider, is whether the Beatles, hunkered over beers in the caves of Germany, would have been as successful in transporting their version of the Buddy Holly sound five years later, to say nothing of the Stones, transporting Holly's "Not Fade Away," if Holly himself were still around to play it, with or without the Crickets?

Though Holly's fate wasn't quite as immediately numbing as Elvis going into the army, it was nonetheless the first mortal blow adolescent baby boom rockphiles had ever suffered. James Dean's death in 1955 was unreal; he belonged to another generation, old enough to get into the movies at night without an adult. Though certain note was surely taken of the Holly crash, it was hardly enough to revive Buddy's own ironically titled "Heartbeat," which was at that moment stalled on the charts at number 82. Nor did his posthumous two–sided single, "Raining in My Heart," backed with a tune by the junior Tin Pan Alley tycoon, Paul Anka, "It Doesn't Matter Anymore," fare much better—or speak well for Buddy's continued creativity in his just–married state of mind at the time.

Of his co–passengers, the Big Bopper capitalized much more on his disfortuitous union in death with Holly than the third member of the party, Ritchie Valens, whose "Donna" peaked at number 3; its flipside, "La Bamba," at 22. Richardson, whose previous claim to fame had been "Chantilly Lace," a few months before, reached number one six months after the crash, as the writer of the eerie western soaper, "Running Bear," as sung by Johnny Preston, and could be heard providing war whoops in the background. Then again, though it took more than twenty years, Valens' life was finally immortalized in a movie— Jerry Lee Lewis and Buddy Holly having already been given the celluloid treatment—and as far as I know, nobody's yet released even a compilation disc on the Big Bopper.

Probably the person who made the most out of the tragedy (Thomas Wayne's prescient "Tragedy" had just been released and was wending its way up the charts when news of the crash crackled across the wires of the Top 40), was the then–unknown Bobby Vee, who in fact sat in with his band, the Shadows, for Buddy Holly the next night on the fated tour, in Fargo, North Dakota. He would have a single on the charts, "Little Suzie," which skied to 77 by the fall, and a prosperous career to come in rock & roll's afterlife, during which he would even dare to put out an album's worth of songs with Buddy's own estranged backup band, the Crickets, among them "Someday (When I'm Gone from You)," which stalled at number 99. (Vee is not to be confused, however, with Tommy Dee, who released his own "Three Stars" a month after the crash, the nation's official acknowledgement of the deaths, along with Eddie Cochran's "Teenage Heaven," which ominously pre–dated his own death a year later. Tommy Dee, on the other hand, should not be confused with Tommy Roe, the Buddy Holly soundalike, whose "Everybody" was the tune interrupted over the radio station in New York City everybody was listening to, when President John F. Kennedy was assassinated in 1963.)

But a belated mourning of Holly did take shape in the surfeit of death songs on the airwaves in 1960, probably as some sort of vinyl repentance at having so readily and cavalierly embraced the cloning of his sound. Along with "Running Bear," "El Paso" by Marty Robbins, and the supposed novelty, "Please Mr. Custer," by Larry Verne— all of them with a John Wayne western motif in which Tinseltown cowboys and Indians died without bloodshed or pummeled each other senseless without getting woozy —the grizzly classics of the lot were Ray Peterson's "Tell Laura I Love Her," and "Teen Angel" by Mark Dinning, both focusing on auto wrecks. Of course, this mini fatal car crash trend may have also been due to the fact that most of us were finally getting old enough to drive our first Chevys to the levee by then. Puberty had opened its gates, and we of the early baby boom years were tumbling on through en masse in Mustangs, Impalas, T–Birds, and Nash Ramblers with the foldback seats. If the black pioneers of R&B had been systematically exploited by an industry of con men, causing a certain raucous and robust honesty to disappear from the American Jukebox forever, this was hardly of pressing moment to the twitching citizens coming under the thrall all at the same time of what certain chord changes could do to one's limber surging loins.

Whether the subject matter was cars or high school or puppy love, the fact that we were all going through it together, in the largest population blip ever to surface on the planet, not only made it news, it made us news, the audience as superstar, the consumer consumed by self. Look what we'd done for Elvis, for Ed Sullivan and Dick Clark. By 1959, having dispensed with the truly dangerous and unpredictable element of sexy R&B and threatening rockabilly, we'd established a tone and subject matter we could all handle: ourselves! In our own high school U.S.A. of the mind, we could revel in the in–crowd thrills and traumas to our heart's content.

And, of course, from 1959 to 1962, the only place to be in high school or in rock & roll, was in good old New York, New York, and I'm not just saying that because I was there. Native New Yorker, Phil Spector, came here from L.A., with his tap shoes, his guitar, and his castanets, fresh from his success with the Teddy Bears. Leiber and Stoller came back here, having established themselves in the R&B hinterlands beyond the Jersey Turnpike. Dick Clark's "American Bandstand" was so close, in Philly, we considered him an honorary New Yorker. Bob Dylan came to New York town in 1960 from Minnesota, ostensibly to meet Woody Guthrie, but modern thinkers now know it was to be near a New York rock & roll high that would never be recaptured. Buddy Holly came here—and met his wife. The previously disdainful Everly Brothers came to New York, in 1959, to record "Let It Be Me," away from the confines of Nashville for the first time. In 1962, they even recorded a Gerry Goffin and Carole King song, "Crying in the Rain." And where did Chubby Checker go, when he wanted to revive "The Twist," and send it to the top of the charts for an unprecedented second time? Where else, but to 45th Street, and the Peppermint Lounge. Even the Beatles, auditioning drummers in the slums of Liverpool, knew about the Brill Building.

"I met John Lennon at a BMI dinner," songwriter Doc Pomus once told me. "One of the biggest kicks I had was when he told me that originally all they wanted to do was reach a point, like Morty [Shuman] and myself, or like Carole King and Gerry, where they could make enough money to survive writing songs."

As supercharged a hit factory as ever there was, the Brill

Building, from 1959 to 1962, was more than the edifice that housed people like Howie Greenfield and Neil Sedaka, Doc Pomus and Mort Shuman, Barry Mann and Cynthia Weil, Carole King and Gerry Goffin. It was a street, an atmosphere, a neighborhood, a social life, a teen–oriented, baby booming industry of personalized three–minute anthems, where Leiber and Stoller worked hand in hand with Morty and Doc, as well as Jeff Barry and Ellie Greenwich, who moonlighted with the baby genius, Phil Spector; it was where the sophisticated pop duo of Burt Bacharach and Hal David were within proximity of the more earthy tones of Otis Blackwell—all of these sounds affecting each other, influencing each other, as they were heard through the walls and the doorways and the hallways, and booming out of Colony Records down the block, as soon as they became national hit singles. There was "Charlie Brown," "Along Came Jones," and "Poison Ivy," by the Coasters, "Kansas City" by Wilbert Harrison, and "Lavender Blue" by Sammy Turner, all of them written by Leiber and Stoller. Jimmy Jones sang Otis Blackwell's "Handy Man," in 1960. Pomus and Shuman hit with "Hushabye" for the Mystics, "I'm a Man" and "Hound Dog Man" for Fabian (the original Vanilla Ice), and the ineffable "Teenager in Love" for Dion and the Belmonts. Neil Sedaka became the hit of Brighton Beach when he followed Elvis to RCA, with "The Diary," which he'd originally written for Little Anthony & the Imperials in 1959. Later he wrote "Oh Carol" about Carole King. Carole wrote "Oh Neil" for Sedaka, but it failed to crack the charts. In 1961, she and Gerry Goffin would write two number one songs, "Take Good Care of My Baby" for Bobby Vee and "Will You Love Me Tomorrow," the Shirelles' biggest hit. They would get so hot that they could (literally) write a hit song for their babysitter, Little Eva ("The Locomotion"). Hal David wrote "Broken

Hearted Melody" for Sarah Vaughan in 1959, with Sherman Edwards. After that, he would save his best stuff for the composer of 1958's epic "The Blob," Burt Bacharach, to be sung by Shirley Alston's stand–in with the Shirelles, Dionne Warwick ("Walk on By," "Anyone Who Had a Heart"). The Shirelles, who would become the biggest selling girl–group of the period, did a Bacharach and David song in 1962, called "Baby It's You." They were Luther Dixon's project, the black man who was the producer, in 1959, of "Sixteen Candles" by the white group, the Crests, one of the prime movers of white do–wop.

As discredited as some of this stuff later went on to be, future time capsules, I am confident, will define our high school experience as forever thus: Freshman year (1959) was the essence of "Teenager in Love," with Dion's dour sexiness at once more accessible and more dangerous than Elvis's solid gold pompadour. While Bobby Rydell unctuously celebrated "Kissing Time," most of us leaned toward Bobby Darin's version of a "Dream Lover," being a gangly fourteen while all the girls around you were counting "Sixteen Candles," by the Crests, and going from "Bobbysox to Stockings," by Frankie Avalon. No wonder the Coasters, as scripted by wiseguys Leiber and Stoller, got so much of our frustrated adolescent attention for their sarcastic "Poison Ivy." It was almost as good a salve as the Bellnotes' "I've Had It," my personal pick as the angriest song of a year that was primarily non–verbal. You could test your body language to the sound of a guitar ("Red River Rock" by Johnny and the Hurricanes, "Guitar Boogie Shuffle" by the Virtues, "Forty Miles of Bad Road" by Duane Eddy, "Sleepwalk" by Santo and Johnny), a saxophone ("Petite Fluer" by Chris Barber), drums ("Teen Beat" by Sandy Nelson), or a Hammond B–3 organ ("The Happy Organ" by Dave "Baby" Cortez), and as rusty as you might have been, it was probably ten times more effective than talking—as Jan and Dean more than amply suggested in "Baby Talk."

Sophomore year brought us the aforementioned slew of death songs, temporarily knocking us off our hormonal kilter. Parents were generally out to accomplish the same thing, as Paul Anka observed in "Puppy Love," and Troy Donohue and Suzanne Pleshette learned in the film *A Summer Place*, whose theme song by Percy Faith covered us in a soapy mush of strings. Dion brought his image another step further with "Lonely Teenager," just before he ruined it by trying out for the Copa with "Where or When." Johnny Burnette seemed to be only white guy who was getting any ("You're Sixteen")—but he was twenty–six at the time; Brenda Lee was far more typical of the average insecure fifteen year old ("I'm Sorry," "I Want to be Wanted").

In our junior year, things heated up, with Carole King and Gerry Goffin writing two hallmark makeout songs, "Will You Love Me Tomorrow" (for the girls) and "Half-way to Paradise" (for the boys), expressing the frustrated, Fifties–mentality, Johnny Mathis–influenced teenage condition about as well as you could, given the constraints of Top 40. Instrumentally, there was Max Crook's legendary musitron solo in Del Shannon's "Runaway," the wacky majesty of "Nut Rocker" by B. Bumble and the Stingers, Dave Brubeck bringing cool jazz briefly to the limelight with "Take Five," Dick Dale previewing surf music with "Let's Go Tripping," and the Mar–Keys previewing Memphis soul with "Last Night." But even with Dion's comeback in "Runaround Sue" and Elvis's hopeful lechery in "Little Sister," some were all too eager to put a sop to our momentum, in "Those Oldies But Goodies" by Little Caesar and the Romans.

Maybe there were twenty–one year olds listening to that tune, who were ready to follow Elvis out to Vegas, and their parents to the rest home, but by senior year, we were ready for a new musical age of social awareness, with Ray Charles at the top of the charts with "I Can't Stop Loving You," and the Crystals bringing Phil Spector's feisty vision of city–rock to gritty reality with "Uptown" and "He's a Rebel." "Telstar" and "Midnight in Moscow" floated in the ether of Top 40, thus the subliminal collective zeitgeist, alongside "If I Had a Hammer" and "Where Have All the Flowers Gone." Women were getting angrier, viz Timi Yuro's triumphant "What's a Matter Baby." Blacks were strutting around a little in Gene Chandler's "Duke of Earl." Dion was strutting around a lot, in his coup de grace, "The Wanderer." Even Elvis hit a philosophical peak, with "Follow That Dream." By senior year, the teenage experience was opening up to some tough truths, as Claudine Clark eloquently expressed in "Party Lights," and Gene Pitney reaffirmed in "Town without Pity."

In most cases, these were the voices and the concerns that would follow us into the next era, but not before all signs and traces of the previous one were expunged in a national disco craze that came to a peak in 1962 with "The Twist," by Chubby Checker—not a remake of his 1960 tune, but the same damn tune that simply refused to die after making it to number one during what would turn out to be a solid year and a half of continuous dancing!

Chuck Berry's "Too Pooped to Pop," which came out in March of 1960, could have seemed an admission that the grand old innovator of R&B to rock & roll was preparing to step aside for a new generation of hoofers, along with the rest of his cronies (he had been in jail for violating the Mann Act, but that's another story), among them, Bobby Bland, who summed it all up in "Let the Little Girl Dance." But by the time Chubby started to do "The Twist," in September, 1960, the song's actual writer way back in 1958, another Chuck Berry protege, Hank Ballard, was already way ahead of him, onto a new move, entitled "Finger Poppin' Time." After which, like competing Vaudeville tap dancers, Chubby and Hank took their separate turns in the spotlight. In September, Hank released "Let's Go, Let's Go, Let's Go"; Chubby responded with "The Hucklebuck." Hank came back in November with "The Hoochie–Coochie–Coo"; Chubby waited until January, 1961, to announce it's "Pony Time." Hank was prepared, with no fear of being redundant, releasing "Let's Go Again," also in January. They both kept pace in March, Hank with "The Continental Walk," Chubby with "Dance the Mess Around." Obviously, they were aware of each other by now, probably sharing the same backup musicians. In June, they continued what must be ranked right up there with the great dancing duels of all–time, surpassing Sammy Davis Jr. versus Stumping Stumpy, or Daddy Hines versus Pegleg Bates, or Gene Kelly versus Fred Astaire, or, later on, Vanilla Ice versus (the then MC) Hammer, with Chubby doing a portamento over poor Hank's head with "Let's Twist Again," which went to number eight, while Hank's "Switch–a–Roo," wound up at number 26 (a tune Hank later admitted to buying off another writer for $25!). You knew then that Hank's time was drawing to a close. His August release, "Keep on Dancing," didn't even crash the Top 40, while Chubby calmly waited until October to put out "The Fly," which went to number six.

Surely, then, it was either a cruel and unusual gilding of the lily or else a supreme gesture of equanimity on a par with Errol Flynn in *Robin Hood* or Bob Hope in *Casanova's Big Night*, tossing the fallen sword back to his rival, when Chubby bolstered Hank's bank account with the re-release of "The Twist," in November, with—get this— the re–release of "Let's Twist Again" (written not by Hank, but by Kal Mann and Dave Appel) on the B–side!

All Hank could muster in February, as a pathetic final attempt to regain an equal footing with his co–conspirator, was the feeble "Do You Know How to Twist?" which hobbled to number 82, while Chubby's February offering was the chance of pace, "Slow Twistin'," which was surely not a sign the Chubster was slacking off. In June, he was back with "Dance Party," and September "Limbo Rock," backed with "Popeye the Hitchhiker," while Hank, no doubt, was somewhere laid up in traction.

This is not to suggest that Hank and Chubby were the only ones Twisting from 1960–1962. In fact, who wasn't twisting? I mean, Count Basie released "The Basie Twist"! You'd have thought he'd have at least recorded it under a false name. Frank "Jungle Music" Sinatra, merely observed the obvious with "Ev'rybody's Twistin.'" Danny and the Juniors, who'd pathetically invited everyone "Back to the Hop" just a few months before, lamely jumped on the bandwagon with "Twisting All Night Long," which lapsed at number 68. The redoubtable Chipmunk, Alvin, had a twist named after him, "The Alvin Twist." The dance went south of the border, with Gary U.S. Bonds's "Twist Twist Señora." The Marvelettes' updated "Twistin' Postman," Sam Cooke tried "Twistin' the Night Away," sax–man King Curtis offered his "Soul Twist," poet Rod McKuen gave the concept a poetic twist, with "Oliver Twist." The Isley Brothers' provided perhaps the only enduring classic of the lot, "Twist and Shout," later revived by the Beatles, who, one imagines, took this all in with knowing smirks as they were honing and refining the final niggling kinks out of their Top 40 act in the caves of Dusseldorf.

In the caves of New York City, the Twist belonged to Joey Dee and the Starlighters, a house band at the Peppermint Lounge on 45th Street, whose "Peppermint Twist" went to number one in January of 1962, immediately

superseding Chubby's endemic sampler, with a pedigree
whose irony would certainly not be lost on Hank
Ballard—a co–writer credit by Henry Glover. It was the
same Henry Glover who ran Hank's record label back in
1958 (the subject of all of Hank's racy Annie songs), who
had staunchly refused to flip Ballard's single of "Teardrops
on Your Letter" over to "The Twist" on the flipside. Even
Glover had joined the ranks of the enlightened by then,
who were all nudging and bumping up against each other,
and the members of the maxi–monde, the jet set, and the
glitterati, who were ushering in what *Life* magazine
dubbed in our honor, The Cult of Youth.

"From one night at the end of September, 1961, I'd say
it took about two weeks before the twist grew into a
phenomenon," said Joey Dee. "You name them, they were
at the Peppermint Lounge. I danced with Shirley
Maclaine. I sat on her lap. Shirley was there every night.
Judy Garland was there every night. Dorothy Kilgallen,
John Wayne, Robert Mitchum, Liberace, a couple of
senators, English royalty."

As a measure of how pervasive and sickening this disco
craze eventually became, even Dion, having semi–
recovered from destroying the Belmonts by singing standards, sank to the level of donning tap shoes and trying to
do "The Majestic." Is it any wonder he went from there
almost straight into Christianity? With new dances coming
out nightly (who the hell was doing these new dances,
apart from the songwriters?) called the Mashed Potato, the
Pop Eye Stroll, the New Continental, the Jam, the Strand,
the Watusi, the Popeye, the Push and Kick, up to and
including, in some weird kind of symmetry, the Dovels
reinterpretation of "The Jitterbug," nearly lost in the
shuffle was the emergence of Merv Griffin, who would later
go on to capture the dancing essence of another era in
Dance Fever, which starred Danny Terrio, the man who

purportedly taught John Travolta how to disco in *Saturday Night Fever*. Merv's contribution to the dancefloor of 1962 was "The Charanga," a Latin sister–in–law of "La Pachanga," which had also usurped the outmoded Cha Cha Cha (just when you'd finally learned how to do it).

The Twist, at least, was supposedly easier to master, though chiropractors debate the issue even now. What is less debatable is how the Twist totally changed the course of modern dancing, separating partners by a good ten feet: our first dance of alienation. Jules Feiffer would have been proud. You didn't even need a partner for the Twist, and at the same time, some guys could successfully Twist with two girls at once, with neither of them realizing it. The Twist, being the creation of the baby boom—or Dick Clark, which is essentially the same thing—was more than a dance, it was a media event, the first of many inspired by the massive coming together of middle class white kids looking for sex and rock & roll. Old enough at last to have a night life, we made the Twist our imprimatur, a dance with no rules, except free expression, partaken primarily in packed communal quarters, to the orgiastic sound of Carlton Latimore's organ.

"We were the first band to be live on Dick Clark's coast to coast network show," said Joey Dee. "We were given almost half an hour, and all we did was three songs. We did the "Murray the K Christmas Show" at the Brooklyn Fox. You were only on ten to fifteen minutes, and 'Shout' was fifteen minutes itself. Once we got involved in it, the frenzy and momentum would carry it."

Carried away a bit ourselves, in the frenzy and momentum, we surfed into 1963 and the tidal concerns of the world outside: The Cuban Missile Crisis, the Cold War, Civil Rights, realities even rock & roll could no longer avoid.

"A lot of promoters thought we were a black act," the

Four Seasons' Frankie Valli told me, "so we did a lot of all-black tours. We were doing a tour with Chubby Checker, right in the midst of the Old Miss problems, and we were playing Jackson, Tennessee, at an armory where they were protesting. We had to cancel the show, pack up, lay down on the floor of the bus, and get out of town."

Only a few miles downtown from the non-stop party music of the Brill Building, in another New York City neighborhood entirely, there was a street sound that moved to a vastly different beat, where the cognoscenti had been aware of exactly what was happening in the south long before most rock & rollers (even those with names like Elvis and Jerry Lee), an audience that was united by a common cause of group harmony even stronger than rock & roll—influenced as much by the underground sound of the dispossessed black man as rock & roll ever had been, but determined to cast it in a message a good deal less frivolous than rock & roll's high school hedonism, one that would become more and more relevant and affecting and inevitable as the short years came to meet it and the generation head on.

Also to be found at the time in quintessential college towns, like Cambridge, Massachusetts and Berkeley, California, and in the Old Town section of Chicago, the Dinkytown section of Minneapolis, San Francisco's North Beach, home of the Beat Generation trading war stories at Ferlinghetti's City Lights bookstore, it was especially alive on MacDougal Street in Greenwich Village, where the Gaslight Poetry Cafe opened in 1959, immediately leading to the appearance of a ragged brigade of older types, post-teenage rebels, who had perhaps danced to the Moonglows in Cleveland, or Elvis in Memphis, but who were now the nefarious potsmoking, long-haired, draft-dodging, commie, radical, pinko subversives—known as folk–singers—who plumbed to the root the anxious soul of acoustic Delta blues, mixed with the strumming sound of Dustbowl populism, to express the existential question mark of the decade about to commence like a sudden sheet of howling hard rain.

"Something happened in this country when they dropped that bomb in Japan," Dave Van Ronk, one of the era's leading figures, commented. "And something further happened when the Russians got the bomb to drop in testing. It was like you were under a sentence of death, suspended. You'd get these incredible, psychotic moodswings—elation, depression, manic activity."

Concurrent with the subversive doings in these college towns and bohemian neighborhoods, in 1960, there was the popular image of the folk singer as well, a collegiate sort of guy, a preppy in a letter sweater, with the keys to his father's Oldsmobile securely in the pocket of his herring-bone blazer. He may have sung Woody Guthrie tunes about the Great Depression and the Plight of the Common Man with his fraternity friends, but the fact he did so in the melodious four–part harmonies of the Four Freshmen, rendered these messages patently harmless. More to be feared was someone like Pete Seeger, a former member of the politically active Weavers, and reportedly a black-listed Communist, which made him about as sympathetic to parents of teenagers as Alan Freed. But, since he was banned from "The Ed Sullivan Show," no one under twenty had ever seen him. Plus, he played the banjo, which hadn't been sexy since 1929. In the meantime, folk singers like the Kingston Trio, the Tarriers, Terry Gilkyson and the Easy Riders, the Brothers Four, the Limelighters, the Highwaymen, Judy Collins, and this new girl with a gorgeous voice who debuted at the Newport Folk Festival in 1959, Mimi Baez's sister, Joan, provided certain precocious high school types an alternative to rock & roll that was a good deal more substantial and energizing than Wayne Newton and Barbra Streisand.

Then, shortly after JFK squeaked by Tricky Dick in the election of 1960, giving us an East Coast President for the first time in fifteen years, Bob Dylan blew into New York, holing up with folksinger Dave Van Ronk, and his wife, Terri, in their apartment on 15th Street, and writing songs as threatening to the status of every comfortable quo as anything produced in the vibrant infancy of the rock & roll era he was only a few years away from altering irrevocably. In answer to what might have been his manager, Albert Grossman's, recurring rhetorical question: "If I could find a white kid who could fingerpick acoustic blues like a black sharecropper, preferably named Johnson, and re-write old English folk tunes into his own socio–mytho-poetic hymns of personal protest, combined with a bit of rock & roll's recalcitrant urban energy, could I rule the middle class market of collegiate and college–bound and otherwise overly–educated baby boom youths, by tapping into their inchoate yet quantifiable yearnings for both artistic license, personal freedom, and an identification with the downtrodden masses, made possible by their parents' unlimited indulgence and deep pockets?" Dylan raged about war and peace, equality, and the bomb, in songs like "Masters of War," and "A Hard Rain's Gonna Fall," "Let Me Die in My Footsteps," "The Ballad of Emmet Til," and "Blowin' in the Wind," where previously folksingers only dallied in green fields and cotton fields, singing of banana boats and the MTA. For every guitar strumming soul on MacDougal Street, Dylan delivered his folk verities and paranoia with a venemous, frenetic, tragi–comic angst, not unlike a gospel–preaching Little Richard struck by lightning.

While the Valadiers were spending a couple of weeks on

the charts with "Greetings (This Is Uncle Sam)" and the jocular Four Preps were doing slightly better with "The Big Draft," in 1962, only on the folk circuit could you begin to understand how soon those draft cards so yearned for by baby boom teens as a symbol of maturity were going to be serving a purpose much more deadly than the procuring of draft beer. This was about the time Phil Ochs was calling Fidel Castro "perhaps the greatest man the Western Hemisphere has produced in this century" and writing his first folk song, entitled "Talkin' Cuban Crisis." Everyone was living under "the shadow of the bomb," crouching under their desks during air raid drills, and slouching along the avenues at night like the characters in John Cassavettes's *Shadows*, while the radio played a Top 40 that was becoming increasingly irrelevant—until Peter, Paul & Mary lifted Bob Dylan's "Blowin' in the Wind" to the top of the charts in 1963, making it not only offical, but commercially profitable, to challenge the established music business authorities.

Suddenly, a generation of musicians awakened by Elvis and inspired to take up instruments by Pete Seeger, started moving to New York, with visions of a new rock & roll frontier. There was Jim McGuinn, the guy smirking in the background behind the Chad Mitchell Trio on several of their albums, moonlighting from his job accompanying Bobby Darin during his Copa phase, at the same Greenwich Village baskethouses as Dylan, and several other future sixties stalwarts like Peter Tork, John Phillips, and John Sebastian—who would each go on to greater fame in rock & roll as members of the Byrds, and the Monkees, the Mamas & the Papas, and the Lovin' Spoonful, respectively.

"I was really shocked when Dylan took off," McGuinn observed. "All I knew was that the little girls liked him a lot."

Which, even in 1962, anyone should have seen as the

ultimate timeless tip–off right there. Politics was getting
sexy. Marilyn Monroe had sung at the President's inaugu-
ral. Under the shadow of the bomb was replacing under the
moon of love, as the ideal place to make out. Late in 1962,
McGuinn's own bosses, the Chad Mitchell Trio, were on
the charts with a satire of "The John Birch Society." Pete
Seeger, the infamous Red, had two songs in the top
twenty–five that year, "Where Have All the Flowers
Gone," by the Kingston Trio and "If I Had a Hammer," by
Peter, Paul & Mary. Woody Guthrie was on the charts as
well, with "This Land Is Your Land," by the New Christie
Minstrels. While it's undoubtedly true that hard core fans
of "American Bandstand" as well as the denizens of Sam
Phillips Memphis Recording Service, or many another
average, hair–combing citizen of High School U.S.A. were
not particularly aware of or concerned about James
Meredith's predicament at the University of Mississippi, in
some precincts along the cutting edge, at least, the nourishment and identification that people once took from that
secret throbbing wellspring where first rock arose, sweaty
and profane, in 1955, in the arms of Joe Turner and Ruth
Brown, was evolving into a commitment.

Though Dylan, like Elvis, was honorably catholic in his
musical tastes, influenced as much by Hank Williams and
Woody Guthrie as Mississippi John Hurt, Buddy Holly, and
the Reverend Gary Davis, the inflammatory issue of Civil
Rights that was about to divide the country during his rise
through the 1959–1962 period posited Dylan's enormous
affect squarely in the blues camps of the North, while the
rockabilly of Elvis generally went South, with Buddy Holly
and Ritchie Valens expiring in 1959, followed by Eddie
Cochran a year later. The Johnny Burnette Trio broke up in
1959, leading to some solo success in 1960 for Dorsey
("Tall Oak Tree") and Johnny ("Dreamin'" and "You're
Sixteen"). In 1964, Johnny would die in a fishing accident.

Patsy Cline found fleeting fame with "I Fall to Pieces" and "Crazy." She would die in a plane crash in 1963. Even the survivors tended toward the bathetic: Brenda Lee's last appearance in the Top 5 came in 1962, with "All Alone Am I," Jerry Lee Lewis started 1959 off with a revealing cover of Moon Mullican's "I'll Sail My Ship Alone," that sailed to number 93 on the charts, one week in January, then sank in the waters of Lake Michigan like the wreck of the Edmund Fitzgerald. Charlie Rich, Roy Orbison, and Elvis Presley delivered, respectively, in 1960, "Lonely Weekends," "Only the Lonely," and "Are You Lonesome Tonight." In 1961, Roy Orbison released "Crying," in 1962, the Everlys recorded "Crying in the Rain." Of them all, the Everlys had the least reason to be sobbing. In 1960, they signed a million dollar contract with Warner Brothers. But pretty soon their career would be gone with the wind, as the pair would crack the Top 5 only once more, with "Cathy's Clown," their first release of the deal. A couple of years later they'd be in the Marines, about as far from representing the draft–dodging predilections of the baby boom as the most abject of Brill Building Top 40 establishment apologists—many of whose works, along with those patented Everly harmonies, would come to form the final defining sound of another quartet waiting in the wings, just across the channel.

Thus, having celebrated nothing so consequential as the spectacle of our historic togetherness, we were now prepared for the next four years, for our college years, to use that togetherness to right all the wrongs of the world. With the safety of our numbers for protection, we united as a group in the harmony of rock & roll.

Three

When the Mood
of the
Music Changes
(1963–1965)

It was like you'd died and gone to harmonica heaven!

From its humble three–piece combo (maybe with the addition of a King Curtis sax) beginnings, the sound of rock & roll grew exponentially during the period from 1963 to 1965, with the best of these sonic revolutions underscored, augmented, highlighted, made the more poignant, the more joyful, the more quintessentially windblown and bittersweet by the sound of a harp, a blues harp in the key of E, a hand–held Hohner, the size of your palm, that any collegiate bohemian could learn to curl his tongue around and sound like a high–plains drifter blowing like a cactus across the campus for a lecture on post–war English lit. In England, John Lennon heard Delbert McClinton's harp on Bruce Channel's chirpingly trivial "Hey Baby," of 1962, and immediately added his own chapter to the legacy on the Beatles' "Love Me Do," which flopped in America, when it was released on VeeJay in 1963. By then everybody was more agog over blind little Steveland Morris, discovered, nine–years–old, in the projects of Detroit, by Ronnie White, a singer with Smokey Robinson's band, the

Miracles, who'd been recording at a new label called Tamla since the turn of the decade, that was hiring up all the indigenous talent. The kid was not just another Johnny Puleo/Jerry Murad eleven–octave jumping clone, harmonica the size of a loaf of French bread. He was real and earthy and down home and, most of all, little, like Walter. They would call him Little Stevie Wonder and put him in the Motortown Review, where he recorded seven minutes of "Fingertips" at the Apollo Theater in New York; the Part II of the tune, where they switch the key from G to C, resulting in the famous cry "What key! What key!" raced up to number one in the country over the course of the summer of 1963.

John Sebastian wouldn't have had to worry about what key. In 1964 and 1965, you could have seen him shambling down the streets of Greenwich Village wearing a belt comprised entirely of harmonicas (wearing jeans as well, of course, and cowboy boots, t–shirt, Prince Valiant hair, and granny glasses, later to be known as John Lennon specs; in 1964, Lennon was but a speck in the consciousness of the bohemians down in Greenwich Village). In all shapes and sizes, these harps came, in sharps and flats and augmented sevenths, too, no doubt. They were the tools of his trade; a harmonica player's son, John could be heard by then blowing billowing fills behind every third folksinger of the era, on albums by Tim Hardin and Fred Neil, Judy Collins, and the very–revered Mississippi John Hurt.

Like almost everything else that was hip in the 1950s and 1960s, the harp had a long and rich tradition among black diminutively nicknamed bluesmen like "Sonny" Terry, "Sonny Boy" Williamson, "Little" Walter, "Junior" Wells, James "Cotton," and the doubly–tiny "Little Junior" Parker—their emotional musical wallop in inverse proportion to their names. Now, brought about perhaps by the unparalleled parity of R&B and pop, do–wop, the

Motown Sound, soul, blue–eyed soul, and post–Twist dance music ("The Jerk," "Twine Time," "Boo Ga Loo," "Do the Monkey," and the incomparable Frug), on the early 1960s record charts, white kids once more found their sustenance and cool moves in the black culture. And before you could say Bo Diddley, there was John Hammond Jr. wailing away on "Who Do You Love," and Mel Lymon first seeing the godhead in the Kweskin Jug Band, Tony Glover, in Minneapolis, forming Koerner, Ray & Glover, John Mayall, in England, fronting the Bluesbreakers, and Bob Dylan blowing his harp through a contraption invented by guitar guru, Les Paul, that attached to his guitar, leading to a momentary boom in that part of the instrument industry easily as big as the previous boom in capos.

The journey from funky bluesy adjunct to a full–scale rock & roll answer to the honking sax of R&B was completed by a couple of Chicago boys named Charlie Musselwhite ("Christo Redemptor") and Paul Butterfield (the Butterfield Blues Band), both of whom could have been found in the early 1960s, like Prohibition gangsters on the lam from polite society, trekking across the psychic and mythic (which is not to say they weren't actual) borders of the black neighborhood, into the black experience, the intoxicating exotica of the Southside: black cat bones, jellyrolls, mojo hands, jujubes, and who knew what else. "Muddy Waters was a spiritual influence on my life," Butterfield one day swore to me. "He encouraged me tremendously. He said, 'You got it, now play.'"

The words of black musicians, from their already hallowed place on that pedestal of rhythm the white world had ceded them, the upside down pinnacle of blues their inherited pigment and condition had guaranteed them, especially to insecure and/or questing white musicians, had always carried much more than their weight in credi-

bility. By 1963, the fruits of this rock 'n' role reversal were
ripening on Vine Streets from L.A. (Hollywood and Vine)
to K.C. (12th Street and Vine); in New York, the Drifters
epitomized black and white city soul in "Up on the Roof,"
written by Gerry Goffin and Carole King. Blue–eyed soul
was about to flourish, in the sound of the Righteous
Brothers of "Little Latin Lupe Lu," while white do–wop
was reaching a peak in "Walk Like a Man" by the Four
Seasons. But the Earls, from the Bronx, were already
casting a long shadow on the future of such an intermarriage, in "Remember Then."

In a baldfaced attempt to recapture that fast fading era
of nonsense syllables and high school dances, Chubby
Checker released "Twist It Up," in the summer of 1963,
undoubtedly trying to hold back time one more time. But
although the tune placed as high as number 25, the
suspicion, at least in these quarters, is that Dick Clark
probably bought up all the copies as Christmas gifts to his
beloved Bandstand dancers, who were certainly the only
ones who could have had a vested interest in returning to
those days of grace and grease. Except, perhaps, for the
Hippies (a pre–bohemian incarnation of the term, meant
to describe a lower class of nightlife swell, high school
dropouts and repeaters, still prowling the streets of several
Eastern cities in 1963, like pompadoured Triceratops in
taps, as everyone else was graduating into leather and
suede) who preferred "Memory Lane," to which only Joe
Franklin danced. But Randy and the Rainbows, out of
Queens, New York, probably understood their motivations,
when they sang "Why Do Kids Grow Up?" It was a
question parents everywhere could have been asking pundits and philosophers like Mitch Miller and Steve Allen
and Pat (author of *Twixt Twelve and Twenty*) Boone, who
had promised them eventual surcease from the plague of
rock & roll; now that Dion and Bobby Rydell were croon-

ers, and Frankie Avalon and Elvis ("There's No Room to Rhumba in a Sports Car") Presley were directing their creative energies toward acting, where was it? Instead, the middle class teenagers of the baby boom had grown right past the high school phase of rock & roll, the puppy love phase, the moon–June makeout phase, and into something much more shocking, fearful, mature, and possibly illegal.

Paul Anka for sure didn't want to see the Golden Era go. Las Vegas–bound, and even if he didn't know it then, author in 1962 of what would become his nest–egg for life, "The Tonight Show Theme" with Johnny Carson, Paul revealed his true feelings in 1963's "Remember Diana." But it was not that no one remembered Diana. It was more like no one from the old neigbhorhood would have recognized her anymore. Stepping out from her pristine Debbie Reynolds/Annette Funicello pink bedroom into college or the real world, in 1963, Diana began to get an identity of her own. It was no easy deal, giving up the privileges of a pom pom girl to become a cycle slut. You had to contend with pop morality, which was not so different at the time from mom and pop's morality. But these pioneering women, who had grown up so much faster than neighboring boys, would prove to be more than competent in leading their emotionally backward brothers into the wild and explicit sexual age that was about to commence.

It didn't seem like this would be possible in 1963, with the Crystals singing "He Hit Me (and It Felt Like a Kiss)." This was after plundering the depths of babydoll mush in "Then He Kissed Me" and "Da Doo Ron Ron." Sometime (uncredited) lead singer of the Crystals, Darlene Love, certainly did not gain any stature among her sisters or independence going solo, as evidenced by "Wait Til My Bobby Gets Home" (shades of Marcy Blaine!) and "Today I Met the Boy I'm Gonna Marry." Suffering Connie Francis! Martha and the Vandellas did at least suggest the rumbling of post–pubescent urges in "Heat Wave." And the Ronettes looked like streetwalkers and sang like cycle sluts, even if they still thought like pom pom girls in "Be My Baby," "Do I Love You," and the pouty "What's So Sweet About Sweet Sixteen." It was nice to hear the Exciters advising girls to be aggressive in "Tell Him" and the Chiffons promoting the value of the soft–spoken guy in "He's So Fine." But, when the lights went down and Johnny Mathis came on the old victrola, all these girls sounded as moral as the Shirelles in "Will You Love Me Tomorrow." Why not? Their songs were being written pretty much by the same people.

Sadly, but not unexpectedly, Caucasian girls were no more advanced in 1963. There was Little Peggy March, declaring obedience in "I Will Follow Him," taking her cue as well as her song from no less a paragon of femininity than England's Petula Clark. Carole King released "He's a Bad Boy," but did not go chasing her rebel to the top of the charts, as the Crystals had the year before, in the prematurely encouraging sidestep "He's a Rebel." Still intent on shrinking into the background, she preferred to remain in the land of nod, like the Murmaids, whose incessantly bubbly "Popsicles, Icicles" was written by a prim and starched David Gates, one of popdom's leading exponents of the whitebread sensibility. Tenafly, New Jersey's Lesley Gore, discovered by Quincy Jones when she was a coddled high school senior, immediately became the incarnation of the whiney suburban princess with "It's My Party;" the follow–up, "Judy's Turn to Cry," with its cat–scratching revenge motif, probably, in and of itself, set feminism back ten weeks. Threatening to create a retrogressive Jersey–sound easily the female equivalent of the latter–day Bruce Springsteen/Jon Bon Jovi axis, Orange, New Jersey's the Angels chose to hide behind a swaggering macho man in "My Boyfriend's Back," obviously the adolescent fantasy of writer/producers Robert Feldman, Jerry Goldstein, and Richard Gottehrer (who would find a way to prolong his girl–group obsession indefinitely, surfacing in the next decade as the producer of Blondie).

As pitifully insignificant as these tunes might seem, they were about all the average American women would be able to sift from the silt of popular sentiment in a year that ended with the image of the Singing Nun plucking our heartstrings with the mournful "Dominique," a French tune that was the beginning of the end of the secular career of Soeur Sourire, and the end of the beginning of Sally Fields's Hollywood post–Gidget apprenticeship, as the flying doer of good deeds. For something tangible, a glimmer of what women were to more widely become, starting as little as six months later, you'd have had to take off your hi–heeled sneakers and don thongs and ride the D train down to Washington Square Park, to catch a glimpse of Maria D'amato, formerly of the Bronx and the Even Dozen Jug Band of Greenwich Village, when she came in from Cambridge, Mass, with the Jim Kweskin Jug Band, to sing "Wild About My Lovin'," "Coney Island Washboard," and, especially the Leiber and Stoller classic ,"I'm a Woman."

If Peggy Lee's 1963 hit rendition of the tune made her out to seem impossibly icy, uptown, and remote, Maria's vision of the latter day Superwoman Syndrome the lyrics imply was so earthy and nonchalant and at the same time so positive and oozing with nectar and sex, uplifting, life–affirming and unstereotypical, that Leiber and Stoller may have had more than a few uneasy moments at home convincing their mates that they weren't in fact card–carrying proto–feminists. With swirling dark gypsy hair and banjo eyes, Maria was a true folk music dreamgirl, in the image of Joan Baez, but not so pretentious, and Mary Travers, but not so lofty; more like Janet Margolin, who only talked in rhymes in *David & Lisa*—but not quite as psychotic. Inspired maybe by Salinger's *Franny & Zooey*, the same mystical waif—almost immediately Hollywood-ized by Cher and Broadwayized by Barbra Streisand—would haunt the careers of Leonard Cohen ("Suzanne") and Bob Dylan ("Spanish Harlem Incident," "Visions of Johanna," "Sad Eyed Lady of the Lowlands"), and almost all the other major and minor lyric poets of the period and beyond, from Tuli Kupferberg and Ed Sanders ("Slum Goddess") to John Sebastian ("A Younger Girl"), Eric Andersen ("Come to My Bedside"), Paul Simon ("For Emily, Wherever I May Find Her"), Mick Jagger and Keith Richards ("Ruby Tuesday"), John Lennon and Paul McCartney ("Lady Madonna"), to Brian Wilson ("Caroline, No").

By the end of 1965, there would be a new kind of woman walking around, the sum total of these fevered dreams, who remembered mournful Arlene Smith of the Chantels, who grew up listening to Brenda Lee, who adapted Darlene Love's power and left the rest alone, who internalized Ronnie Bennett's strut and discounted the spectre of Phil: the ineffable, nasal Cher, decadent, throaty Marianne Faithful, snotty Mary Weiss of the Shangri–Las, defining the neighborhood tease, Janis Joplin's wild–haired and bourbon–soaked dementia, Linda Ronstadt's adenoidal folkie tribute to Connie Francis, smokey–cool Dusty Springfield and kooky Barbra Streisand's pipes and thrift shoppe chic, Laura Nyro's subway evangelism—Bonnie Raitt, Stevie Nicks, Patti Smith, Chrissie Hynde, Debbie Harry were all listening to them.

As if willed into being by the collective subconscious desires of a male collegiate generation ready to break the bonds of their 1950s (if not eternal) suppression, these new voices often transcended their material, finding substance where there may have been none, by the force of their presence, achieving self–knowledge out of what might previously have passed for casserole recipes. The Lesley Gore of 1964, a freshman now, stood proud and fast in "You Don't Own Me," "Maybe I Know," "I Don't Wanna Be a Loser" and "Sometimes I Wish I Were a Boy." Dusty Springfield spoke up against passivity in Bacharach and David's "Wishin' and Hopin'." Even Dionne Warwick got tough in the same team's "Walk on By." But Mary Weiss was the cycle slut personified, in a slit skirt, beehive, trampy blue eyeshadow, in "Leader of the Pack," the biggest of several epic Shangri–Las psychodramas ("Out in the Streets," "Remember (Walking in the Sand)," "Give Us Your Blessings," "I Can Never Go Home Anymore"), co–scripted by Jeff Berry, Ellie Greenwich, Phil Spector and Shadow Morton, that would eventually leave Mary disgraced, winded, upended, and contemplating her eventual suicide.

But the true commercial realization of the Maria Muldaur nee D'amato promise of 1963 found full flower in Canadian Gale Garnett's "We'll Sing in the Sunshine," breaking on these shores three solid years before the fabled Summer of Love, in which Gale depicts a nascent flower child readily able to live with a man out of wedlock —in fact, she doesn't even want to marry him! She's perfectly willing to depart after a year or so! Now, topless bathing suits and see–through blouses were becoming marketable items in 1964, inklings of the outrageous excesses to follow, but certainly nothing your average book–laden brown–noser was apt to bump into in Brooklyn. *Playboy* magazine hadn't as yet invented pubic hair. The practice of rampant free love, as occasionally discussed in fraternal lodges and college cafeterias, was a phenomenon that took place only among certain lust–crazed, tanned, and Godlike fringe elements coalesced in wife–swapping clubs clustered in sea coast towns in California, not unlike surfing. Here in the East, we made do with periodic forays down to Greenwich Village, to see Maria and then to check out the underground films of Andy Warhol, Ed Emschwiller, or Harry Smith (*Flaming Creatures*), where you got a chance to ogle naked bodies who were not playing volleyball, as they did in all the nudist epics of adolescence.

But, Gale Garnett also *wrote* "We'll Sing in the Sunshine" herself (it won a Grammy for best Folk Recording), not someone like the retrogressive record producer, Richard Gottehrer. If this was the drift and the gist of female thinking, it seemed the only logical alternative, if you were a baby boom male, free, white, and old enough to fantasize, was to indulge, like John Phillips did in the winter of 1963, in some heavy "California Dreamin'."

By all accounts Disneyesque, home of the Hollywood version, edited for television, purveyor of Ozzie & Harriet and Frankie & Annette, and products that worked, an America that worked, where Richard Nixon swore his first oaths in office, and Ronald Reagan came to ultimate power and ultimate fantasy, California, in 1963, was "Surf City," "The Surfer's Choice," the epicenter of "Surfin' USA," an endless "Surf Party" or "Surf Hootenanny," where there were two girls for every boy (Annette Funicello and Cher), and everyone lived the hedonistic credo of "Louie Louie" to the hilt. The Clampetts had moved to Beverly Hills, predating the arrival of the Fresh Prince, Will Smith, to Bel Air, by some twenty–seven years. In California, *American Graffitti* was being written on the subway walls of cities with no subways nor pedestrians, celebrating the American verities of sun, fun, and suburban sprawl, the state's principal industry. The Beach Boys were dead serious in "Be True to Your School," Paul Petersen, Donna Reed's son, shamelessly extolled "The Cheerleader," in 1964, the same year the Ripchords immortalized the "One Piece Topless Bathing Suit," and the Hondells recorded "Little Honda," snazzy and effective as any TV commercial. Cars being as essential to the breezy California lifestyle as car–songs were to rock & roll, California, again, proved itself up to the task, with "GTO" by Ronny and the Daytonas, "409" by the Beach Boys, and "Drag City" by Jan and Dean, cowritten by Brian Wilson. But there were dangers on the road, especially when you could get your driver's licence in California at about the age of eight, as we heard in the unflinching and prophetic story from Jan and Dean, of "Dead Man's Curve"—where Jan Berry would lose most of his mental faculties, in a Corvette in 1966.

Eventually, Phil Spector returned to California, with his true love, Ronnie, to Gold Star Studios (now a shopping center), to surround her with a Wall of Sound—mortar of strings and overdubbed guitars, impossible castanets, plastered with saxes, two coats of drums. So far as I know, neither of them ever saw the sun. Dick Clark moved his Bandstand to L.A. in 1960, lock, stock and Top 40, a move nearly as devastating to some as the earlier exits by the Dodgers and the Giants. John Phillips, newly married to Michele, came out West after the demise of the Mugwumps, to form the Mamas and the Papas, but nearly handed his franchise dreamsong to Barry McGuire in 1965 to follow up "Eve of Destruction" (and what a mind–numbing juxtaposition "California Dreamin'" would have been to that). Brian Wilson had taken to his room by 1964, suffering from a nervous breakdown from which he would never entirely come back. But it didn't stop him from composing, in between the statutory public affairs announcements, like "Fun Fun Fun," "Dance Dance Dance," "I Get Around," and "California Sun," epics of lost loneliness that were almost East Coast in their angst

("When I Grow up [to be a Man"]). It was about this time the Beach Boys recorded Dylan's "The Times They Are a–Changing," the same year Cher was singing Dylan's "Blowin' in the Wind."

Spearheaded by Bob Dylan's rise from gutter boy to prophet laureate in the wake of a presidential assassination, an assassin assassination, a covert war uncovered in Southeast Asia, as well as church bombings and murders in southern America, Greenwich Village, during the 1963–1965 period, became a kind of mini Paris in the 1920s for a whole assortment of poets and musicians and musicians working in the mode of poets and poets operating in the image of rock stars, in a conspiracy of creativity and competitive bloodlust summed up to me by Phil Ochs, in a 1974 interview, only two years before he killed himself.

"That period in the Village was incredibly exciting, supereuphoric," he said. "There was total creativity on the part of a number of individuals that laid the bedrock for the next ten years."

It wasn't only Ochs and Dylan who were at each other's creative jugulars and also incidentally the world's. Like some kind of Calder 3–D realization of Lawrence Ferlinghetti's *A Coney Island of the Mind*, the 1960s revision of Greenwich Village, long a mystical watering hole for bohemian dreamers, during this period especially, became a magnet and an oasis (complete with mirage) for every Kerouac–inspired, "Howl"–quoting, fellow traveler who'd ever flirted with iambic pentameter (or used it as a substitute for flirting). Add to this the fact that there were more white middle–class boom babies attending college at this time than ever in the history of higher education, thus, more acoustic guitar–strumming folk/poets putting that particular elitist view of world events into rhyme in the manner of Phil and Bob, and it's easy to understand why there weren't coffee houses enough to hold their surging idealistic ivy–covered audiences. By 1964, when Dylan released his third album, *The Times They Are a–Changin'*, and appeared on the covers of *Life* and *Newsweek*, MacDougal Street alone would have about a dozen (selling grenadine at $1.25 a pop).

Few of these poets had the good fortune to be managed by Albert Grossman, who may not have then, but certainly by the time he began to sport his legendary grey ponytail, had acquired an impressive clientele, including Dylan, Peter, Paul & Mary, Paul Butterfield, Janis Joplin, Richie Havens, and the Band. It was through the Peter, Paul & Mary connection (with politely harmonic versions of "Blowin' in the Wind" and "Don't Think Twice" for public consumption), that Bob was able to leap from the coffee house circuit onto the platform of world events, like some diffident Benny Profane, jumping out of the pages of Thomas Pynchon's grandiloquent V, a reading generation's first anti–hero, bringing the Kerouac/Salinger essence hinted at in "Talking Bear Mountain Picnic," "Song to Woody" and the anti–bomb shelter lament, "Let Me Die in My Footsteps," to withering fruition on "Masters of War," "Talking World War III" and "Hard Rain's Gonna Fall," from his May, 1963 release, *The Freewheelin' Bob Dylan*.

Out of the grey flannel miasma of the Eisenhower epoch, the Kennedy promise of an elevated discourse seemed finally to be taking flesh: Joannie and Bobby, an item at all the sit–ins and marches, like Jackie and Jack. Joannie's sister, Mimi, was married to Richard Fariña, who'd gone to Cornell with Pynchon, and who was working on a novel of his own, Black Humor, of course, like Pynchon (and Joseph Heller, Philip Roth, John Barth, Donald Bartheleme, Bruce Jay Friedman, Terry Southern, Thomas Berger, and Stanley Elkin), tying the ludicrous discrepancies of the modern world into prose styles as radically individual as they were at times impenetrable. Now that Krushchev's missiles were beaten back at Castro's door, it seemed like a writer was once again something to be, whether you went for Theatre of the Absurd (Beckett, Ionesco), New Journalism (Tom Wolfe, Jimmy Breslin, Pete Hamill) or Protest Music. And if the prevailing forms were too confining, the airspace of entrenched public preconceptions too narrow for the thought–dreams of experimentation, why, you'd just have to plow through them, break new ground.

"My thought throughout this whole time period was," Ohio State's Phil Ochs suggested, "all right, here we have the form of a song. How important can a song be? Can it rival a play? Can it rival a movie? Can it make a statement that's as deep as a book? And by making a simple point, can it reach more people than a book ever can? Being a socialist, I thought, what political effect can these songs have? I saw it with my own eyes. I was writing about Vietnam in 1962. I sang the songs, and I saw they had a political effect on the audience."

To which Eric Andersen at Hobart College and Buffy Sainte–Marie at UMass and Tom Rush at Harvard and Paul Simon at Queens College, Jim McGuinn out of the Oldtown School of Folk Music, and Tuli Kupferberg, years out of Brooklyn College, and thousands of other idea–devouring college kids already hopelessly caught up in the mythos of group harmony, would necessarily concur.

Although the purported fathers of the folk scare, the Kingston Trio, claimed not to give a damn (or, depending on what radio station you listened to, a hoot) about a greenback dollar (or whether or not Pete Seeger ever got to play on *Hootenanny*), on the record charts, folk music was as big a business as it was ever going to be when the leading edge of the baby boom began to hit college in 1963: the Rooftop Singers hit number one in January, with "Walk Right In," Peter, Paul & Mary nearly got there with "Puff,

the Magic Dragon," a few months later; Trini Lopez
brought Pete Seeger's subversive campfire hymn, "If I Had
a Hammer," to the top five in September, around the same
time "Blowin' in the Wind" was cresting on the airwaves,
and "Green Green" by the New Christy Minstrels was
peaking in the top twenty. On November 9th, culminating
an unprecedented year of Civil Rights conflict and confrontation, from the bombing of a Birmingham church to
Martin Luther King's Washington D.C. "I Have a Dream"
speech (which wouldn't become a hit single until 1968,
the year he was assassinated), "We Shall Overcome" by
Joan Baez, entered the charts at number 90. Probably with
a bullet. Maybe it was mentioned that week on TV on
David Frost's satirical *That Was the Week That Was.*

And then, one morning a couple of weeks later, while
Tommy Roe, still trying to make some money as the new
Buddy Holly, was singing "Everybody" on Top 40, a
bulletin with a bullet that stopped the radio exploded out
of a secondary market known as Dallas, Texas, killing the
tranquility with a series of events that belonged in some
emerging Third World dictatorship (if not on "The Twi-
light Zone"). And in the days that followed the Kennedy
assassination, a generation brought together in the gloomy
aftermath—during which Connie Francis released "In the
Summer of His Years," one of her biggest hits since "If My
Pillow Could Talk"—could feel a certain existential universal vulnerability beyond anything it had been prepared
for in its collective life. Leaderless—godless? parentless?
—we might have fallen prey to anarchy, communists in the
quads, Billy Graham on the tube. Kennedy–Oswald–Ruby
–Johnson–The Warren Report. It was Theatre of the
Absurd/Black Humor/Protest Music in real life. As far as
the baby boom collegiate constituency went, only one
fringe group of players could have had the will, the wit,
and the cynicism to translate this potential for alienation,

paranoia, chaos, into life–affirming, anti–authoritarian tunes for a generation about to make a huge turn toward the left of center.

In 1964, Dylan wrote "He Was a Friend of Mine," "The Times They Are a–Changing," "Chimes of Freedom," and "I Don't Believe You." Richard Fariña wrote "Pack up Your Sorrows" and "Birmingham Sunday." Pete Seeger hit the charts with Malvina Reynolds's "Little Boxes." Buffy Sainte–Marie wrote "Universal Soldier" and "It's My Way." Phil Ochs wrote "Too Many Martyrs" and "Bound for Glory." Tom Paxton wrote "Rambling Boy" and "I Can't Help But Wonder Where I'm Bound." Paul Simon wrote "Sounds of Silence" and "He Was My Brother." If ever there was a time ripe for a true musical revolution, born of the collective voice of the idealistic settlers along the New Frontier, it was in 1964.

But then, somehow, embodying Pete Seeger's adaptation of the Book of Ecclesiastes—which was turned into a number one summertime hit by the Byrds in 1965 under the title of "Turn! Turn! Turn!"—about everything having its season, and every purpose having a time, what finally came over the radio, as soon as the radio started playing songs again, came not from the folk music of the left, the anarchic rebel energy of Black Humor and New Journalism, experimental films and Theatre of the Absurd loose in the land, but from across the pond in England, where, suddenly, after years of dues and demos and moldy dates in the caverns and caves of Europe, it was deigned time for the Beatles to resurrect the humpbacked carcass of American pop!

Hollyesque, named in tribute to Buddy's band, the Crickets, with Everly Brothers' harmonies, Little Richard shrieks, and Carnaby Street suits, Eton haircuts, Alistair Cooke–hosting–*Omnibus* accents, and Brill Building aspirations, it was the Beatles mission, it seemed, to restore on the airwaves and thus in the intuitive, subterranean psyche of the culture, the kind of above–the–waist, below–the–neck, loves–me–loves–me–not equanimity we had before the shootings; way before the shootings, in fact—before the victim ever rose to power—all the way back, if you must know, to 1959, arriving here on a transatlantic flight on February 7, 1964, exactly five years to the week after their nearly–namesake band's leader went down in a much smaller plane over a field in Iowa.

Who was greasing the wheels while the Beatles dominated the pop charts of 1964 like no act since Elvis, expunging even the name of Elvis from the ranks of the top ten for the first year since 1956—Alan Freed's tax accountant? Barry Goldwater's press agent? If we were so hungry for British pop, how come Cliff Richard took twenty–seven years to make it over here, and Cilla Black couldn't penetrate the top thirty on the Beatles' tailored coattails? How come the great Hank Marvin and the Shadows couldn't make it across the water at all? I mean, it took Lonnie Donnegan five long years to follow up his 1956 skiffle fluke, "Rock Island Line," with "Does Your Chewing Gum Lose Its Flavor on the Bedpost Overnight," in 1961, so it wasn't as if yodelin' Frank Ifield's 1962 ditty, "I Remember You," suddenly unleashed a tribal flood of Rita Tushingham fantasies on an adolescent nation that still referred to Acker ("Stranger on the Shore") Bilk as Mister. Otherwise, why would Ifield have stiffed on the charts of 1964 in January with the hardly subtle entreaty "Please"? Actually, it was more like the kind of demented irony you'd find lampooned on "The Goon Show." Or else, I suspect, it had to be the work of Bond. James Bond.

Suggesting a refined soothing of the Beat, rather than junior Beatniks, the sassy badinage with which the Beatles greeted the members of the working entertainment press (the police reporter bringing along his adolescent daughter as interpreter) may have been nothing compared to Dylan's already daunting sarcasm—which would be brought to high performance art on his subsequent *Don't Look Back* tour of England in 1965—but it was certainly more chipper than anything a pre–Beatles rock neanderthal might have been permitted to utter. And although their surface output may have contained enough ersatz versifying to fill a Hallmark hackies quota for a decade of Valentine's Days, it was nonetheless at least the equal of a dozen separate Brill Building partnerships. They'd done their homework, as good little Preppies should, peppering their club act with Chuck Berry covers, Little Richard covers, Brill Building and Motown covers. As Liverpudlians, they were even more exotic and lower in class, yet far safer than blacks—so who better to reinvent the dangerous delights of rock & roll without the actual danger?

No need to censor the Beatles; in the midst of America's covert war buildup, they weren't even draftable. They filled 1964 with the sound of "Yeah, Yeah, Yeah . . . " Every label that had previously rejected their demos rushed to the cutout bins to reclaim and release their abandoned product, creating a logjam at the top of the charts that resulted in the Beatles occupying, during one week in April, numbers one through five on the Top 10—a week that, apparently, even sainted Bob Dylan, who had never previously admitted to owning a radio, took note of, briefly, in between ceaselessly firing out prolix gems of eloquent confusion, astonishing verbosity and meter, even a 144–line tone poem to Woody Guthrie that he recited one night at Carnegie Hall, raging, ravished verse no greeting card honcho could ever have concocted a holiday for. There were battles coming, he prophesized, just up the road, that would rattle the walls of the city—to which the Beatles responded "I Want to Hold Your Hand." There were these shipwrecked alienated refugees of American corporate splendor that Dylan perceived growing like a crowd around the scene of a grizzly accident, spreading like a contagious giggle at a gravesite. To them, and to their mistreated, hung–up compatriots, just coming into being every Saturday night in front of Feejons or the Kettle of Fish, the visiting Beatles crooned "Love Me Do," with John Lennon's neat harmonica part evoking 1962.

Love being just another four–letter word to Dylan, who was in the middle of inspiring a multitude of peers to not only jump off the wedding cake but out of the socialization process entirely in "It Ain't Me, Babe," it's hard to imagine what kind of chuckles were running through his mind as he hummed "Can't Buy Me Love" in the Waverly Theatre, watching the Beatles cavorting across the screen in *A Hard Day's Night*. Like Elvis, one of the Beatles' instant American Dream perks was the ability to be cast as themselves in a movie. Elvis, in fact, was still at it, starring that year in *Viva, Las Vegas,* which I'm certain the Beatles meant to see if and when they got a chance. But it was with the wacky Marx Brothers' cum cinema verite slapstick of the Richard Lester flick, in fact, that the Beatles began to gradually win over the first recalcitrant converts from the academia of folk politics and poetry, to their world plan; namely "I Feel Fine." Dylan's own eventual filmic debut in D.A. Pennybaker's *Don't Look Back* (which was not released until 1967), revealed a persona closer to Karl than Harpo, but maybe not so much unlike Groucho after all. Of course, by then, he'd long since become anathema to any sort of happy media head, having walked off "The Ed Sullivan Show" and roundly excoriated TV talk show host Les Crane and his earnest Hollywood crooner/actor guest Tommy Sands, when Les had the temerity to book them both on his evening chat–fest, soon after the release of *Bringing It All Back Home* in 1965, about the time the Beatles were making their second movie, *Help!* and Elvis his eighteenth and nineteenth (*Girl Happy* and *Harum Scarum*).

Actually, for all the average American (even the average baby boom teenager) needed or noticed the denizens of the Greenwich Village folk scare, the Beatles had the popularity contest won from the beginning, on the only place where it counted, the radio, hands down. After a year of "Yeah, yeah, yeah," the Empire was thought to be pretty much restored, *Dr. Strangelove* notwithstanding. Goodbye Marilyn Monroe, hello Mandy Rice–Davies. But oddly enough, all the stuff we imported from England in the rush of profit–taking that accompanied the Beatles emergence as a force for good retrogressive corporate rock & roll in the image of Dick Clark, albeit slightly more hirsute, was in actuality the work of desperate pockmarked souls who lurked down by the local docks in search of American blues albums whenever they came in on black market boats, purloining discs like they were Spearmints and Lucky Strikes from an earlier generation of American GIs. Forget surf music, in Brighton the locals kept their coats on even at the beach (although they'd sometimes change into their bathing suits underneath them, a fashion quirk that would be quickly co–opted and expanded upon in San Francisco within the year). Forget anything resembling a vibrant rock & roll culture: in England there was one radio station, the BBC, virtually the voice of the conservative government. Anything revolutionary, or even remotely dicey, simply never made the cut. When it came to your buttoned–up essence of prudery, England was Boston's guru in the cause of right–thinking seventeenth–century morality.

Where the Beatles brand of blues generally went no further than Little Richard and Chuck Berry, many of their cohorts on the same circuit started there. The Rolling Stones were into Muddy Waters's "I'm a King Bee" and "I

Just Want to Make Love to You," Memphis soul from Rufus Thomas ("Walking the Dog"), R&B from Marvin Gaye ("Can I Get a Witness"). They probably smoked cigarettes and slept with older women. The Animals' lead singer, Eric Burdon, sounded black, and looked like a longshore-man. He reached into folk antiquity for "House of the Rising Sun." You could imagine him being a bouncer there, in New Orleans, shining Fats Domino's shoes. In 1965 they took John Lee Hooker's "Boom Boom" to the top 40. Manfred Mann was partial to Howling Wolf ("Smokestack Lightning"), Muddy's "Got My Mojo Work-ing," Willie Dixon's "I'm Your Hoochie Coochie Man." The Yardbirds were ahead of all of them. This was the band that featured in succession the cream of England's white blues guitarists: Eric Clapton, Jeff Beck, and session-hound, Jimmy Page (there wouldn't be a black blues guitarist coming out of England until they imported James Marshall Hendrix from Seattle in 1966, managed by Chas Chandler, ex–bassist of the Animals) and let them loose on "Good Morning, Little Schoolgirl," Howling Wolf's "Five Long Years" and "Smokestack Lightning," and Bo Diddley's "I'm a Man," in endless orgiastic flurries of liberation from the blue–nosed outside world, called rave –ups, during which, one undoubtedly drizzly night, the notion may have emanated from the bandstand that Eric Clapton was, much to his eventual consternation, if not embarrassment, God.

God was replaced in the Yardbirds by Jeff Beck, and moved on to John Mayall's Bluesbreakers, an even bluesier outfit, where his playing was sufficiently otherworldly and yet rootsy as the very Deltas of Stratford–on–Avon. In the meanwhile, Peter & Gordon, who looked like a couple of Oxford loafers, were enjoying the number one position on the charts, with a decidedly unbluesy Lennon and McCartney tune, "A World without Love." But even they, on their own private victrola, were learning American folk songs like "All My Trials," "Five Hundred Miles," and "Trouble in Mind." Of course, the market for pop being what the Beatles were designated by the vicissitudes of 1964 to represent, like grateful and gracious Miss Americas, blues leaning, folk sympathizing, rowdy or raucous specimens of the English demi–monde fell by the wayside in favor of the Newbeats ("Bread and Butter"), J. Frank Wilson and the Cavaliers ("Last Kiss"), the Zombies ("She's Not There"), the Dave Clark Five ("Because," "Bits and Pieces," "Glad All Over"), Gerry and the Pacemakers ("Don't Let the Sun Catch You Crying," "How Do You Do It"), the Kinks ("You Really Got Me"), Chad & Jeremy ("A Summer Song"), Billy J. Kramer ("Little Children," "Bad to Me"), the Bachelors ("Diane") all sharing the top ten (Herman and the Hermits peaked at number 13 with "I'm into Something Good," written by Goffin & King) with eleven different Beatle tunes (twelve if you count Peter & Gordon's cover). The Stones finally joined the party in December, with "Time Is on My Side," but not before striking out with "Not Fade Away," written by Buddy Holly. Manfred Mann's journey to number one with "Do Wah Diddy Diddy," by the Shangri–Las' godparents, Jeff Barry and Ellie Greenwich, had to be a bittersweet victory to their fans. But if establishment acceptance was even the least bit in doubt, before the summer was over, you'd have the Hollyridge Strings and their Musak version of "All My Loving," and the venerated Boston Pops, under the baton of Arthur "Meet Me at the Marquee" Fiedler, covering "I Want to Hold Your Hand." By December, sensing the drift, the Village Stompers left Washington Square and recorded "Fiddler on the Roof."

So, folk music was dead on the charts. But blues was alive. And magic was afoot. James Brown was getting back on the good foot. And B.B. King was appearing live at the

Regal in Chicago, where Michael Bloomfield and Paul Butterfield, and National Merit Scholarship refugee Elvin Bishop were somewhere within earshot. John Hammond Jr. was routinely being mistaken for the pale ghost of Robert Johnson at coffee houses up and down the eastern seaboard, where his sideman, Jimmy James, late of the Isley Brothers band and Joey Dee's band, played guitar behind his back and with his teeth, like the second coming of T-Bone Walker, who was himself picking up spare change at private parties hosted by Steve Miller's father. Young Steve sat in sometimes on guitar over at Pepper's, on Chicago's Southside, and the regulars, like Buddy Guy and Hubert Sumlin, Otis Rush, Muddy, and Howling Wolf accepted him, adopted him, like they did Tracy Nelson, when she came down from Madison, to record her album, *Deep Are the Roots*, which opened up with "Starting from Chicago."

But in Detroit, in 1965, as well as in Newark, as well as in Watts, and elsewhere, in the wake of Lyndon Johnson's mandate for a Great Society, with liberty, equality, and racial justice for all, there were the opening salvos of a televised revolution, in living color, in which the separation of blacks and whites started to get vivid. Luckily, at Motown Records, the writers did not reflect in their lyrics a distinctly black attitude or experience. Neither did they reflect the writer's own attitude or experience. Or even the performers'. The performers could have been interchangable. Smokey Robinson & the Vandellas. The Four Temptations. Diana Reeves & the Marvellettes. Little Stevie Supreme. Not that the tunes weren't great, a super-fine assembly–lined pop/R&B operetta, mainly written by the Holland brothers, Brian and Eddie, and Lamont Dozier—former Atlantic recording artist with the Romeos —who reported dutifully for work from nine to six each day, from 1963 on, crafting, out of a cubbyhole office above the recording studio in the main building that came to be dubbed Hitsville, USA, approximately a hit a week, starting with "Locking up My Heart" and "Come and Get These Memories," the stuff of endless K–Tel repackagings. In their own invigorating, bass–dominated way, they were right up there on a par with Lennon and McCartney 1964, as locked in as the Brill Building 1959–1962. No wonder the Beatles made sure to schedule a tour of Motown. Even Bob Dylan, allegedly so far above the mundane fray to be bothered with such things, came by for a lunch, and left calling Smokey Robinson America's finest poet since Nick Kenny.

Motown never pretended to be anything other than a factory, the only difference being that blacks held the keys to the executive washroom, and shared, maybe, in the profits. In attempting to redress the imbalance blacks had experienced in recouping the riches that were their rightful share of the American rock & roll pie, Berry Gordy Jr. went to great pains grooming his progeny, fixing their diction, while giving them dictation, offering choreography lessons in the mail room, backup singing gigs after school, the Motortown Review after graduation. There were makeup people, sound people, engineers, producers. Why, I couldn't exactly pick him out, but you could have taken a black Fabian off the streets of Detroit in 1964 and 1965 and, with the help of a Smokey Robinson, a Lamont Dozier, the Holland brothers, Bennie Benjamin, and James Jamerson, turned him into minor national legend.

So, while the Civil Rights Movement was going the way of folk music, and "The Beverly Hillbillies" was the top show on the tube, Diana Ross & the Supremes were going from "Stop! In the Name of Love" to "Back in My Arms Again" to "Nothing but Heartaches" to "I Hear a Symphony"—to the very selfsame Copacabana in New York that devoured Bobby Darin and the rest of Bronx's best apostles of do–wop back in . . . wait, don't say it . . . that halycon year of 1959.

Elsewhere, however, in black music, more authentic heads were attempting to prevail. The Impressions brought some gospel perspective to "Amen," "People Get Ready," and "Meeting over Yonder." In Memphis, the spirit of black pride in the face of adversity was embodied in 1963–1964 by Rufus Thomas's adventures with his dog ("The Dog," "Walking the Dog," "Can Your Monkey Do the Dog," and "Somebody Stole My Dog") and in 1964–1965 by Otis Redding's epic journey from "Security" to "Respect," James Brown's trailblazing off–the–beaten funk of "Papa's Got a Brand New Bag," Marvin Gaye ("I'll Be Doggone," "Ain't That Peculiar"), Wilson Pickett ("In the Midnight Hour"), and Aretha Franklin ("Running out of Fools"). Sam Cooke answered Bob Dylan's "Blowin' in the Wind" with his own wistful "A Change Is Gonna Come," released posthumously, after Sam was shot on Christmas Eve, 1964.

Sure enough, in 1965, the inevitable change did come, in spite of the best efforts of the keepers of the status quo to forestall it, via Bob Dylan's collaboration with the members of Paul Butterfield's Blues Band ("Born in Chicago," "Mystery Train") at the hallowed Newport Folk Festival. The same steamy summer when Phil Ochs was writing things like "In the Heat of the Summer," "Here's to the State of Mississippi," "I Ain't Marchin' Anymore," and "Draft Dodger Rag," and Eric Anderson wrote "Thirsty Boots," the Beatles dropped their love song fetish to cry for "Help!" because the eastern world was exploding at the top of the charts in Barry McGuire's "Eve of Destruction."

Living under the same sky as the rest of us, the glorious incessant sway of Motown, the Beatles, Phil Spector trying to reclaim, or at least retain, that lovin' feeling, and, especially, the Byrds' transforming "Mr. Tambourine

Man" into a national hit, Dylan came to realize the awesome power of rock & roll (as well as, not incidentally, the rock & roll constituency, i.e. the educated white baby boom bandstand graduates). His subsequent assault on the pristine ears of an acoustic generation passing away in front of his eyes like Mississippi John Hurt was his parting shot to the moldy figs who'd nurtured him like a prize begonia. He would cast his lot with the Chicago blues folks up North, the rock/folks out West. With Dylan's urban subterranean blues nightmares plugged into the anthem potential of rock & roll, why, there was nothing to prevent him from feeling like a Beatle, or better, just like a rolling stone.

Four

The Walls of the City Shake

(1964–1966)

As in tune as he was in most other regards relating to the unseen psychic dreamwaves of the multitudes, by forming a rock band in 1965, Dylan was just slightly behind the rest of his contemporaries, approximately 98 percent of whom came to that decision on the morning after the night they saw the Beatles on "The Ed Sullivan Show," in February, 1964.

Despite the mush they were lip–synching ("'Til There Was You"!), there was something about their collective tongue–in–cheek persona, Ringo's bobbling head maybe, the implicit wink in John and Paul's onstage communication, that suggested the possiblity that the job of a player in a rock & roll band might not be too awful a middle class fantasy after all. Looking at their clothes, especially their hair, you got the feeling you really wouldn't have to be Danny & the Juniors, in a baggy zoot suit, working nights and New Year's Eves, and eating leftovers in the kitchen while the bride danced the kazotsky with her father–in–law. No, in the image of the Beatles was suggested all things suave and scintillating. They were humorous; they were literate; collectively they'd not only read a book, John Lennon had written one.

For the working musicians of the time, of course, the issue was a bit more pragmatic. "I remember walking down the street just before I left New York," Dylan's mentor in this regard, Roger McGuinn, Jim at the time, recounted. It was 1964, and he had bangs like John Sebastian and acoustic guitar chops like Pete Seeger. He'd just electrified his twelve string because he saw George Harrison playing one like that in *Help!* "There were these club owners who said, 'What we need is four of him.' That's when I knew I had something that would work." That's when he left his secure position in Bobby Darin's backup band to set out for California to form the Beefeaters, which later became the Byrds, the first of the folk–based bands to use rock instruments in the service of their utopian vision of electrified group harmony, aka Dylan's "Mr. Tambourine Man."

With much the same reasoning, many of McGuinn's Greenwich Village baskethouse confreres were also assessing their future direction, among them John Phillips, who put together the Mugwumps, with Zal Yanofsky; John Sebastian, the first–call harmonica hand, who sometimes sat in with them, stayed home, eventually stealing Zal for the Lovin' Spoonful, leaving Phillips free to split with Michele for the Virgin Islands, where they would form the Mamas and the Papas with John's folk scene pals, Cass Elliot and Denny Doherty; Steven Stills, who wended his way west for his fateful encounter with Neil Young's hearse in a Los Angeles traffic jam that resulted in the formation of Buffalo Springfield; Peter Tork, a Maynard Krebsian banjo–picker who'd flunked out of the same school twice in Wisconsin, plucked from the Tuesday hoot at the Gaslight, dusted off, and shipped, like a Beverly hillbilly, to become a Monkee in Hollywood; Paul Simon, who'd been knocking his brains out with one stiff after another since junior high, finally reverting to the accounting firm handle of Simon & Garfunkel for a pitiful stab at commercial folk music a la the Kingston Trio in a suit and tie ("You Can Tell the World," "Go Tell It on the Mountain," "Last Night I Had the Strangest Dream"), before buying a plane ticket to England, where he was fully prepared to live out the rest of his life as a folk–singing busker.

And so, riot–torn 1965 produced as fine a white AM radio summer at the top of the charts as a college–age audience of rock & roll literate, cynical, slightly hirsute soulmates could ever have wanted, most of them receiving it on their transistors as they hitchhiked from east to west to the tune of "Cast Your Fate to the Wind" by the Vince Guaraldi Trio, dragging knapsacks and harmonicas, reliving Kerouac approaching mystic Denver, high on electric energy and endless possibility, starting in June with the Byrds hitting number one with "Mr. Tambourine Man," followed by a month of "(I Can't Get No) Satisfaction" by the Stones; "I Got You Babe" by Sonny and Cher, displaced the regrettable "I'm Henry VIII, I Am" by Herman's Hermits in August, followed by "Help!," "Eve of Destruction," and Dylan's six–minute, rule–shattering epic, "Like a Rolling Stone," the organ part by Al Kooper of the Royal Teens, straight out of Max Crook cum Carlton Lattimore, whose peaking at number two represented a moral victory of such magnitiude that the song may as well have gone the final inch.

The rest of the year wasn't too shabby for Dylan, careerwise, either. Both Cher and the Byrds had hits with "All I Really Want to Do." The Turtles, previously better known as the Crossfires ("Santa and the Sidewalk Surfer," 1963) blasted to the top 10 with "It Ain't Me, Babe." The Wonder Who revived "Don't Think Twice," with a Frankie Valli falsetto. Even Elvis recorded Dylan's "Tomorrow Is a

Long Time," for inclusion in the movie *Spinout*. By the end of the year (which had opened with the serendipitous and eminently quotable "Subterranean Homesick Blues"), Dylan had scored again, with the acerbic "Positively 4th Street." And although that tale purportedly put down many of his so–called backstabbing so–called friends, Dylan's commercial success was nothing if not egalitarian; the wealth cascaded down the streets of Greenwich Village. Joan Baez hit the charts with "There But for Fortune," by Phil Ochs. The Spoonful's "Do You Believe in Magic" went to number seven in October. Glen Campbell made a hit out of Buffy Sainte–Marie's "Universal Soldier." By then, even Andy Warhol was sponsoring a rock & roll group, hiring the Velvet Underground to provide an underscore for his experimental films. By then, even crotchety word–poets like Ed Sanders and Tuli Kupferberg had begun to sense the power of a rock & roll beat to transform the merely linear into the stuff that could make the young girls cry. Leonard Cohen, the Canadian poet and novelist, was reportedly seen, a guitar on his back, looking for a room at the Chelsea Hotel in which to store his typewriter. Richard Fariña was completing his novel, *Been Down So Long It Looks Like Up to Me*, along with the second Dick and Mimi folk/rock album, *Reflections in a Crystal Wind* (the Judy Collins version of Fariña's "Hard Lovin' Loser" would make the top one hundred in 1967). And among everybody else who hung out in front of the Night Owl Cafe, at the corner of MacDougal and West 3rd Street, seventeen hours a day, six days a week, the redeemed believers in the magic of their own homegrown kind of rock & roll, close friends of Buzzy Linhart, Freddy Neil, and Tim Hardin, who'd left that corner only once in their lives, to journey uptown to pack Carnegie Recital Hall the night Richie Havens played there (Richie's cover of the Beatles' "Here Comes the Sun" would hit the top twenty in 1971), it was safe to say, a monumental evolutionary consensus had been reached.

"Yeah," the Byrd, McGuinn, explained, summarizing the historic moment, "Dylan was real and the Beatles were plastic. Then the Beatles got more authentic and Dylan got more top 40."

Part of the credit, many believe, must go to the brand of hallucinogens the Beatles were ingesting, bestowed upon them by McGuinn, when the Byrds, posing as "The American Beatles" (for whom we got in return, Donovan, "The English Dylan"), toured England for the first time, and, as "John Lennon's favorite American band" got an audience with the fab four.

"We'd seal ourselves up in a bathroom, get the security guys out of there, and all take acid and sit on the floor and play guitars," McGuinn recalled nostalgically.

With the year 1965 coming to an AM finale, culminated by "Yesterday" by the Beatles, "Get off My Cloud" by the Rolling Stones, and "Turn! Turn! Turn!" by the Byrds, written by Pete Seeger, followed by Paul Simon opening up 1966 by being summoned back from England to find "The Sounds of Silence" a folk–rock hit, and the Beatles finishing January off with "We Can Work It Out," it was easy to see why the enormous, white, college–bound or majoring in liberal arts, baby boom audience, formed from the alliance between Dylan and the Beatles—folk/rock—started about then to entertain thoughts of a universal bohemianism, and all the exotic delights lurking therein, by dumping college entirely, for the free–spirited neo-beatnik dream of sex, dope, and rock & roll.

It was at this time that you began to see, one to a neighborhood at first, then multiplying like the miraculous, instant sales of a hit single, guys appearing on the periphery of events, watching the weekly softball game from outside the chain link fence, say, or several seats

down from you on the subway, who had obviously not paid
a visit to Tony or Mario or Nunzio at the barber shop in a
year, years, who had sideburns like Abe Lincoln, like
Ozark Ike, muttonchops, and hair way past the artsy
unkempt boy–genius level, to the shoulders, in a page boy,
like Doris Day!

Now, despite a legacy of ducktails, slicked back with
Max Factor's Crew Cut, as a still basically God–fearing,
government–fearing, parent–fearing, cop–fearing, teacher–fearing, dream–fearing, impulse–fearing, shadow–
fearing generation of conformist young men, hair, to the
baby boom crowd, was in 1964 and into 1965, as it had
been in 1959 (did Kookie lend Connie Stevens his comb?
He did not!)—as it had been in the days of Delilah—a
symbol as much as a statement, of manhood, maybe, cool,
possibly, but more than any of that, of true, staunch,
steadfast, regular guyness. It was at the barber shop that
boys and men alike sought refuge from the indignities of
heterosexual domesticity. Where brother and brother,
where father and son (and often grandfather, if only for a
trim), where teammates, buddies, neighbors, and total
strangers huddled together telling dirty jokes and making
locker room noises, leafing through worn copies of *Saga*
and *True Detective*, and occasionally ogling babes as they
passed by the plateglass window on their way to the A&P.
At the barber shop you got to be a redneck once a month,
for a dollar, in those days, plus tip. It was a rite of passage,
not unlike going fishing or getting a tattoo—only it was a
lot less smelly than the former, and certainly more revers-
ible than the latter.

Imagine, then, the terrible tremors of guilt the first time
you passed by the barber shop, your dollar clutched in
your hand, to waste it on eggcreams instead of your
monthly scalping, the elemental childhood memories
wrenched out of you, of camaraderie and belonging,

parental to say nothing of female approval. All brought on by the Beatles, who weren't even American, and risked nothing with their moptopped conceits. It wasn't John or Paul or George or Ringo who had to one day muster up the incredible courage necessary to ask Nunzio to let their sideburns grow. Who had sideburns after all in those days but grease monkeys and people on the lam, and kids with commercial diplomas? It was these lonely longhaired freaks, not the Beatles, not even Dylan, who were the generational avatars, the vanguard of societal progress down the ladder of propriety into the spiraling whirlpool of utter and ultimate deviance. Once hair edged out past the collar toward the middle of the back, crossing the line between merely needing a haircut and the conscious decision to let it grow, and people began to revel in the feel of it, and even the look of it, and were willing to take their lumps and get kicked off the team or thrown out of school just to keep it, there was virtually no predicting where it would end, no bottom, no limits, no ties (no neckties). If a president could be murdered, after all, his purported killer murdered on television, and the double murders covered up, what was the point of following the middle class rulebook anymore in a world where no one else did?

We were out of the house now, in college, and having sex with Joannie and Maria and Marcy Blaine if we damn well felt like it, or dropped out of college and living with all three of them, in a four room apartment, and paying the rent with money from home, or panhandling to make up the deficit. We celebrated our massive independence to the sound of an electric blues guitar renaissance, sending cataclysmic decibels into the black night of the Delta moon, accompanied by approximately a hundred thousand tambourines, Richie Havens's stomping right foot, John Sebastian's twinkling autoharp, Lothar (John Emelin) & the Hand People's theramin, and a garage band Farfisa organ explosion seemingly out of every basement window. Parents no longer ruled our world (only their checkbooks); rock & roll did, LSD did. We could go into the bowling alley any time we wanted now, day or night—and we didn't want to go! They wanted us in the army, but we didn't want to go there either. In the new order, there would be no more war! Since the old order was still nominally in effect, however, we would have to outsmart it. As the most intellectual generation ever to occupy the planet all at the same time, some of us did this merely by uprooting our lives and moving to Canada, or staying in school for a Ph.D. in Earth Science, or simply ingesting so many drugs we went crazy.

Certainly the folks in the record industry seemed to be staunch devotees of the latter course of action, laying wheelbarrows full of money at the doorsteps of former business majors lately sprouting full beards and Vox amplifiers, philosophy majors playing tambourines and writing mantras, sociology dropouts on wacky weed imitating Ma Rainey in front of amphetamine guitarists and a blissfully snoozing and/or grooving outdoor assembly, who would then rush home and plunk down a ten spot for the album.

"I walked into an office and the guy asked me what I wanted," said Marty Balin, when he went to L.A. to negotiate the Jefferson Airplane's first contract in 1966, with RCA records, undoubtedly with some feathered protege of Steve Scholes, who'd given Elvis all that money in 1955 and Neil Sedaka, hopefully, something less, in 1959. "I said, 'We want fifty thousand dollars.' He said, 'Okay, what else do you want?' Done. I had said it off the top of my head, jokingly, and he said okay, what next? I didn't know what to say."

What could you say? (Actually, you have to wonder what Marty Balin did say when Steve Miller, only a year or so later, was handed a reported six hundred grand by another toadying chump for his unproven and largely illusory talent.) Spoiled by our parents as kids, and accustomed to getting our way, and having our every move turned into evolutionary rhapsodies in the press, this middle class takeover of rock & roll was more than just the latest Twist in our epic adventures in self–absorption; it was, for all extents and purposes, designed to be the end of rock & roll—and the start of our own form of it, called rock. With egos sky high, our birthright would be the challenge of remaking the world in our own image! Compared to that, avoiding the draft, stopping the war, creating a blissful utopia according to an as yet unformed but certainly rock–inspired agenda, would be a piece of cake.

The first official reflection of the elevation of rock past rock & roll and into the artsy, occurred in 1966, with the ushering in of the Album Era. There was such an onslaught of provocative, folk–tinged, blues–powered, pop–informed, and at least somewhat English Lit 101–influenced music coming from our leading artists in the album format that a delirious fan albeit on a fairly unlimited budget would have had to give up pizza and Ritalin for a month to keep abreast of it. It was here that the Beatles professionalism and craftsmanship and sheer glorious abundance finally lifted them beyond a doubt past the pop prodigy stage, into the realms of the mythical. In *Rubber Soul* (released in December, 1965), their breakthrough could be heard in "Think for Yourself," "The Word," "I'm Looking through You," "Run for Your Life," and especially in John Lennon's poignant "In My Life," and quizzically near–eastern "Norwegian Wood." In *Yesterday and Today* (June, 1966), social satire surfaced with "Nowhere Man," "Dr. Robert," "Day Tripper." In *Revolver* (August!), the drug culture was upon us: "Yellow Submarine" (a code for LSD, of course), "Good Day Sunshine" (Sunshine was another brand of potent lysergic acid), "Tomorrow Never

Knows" (had they met the Swami by then?), "Taxman" (protest music) and the lovely "Eleanor Rigby" (humanistic character portrait, complete with a string of trumpets).

The Rolling Stones, suitably impressed, followed up their singles collection, *High Tide* and *Green Grass* (March, 1966), with the June release of *Aftermath*, with the more courtly, almost Elizabethan, "Lady Jane," balanced by the properly noxious "Under My Thumb," the angry, sitar–dominated "Paint It, Black." Peter Townshend, holed up in a flat with two tape recorders and plenty of LSD, was listening intently. Encouraged by his manager, Kit Lambert, and the optimistic tenor of the times, he was already contemplating rock operas while writing "My Generation" and "The Kids Are Alright." There was a mini opera, "A Quick One While He's Away," on the *Happy Jack* album of 1966, of which Paul McCartney himself took note, pausing in the Beatles' efforts toward the millennial *Sergeant Pepper*, to tell Townshend he'd heard his work and been affected by it. Which is not to say Townshend ever returned the compliment.

"I was never influenced by them," he told me a few years later. "I mean, musically, a lot of it was melodic in a way that, although it sounded great when they did it, when you tried to find out what it was that made it tick, and react to it musically, it was very much like Italian lovesongs. How can you be influenced by that?"

On the other hand, how could you not be influenced by it, at least by the widespread acceptance of the Beatles far–reaching musicality, with which Dylan and his subjects gave voice to otherwise verboten material, the popular form exploding into total contemporary relevance, outstripping, for a time, with its speedy pipeline to the marketplace, all the other experimental forms rampant in the fertile and accepting, college–dominated landscape— plays, poetry, books, journalism, films—as the most vital and immediate artistic response to current events. In January, Dick & Mimi Fariña's *Reflections in a Crystal Wind* contained the rousingly cynical "House Un–American Blues Activity Dream," the eerie, perceptive "Mainline Prosperity Blues." In February, Eric Andersen came out with *'Bout Changes & Things*, with his two classics, the post–coital (and/or post–trippy) "Violets of Dawn," and the Civil Rights marching song, "Thirsty Boots." At the same time, the Byrds, on *Turn! Turn! Turn!* sang Dylan's "He Was a Friend of Mine" and "Lay Down Your Weary Tune." They added their own contributions to folk/rock's liberating oeuvre: "Set You Free This Time" and "It Won't Be Wrong." Phil Ochs, caught live in his April release, sang his latest outrageous editorials, detailing stuff still deemed unfit for newspapers like the *New York Times* to print: "The Marines Have Landed on the Shores of Santo Domingo," "Cops of the World," "The Ringing of Revolution," and the not–so–tongue–in–cheek, "Love Me, I'm a Liberal," presciently predicting the imminent demise of the baby boomers' favorite political stance, less a party than a Party. *The Fugs* and *Virgin Fugs* (comprised of their early stuff) came out, adding apocalyptic, if not apoplectic, tunes like "Group Grope," "Kill for Peace," "Morning Morning," and "Saran Wrap," "Coca–Cola Douche," "My Bed Is Getting Crowded," "CIA Man," and "I Saw the Best Minds of My Generation Rot" to their abundant repertoire of eminently scatological sociology.

And then, in May, predating the release by at least a month of Elvis Presley's latest flick, *Paradise Hawaiian Style* (featuring the enduring "Queenie Wahine's Papaya"), Dylan's four–sided *Blonde on Blonde* and the Beach Boys' *Pet Sounds* both hit the stores. The Lovin' Spoonful's latest, *Daydream*, came out that month, as well, propelled by the good–time title hit, their credo, "Jug Band Music," and "You Didn't Have to Be So Nice." But *Pet Sounds* was on another level; Brian Wilson, like Phil Spector before him, and Captain Video before him, attempting to become a master of his spaced out universe. Permanently off the beach, Brian devoted himself to the sounds rumbling in his head like far–off waves, slicing, dicing, overdubbing like a madman—twelve violins, four saxes, two basses on "Let's Go Away for a While"—reaching for everything he'd ever remembered from music appreciation—oboes, flutes, french horns, bass clarinet, harpsichord, accordian, theramin (later to turn up on "Good Vibrations," which he was writing at the same time), including the voices of his favorite pets, the dogs Banana and Louie on "Caroline, No"—even going so far as to record a couple of tunes at Spector's Gold Star studios. Lyrically, his collaborators interpreted his increasing agitation—possibly brought on by his increasing exposure to mind–opening/altering/ruining drugs—which mirrored our own: "Here Today," "God Only Knows," "I Know There's an Answer," "Wouldn't It Be Nice" and the sadly ironic "I Just Wasn't Made for These Times" (ironic either in that he was too advanced for his time—the album wasn't one of his biggest sellers, "God Only Knows" and "Caroline, No" barely made the Top 40—or not advanced enough—as an album artist, world class composer, and philosopher king, this was his peak). On the other hand, Paul McCartney, fresh from contemplating *Happy Jack*, and still working on his own magnum opus, pronounced *Pet Sounds* "the album of all–time."

Many others save that kudo for *Blonde on Blonde*, in which Dylan went over whatever lines he himself had drawn in the sands of perception. If "I Want You," "Rainy Day Women #12 & 35," and "Leopard Skin Pillbox Hat," clung to an accessible urban bluesy framework, in "Visions of Johanna," "Memphis Blues Again," "Just Like a Woman" and "Sad Eyed Lady of the Lowlands" he was almost

certainly, in sports lingo, "out of his mind." Merging the
Black Humor of everyday anti–authoritarian middle class
outlaw existence in the war zone of emotional, social,
governmental, and sexual politics, the stark poetry with
which he illuminated his own and the thinking public's
psychic landscape, was a brand of personal reportage that
leaped past New Journalism straight into Gospel, with a
cinemascopic vision that was less the product of specific
drugs, than the same heavy drug of immense fame the
Beatles were sniffing daily in the air like morning dew, the
mantle of poet laureate embedded with Shakespearean
sweat on the collar, living legendhood like an elixir, the o.j.
of the left brain. Could you drive a motorcycle, drunk on
that stuff?

Hardly had the free, white, and twenty–one–and–
under world time to absorb what would prove to be Dylan's
last gasp as leader of rock & roll's expanded consciousness
and literary utopian protest movement, than the Jefferson
Airplane's first album came out in August, RCA's fifty
grand investment resulting in a paltry indication of what
was going on in San Francisco, with its proto–folkie
laments like "Come up the Years," "It's No Secret," and
the hymnal, "Let's Get Together," purportedly written by
the nefarious sea–dog, Dino Valenti. More germane to the
attitudes implicit in the fault lines, was the work of a
banker's daughter named Grace Slick, her husband Jerry,
and his brother Darby, in a band called the Great Society
(an ironic tribute no doubt to Lyndon B. Johnson), who
were singing nose–thumbing drug–drenched folk/blues
like "White Rabbit" and "Somebody to Love." Or Janis
Joplin, the Texas blues singer auditioning on Henry Street
for a garage band called Big Brother & the Holding
Company. Or the original space cowboys, the Charlatans.
Or the Grateful Dead, known then as the Warlocks,
guitarist Jerry Garcia's fourth generation disciples of B.B.

King and Owsley Stanley, who were willing volunteers at novelist Ken Kesey's Trips Festivals, where they spiked the punch with LSD, and all other such loopy, avant–garde examples of merry pranksterism (as immortalized in Tom Wolfe's New Journalism classic, *The Electric Kool Aid Acid Test*) for the remainder of the decade.

Urged by an intensity much too manic to merely be an adjunct of the marketplace, or, even if it was, it was an adjunct of a new marketplace, for a new audience of baby boom rockers, with a new, lunatic sensibility, inspired more by Lenny Bruce than Jerry Lewis, the next month saw the release of the Byrds' *Fifth Dimension*, which contained another alleged Dino Valenti tune, which may have been written by Chet Powers or Billy Roberts, "Hey Joe," their own "Mr. Spaceman," and the Coltrane–inspired ode to space travel, "Eight Miles High," which had been the victim of a radio boycott as a single only a few months before, for allegedly being a description of a drug experience (and this while the Association's "Along Comes Mary" made it all the way to number seven a couple of months later)!

And still more product was on the immediate pipeline, reflective of the wide open nature of the new bohemian age, being created by the generation's own musicians, instead of by the hourly Brill Building conscripts of yore, and bearing their distinctive baby boom middle class signature, for the consumption of their peers. But most of it, despite its cosmic significance, was stuff you'd never get to hear on the narrowly defined world of AM radio, because it was deemed too esoteric, too deep, too strange, Dick Clark didn't have a piece of it, or, it was simply too long for existing formats—in other words, not ready for prime time. Not yet.

Instead, what was being played on the radio, as far as singles went, generally went only as far as your average teenybopper could digest. Through 1965, this was a not insubstantial legacy, mainly because of Dylan, the Beatles, and the Stones, and everyone they inspired, meaning virtually everyone else, save Nancy Sinatra. But in 1966, the sanctity of the three–minute form was suddenly cast into grave doubt, along with the livelihoods of those Brill Building barons who short years before must have thought their run would go on forever, putting down mortgage payments for spacious split–levels in Ronkonkoma and Upper Saddle River and sending their kids to private schools in France and Switzerland and Teaneck, New Jersey.

You could have heard the echoes of something ominious, almost retaliatory, in 1965, in tunes like "Are You a Boy or Are You a Girl" by the Barbarians (though they would redeem themselves somewhat the next year in the garage band classic, "Moulty") and "Dawn of Correction" by the Spokesmen, the premature answer to "Eve of Destruction," written by the same team that wrote the now hopelessly fascist "At the Hop"). In 1966, AM radio unmasked its true intent to reflect the anti–hip, unhip, Goldwater conservative, working class, American–and–proud–of–it mentality, exemplified by Marine Staff Sergeant Barry Sadler's "Ballad of the Green Berets" and "The A–Team" and Frank Sinatra's "It Was a Very Good Year" and "Strangers in the Night," as well as "These Boots Are Made for Walking" by daughter Nancy, "I Fought the Law" by the Bobby Fuller Four, "Kicks" by Paul Revere and the Raiders, "They're Coming to Take Me Away, Ha, Ha," by Napolean XIV, and the strangely ominous, "I Spy (for the FBI)" by Jamo Thomas.

Certain writers, like Bacharach & David, pretended to take the public pulse in 1965, with "What the World Needs Now Is Love" by Jackie DeShannon. A year later, they began to look toward Hollywood and Broadway for further work. Leiber and Stoller tailed off dramatically after 1963, devoting much of their time to producing albums for outmoded acts like the Exciters, the Ad–Libs, the Dixie Cups (as well as the Soul Brothers, Joan Toliver, and Steve Rossi). They offer the entire year of 1966 as a black hole in their epic discography. Doc Pomus could manage only "Do the Freddie," for Freddie and the Dreamers, in 1965. Soon after that, his partner, Mort Shuman, left him to discover Jacques Brel, alive and well and living in Paris. The newlyweds, Jeff Barry and Ellie Greenwich, and Gerry Goffin and Carole King, probably spent a lot of sleepless nights on separate beds, blaming each other for the cold spell. Carole began to sense the inevitability of a recording career, if she ever wanted to hear another single of hers on the radio. Jeff and Ellie formed the Raindrops, but couldn't make it into the Top 40 (at least they were getting a little "Hanky Panky," courtesy of Tommy James and the Shondells). The newlyweds, Barry Mann and Cynthia Weil, did a whole lot better, but even then Barry was thinking about the eventual solo album he'd one day get to record, whose failure would haunt him for years thereafter. Gerry Goffin had a kind of professional breakdown as well, pondering the very essence of his creative soul.

"I mean, first it was just sort of pop lyrics," he painfully ruminated when I spoke to him about it, "then, all of a sudden, poetry got involved, and there's a big difference between being a poet and being a pop lyricist, which blew my head a whole lot. Being a poet is a lot harder."

The Greenwich–Barrys may have begun to sense that their mentor, Phil Spector, was a little nutsy, beating a dead horse with the symphonic "River Deep—Mountain High," his pet project of 1966, that would eat him out of house and home. Phil himself may have been thinking twice about his own lovely bride, Ronnie, after "I Can

Hear Music" by the Ronettes bombed at number 100 on the charts in 1966, an insult worse than "Just Once in My Life" barely scraping the Top 10 for the Righteous Brothers, right after the majesty of "You've Lost That Lovin' Feelin'," of 1965. "Hung on You" did even worse, not even making the Top 40. When "River Deep—Mountain High" by Ike and Tina Turner, failed in June, Phil took to his palacial mansion with Ronnie, to ride things out.

Mann and Weil stayed hot—and married—during the period, following up "You've Lost That Lovin' Feelin'" with "(You're My) Soul and Inspiration," for the Righteous Brothers, and "Kicks" and "Hungry," for Paul Revere and the Raiders (one of Dick Clark's house bands, on "Where the Action Is," in case Clark's accountant was getting worried). But Neil Sedaka endured the drought with his parents living right across the street from Neil Diamond's parents in Brooklyn. Neil had just started his own rise to eventually selling out the Greek Theatre in L.A. on a regular basis, by selling a song called "I'm a Believer," to Sedaka's mentor and publisher, Don Kirshner, for the Monkees—Kirshner's canny ploy to keep his staff writers earning back their six–figure advances.

The advent of the Monkees, the new "American Beatles," supplanting the Byrds (who reputedly took drugs), could have been seen as just another example of good old American ingenuity at work. With the Beatles already having their own Saturday morning TV cartoon, why not do the next best thing by creating a sit–com for a quartet of suitably goofy–looking American stand–ins, thus, as Ricky Nelson had proven a decade before, assuring quick access to the top of the charts for a succession of tailor–made singles, most of them written in–house, by indentured Kirshner employees, starting off with "Last Train to Clarksville" by Tommy Boyce and Bobby Hart, moving right along with Diamond's "I'm a Believer," and into 1967 with "(I'm Not Your) Steppin' Stone" by Boyce and Hart, "A Little Bit Me, A Little Bit You" by Neil Diamond, "Pleasant Valley Sunday" by Goffin and King, "Words" by Boyce and Hart, and "Daydream Believer" by John Stewart, on hiatus from the Kingston Trio. In 1968, you could even stuff them into a wild movie with a one–syllable title beginning with an H (*Head*, not *Help!*. *Hair* was already being used on Broadway), in which there was a Gerry Goffin and Carole King song, "The Porpoise Song," as well as a Toni Stern and Carole King song, "As We Go Along," presaging the sad breakup of America's once–pre–eminent songwriting team.

But, when observed in the context of producing music that catered to the part of the record business tied into AM radio's overweening desire to restore, all by itself, for a new generation of sub–teens, not only America's competitive trade imbalance with England, but the whole set of apple pie promises this influx of new talent seemed to have mysteriously undone (when the pop success of the Beatles was supposedly engineered to bolster those Boy Scouts of America promises in the first place), it looks insidiously like a plot was at hand, to erase, along with all this new talent inspired by the Beatles, the moral order their longer, intense, questing, and questioning works presumed, with a barrage of pop platitudes, designed to once again move back the clock to a time when Eisenhower was in the White House, and Tricky Dick was getting eggs thrown at him in Venezuela. This possibly hidden, but surely not coincidental, agenda was initially inconsequential in de-railing the righteous express of the white middle class nascent album market. It only succeeded, in fact, in driving it, as early as the summer of 1966, to the vast, undiscovered wasteland of the FM band, en masse, like citizens of a new nation, annexing stations, sounds, atti-tudes, as one unified (counter) culture.

As far as removing black music from the upper echelons of hitsville, however, the AM conspiracy was much more effective. After gaining a foothold in 1960, when 25 percent of the year's biggest hits were by black artists, from 1961 to 1963, during the reign of JFK, there was an R&B heyday in which (by my own approximation) some 104 songs made that pinnacle, or nearly 34 percent of the era's top–selling singles. After Kennedy was shot, and coinciding with the period of greatest promise for progress toward black equality, combined with greatest unrest in the inner cities, the next three years produced only 62 songs that achieved major hit status, a dropoff of 40 percent! When you also consider that 34 of the 62 hits came from one company, Motown Records, already considered by AM radio as the next best thing to white in their advocacy of the status quo ("You Can't Hurry Love," "You Keep Me Hangin' On," "My World Is Empty without You" by the Supremes, "Reach out, I'll Be There" by the Four Tops, "Uptight (Everything's Alright)" by Stevie Wonder), unthreatening enough to form the nostalgic core of the baby boom's big chilling–out period of later years, with virtually no alternate cultural component, then the loss of an authentically subversive black voice during this time is even more unsettling, especially when you think of how essential black music has always been for providing white teenagers and musicians a creative wellspring from which to draw sustenance, inspiration, compelling rhythms, if not complete tunes. Nineteen sixty–six, in fact, had fewer black songs at the top of the charts than at any time since . . . 1959 (obviously, a paradigm year of corporate pop perfection); and if you remove Motown product from that number it dwindles to the lowest total in the history of the rock era!

Was this unfortunate gulf reflective of anything more sinister than the coincidental ebb and flow of product? Or was there, perhaps, in our own baby boom midst, a portion of the audience, maybe a significant portion, that was not idealistic, pacifistic, into Civil Rights, and against the war? Could there in any way be a silent majority, absolutely silent during Goldwater's humongous defeat, but just starting now to rumble deep in the country's sagging gut, who were as threatened as AM radio thought they were by the implications of Watts, the legacy of Cleveland?

Or was it just that AM radio was becoming as increasingly calcified and irrevelant as the sentries on the hip frontier assured us? In 1966, the black voice was still being heard, by those of us musically pure enough to ferret it out, in John Hammond Jr.'s fourth album, *Country Blues*, featuring Muddy Waters's "Seventh Son," Robert Johnson's "Traveling Riverside Blues," and the classic, "Statesborough Blues." The Blues Project, finally breaking through with an album recorded in Greenwich Village, highlighted Danny Kalb's amazing electric guitar chops on "Back Door Man," "Alberta," "Spoonful," and "Jelly, Jelly, Jelly." The Paul Butterfield Blues Band's second album contained more of Michael Bloomfield's legendary assaults on the pentatonic scale ("Walking Blues," "I Got a Mind to Give up Living," "All These Blues"). In England, Eric Clapton was putting a shine on his godly rep, with versions of "Stepping Out" and Freddie King's "Hideaway." In the Yardbirds, Jimmy Page ("Over, Under, Sideways, Down") and Jeff Beck ("Shapes of Things," "Jeff's Boogie") were confirmed blues addicts. There were albums out and being devoured by like–minded white kids over here, by Junior Wells and Buddy Guy ("Messin' with the Kid," "It Hurts Me, Too"), Otis Rush ("So Many Roads, So Many Trains"), John Lee Hooker ("Sugar Mama," "Decoration Day"), Howling Wolf ("Killing Floor," "Evil"), Mississippi John Hurt ("Coffee Blues"),

Muddy Waters ("Rolling and Tumbling," "Mannish Boy"), and Lightning Hopkins ("Nothing But the Blues").

Whether the black audience, middle class, and of college age, or the other black audience, shooting hoops, shooting up, or running riot in the shopping centers of the American white suburban collective imagination, had any use for Muddy Waters and Howling Wolf, to say nothing of Michael Bloomfield and Eric Clapton, Danny Kalb, or even the massive spectacle of Jimi Hendrix about to unleash his ferocious power on the planet, is not to discount the sincerity of the white blues fan, nor to dismiss the worthiness of the concommittant black rage. If in 1966, Otis Redding was singing the Stones' "(I Can't Get No) Satisfaction" and Stevie Wonder Dylan's "Blowin' in the Wind," primarily to attract a white audience, wasn't it merely a classic payback for 1956? Surely James Brown was talking to some of his own people, in "Don't Be a Dropout," as well as in "Money Won't Change You," "It's a Groove," and "It's a Man's, Man's, Man's World." Soul music from Memphis had a huge black audience, swooning to Otis's "Fa Fa Fa Fa Fa," "Hold on (I'm Coming)" by Sam and Dave, "B–A–B–Y" by Carla Thomas, Eddie Floyd's "Knock on Wood," and Percy Sledge's "When a Man Loves a Woman," even in the midst of turmoil, affirming some essential verities. At Motown, the Temptations ("Ain't Too Proud to Beg," "Beauty Is Only Skin Deep") were making their move toward putting more soul in their sound than their cloistered, ethereal brothers, Smokey and the Miracles ("The Tracks of My Tears").

As much as AM radio tried to ignore them, the desires of middle class tastemakers would ultimately prove too tempting for them to entirely resist trifling with, as evidenced by the garage band sound of 1965–1966, a suburban eruption more poignant and prominent than a pimple

on prom night. With the Kingsmen's "Louie Louie" as
model, the skies of AM America soon became filled with
the Friday night Frat House sounds of "Hang on Sloopy"
by the McCoys (from Ohio), "96 Tears" by ? & the
Mysterians (from Michigan), "Wooly Bully" by Sam the
Sham and the Pharoahs (from Texas), "Laugh Laugh" by
the Beau Brummels (from California), "Good Lovin'" by
the Rascals (from New York), "Wild Thing" by the Troggs
(from England), and "Dirty Water" by the Standels (who
everybody thought were from Boston, but were from L.A.),
a rough–hewn, and slightly off–color, and decidedly
macho brand of rock & roll—admired by Beatlemaniacs
and folkies alike ("Satisfaction" by the Stones and "My
Generation" by the Who are considered proto–garage
rock anthems)—but hardly as threatening as the deviant
behavior found just out of earshot.

At the same time, in the work of the baby boom's
original middle class rocker, Paul Simon, a sort of compromise was effected, in Simon & Garfunkel's September
album release, *Parsley, Sage, Rosemary & Thyme*, whereby
some of the college generation's concerns were translated
into a rock & roll language AM radio could accept: "The
Dangling Conversation," "Feelin' Groovy (the 59th Street
Bridge Song)," "Homeward Bound," and "I Am a Rock."
Caught somewhere between Dylan and Dion, Simon, like
most of his cautious, East Coast, alienated peers, would
never make it either as hood or hippie, probably because
his hair curled up too funny in the back whenever he let it
grow, but tunes like "Scarborough Fair," "Patterns,"
"Cloudy," and "7 O'Clock News/Silent Night," perfectly
defined the mood of the precise leading edge of the baby
boom blip, epitomized by Dustin Hoffman's celluloid
portrayal of Benjamin in *The Graduate*, that would continue to define rock culture long after they'd changed

out of their t–shirts for business suits (though that change itself would not occur until long after their parents stopped sending them money from home).

In October, Frank Zappa's Mothers of Invention were obviously not in it for radio airplay, surfacing with *Freak Out*, which moved the envelope another notch toward the psychotic with "Who Are the Brain Police," "Trouble Comin' Every Day," about the second round of riots in Watts that summer, the pre–psychedelic pyschedelia of "Help, I'm a Rock," and the epic frustration of "You're Probably Wondering Why I'm Here."

That same month, Judy Collins introduced her more sedate audience to Leonard Cohen's quintessential hippie chick, "Suzanne," who was by then already sublimely defined as one part Michele Phillips's doe–eyed somnambulism, one part Grace Slick's stoic cool, another part Janis Joplin's weatherbeaten funk, and the last part legendary San Francisco topless go–go dancer Carol Doda's silicone perfection. As the living culmination of the journey begun by Gale Garnett's wayward flower child of 1964, "Suzanne"'s implicit promise of unembroidered erotic bravado, unencumbered and untainted by thoughts of race—the rat race, the space race, the arms race—creed, or color (multiplied by Acapulco Gold) would be all the invitation the leading edge would need to fling off the last of their inhibitions, and jump, libido first, into the new sensual consensus of dope, sex, and rock & roll (in any old order you chose it).

At the ramshackle Animal Houses along the increasingly outmoded and deserted borders of Fraternity Row, 1966, AM radio still played the messages of warning they were able to glean from the singles racks: "Lies" by the Knickerbockers, "Psychotic Reaction" by the Count Five, "Kicks" by Paul Revere & the Raiders, and "The Pied Piper" by Chrispian St. Peters. But even on AM, the sounds of the inevitable changing of the moral guard were impossible to entirely squelch: "Rainy Day Women #12 & 35" by Bob Dylan, "Day Tripper" by the Beatles, "19th Nervous Breakdown" by the Rolling Stones, "California Dreamin'" by the Mamas and the Papas, "Along Comes Mary" by the Association, "Blowin' in the Wind" by Stevie Wonder, "Shapes of Things" by the Yardbirds, and "Eight Miles High" by the Byrds. Finally, the virginal Beach Boys, in "Wouldn't It Be Nice," got laid; two months later "Good Vibrations" went to number one.

With the blissful promise of a Sexual Revolution clouding up everyone's peripheral vision, depth perception addled by THC, it's possible only now to understand how otherwise intelligent observers may have been too preoccupied to notice when Richard Fariña killed himself on a motorcycle returning home from a book signing party, and when Jan Berry nearly killed himself swerving through the fast lane in a hot rod, or when Bob Dylan, still fervently booed from coast to coast for the high treason of "Like a Rolling Stone," broke his neck and his artistic momentum, a couple of months later on a motorcycle. On a tour of America themselves, in the midst of this, the Beatles must have noticed. John Lennon, especially, had discovered the wrath his expanded–minded honesty could provoke in the hinterlands. Did he want to be similarly cruxified? And so, after pulling up stakes at Candlestick Park in San Francisco that August, the Beatles formally announced that they would no longer be a touring band.

With our two major organizations for social change effectively ruling from the tower rather than the street, the legions of potential unrest were left without reference point or focus, staggering between singles and albums, between albums and live performances for meaning and direction, uniquely vulnerable to the fickle whims of the marketplace of ideas. And while it's true that both of these extended self–preservationary forays would prove fruitful for the principals in the short run as artists (Dylan began work on the fabled *Basement Tapes*, the Beatles mastered their studio craft at least three times over), in the longer term, for them and for us, their actions were tragically insufficient in heading off the inevitable descent.

Five

The Whole World Is Watching

(1967–1970)

Seven years after it, on the crest of another Disco era in 1975, as I was sitting with the program director of a tiny secondary market radio station, sampling sides, my assignment being to test his reactions to a typical week of single releases, to see if my taste (i.e.,"taste") had anything to do with what actually found its way on the air, even in the boondocks—during a week when Simon reunited with Garfunkel and a Kurt Vonnegut lyric appeared on a chartbound tune by Ambrosia and every third record was a calculated remake of "The Hustle"—easily his most revealing response was to a slow, droning, philosophical dirge called "The Aging," by an unknown band from the Midwest named Blackberry Winter. Listening to the requisite thirty seconds, he removed the needle from the disc, and dismissed it with the authoritative pejorative, "Too 1968."

Like everything else it represents in the mind's evil eye, 1968 was a year in which the musical and mystical forces that collided in the atmosphere so unnerved and divided the country that years later its mere mention would signify

113

a rebuke far more dire and unforgiving than your typical radio programmer evasion. For those on either side of the moral and musical debate, which was one and the same thing, it was still too soon, in 1975, to have those particular 1968 nightmares brought vividly back to the roiling squall of the national soundscape, about to become awash as it was in the processed hum of synthesizer and drum machine. Like movies about the war in Vietnam, it would be many years before any sort of objective distance on the musical self–destruction of the baby boom could be approached, let alone achieved.

If not the worst calendar year in the entire history of rock & roll, then easily the angriest, in 1968 the country seemed to be unraveling, daily, with the whole world watching, on television, in the streets, at rock concerts, for free. Not only musically, but politically as well, it was a year when confrontation was the rule, compromise the exception. And every confrontation resulted in further deep divisions that would never entirely heal. Surely, if you were part of the solution, you were also part of somebody else's problem.

By my informal count, there were at least twenty–two musical confrontations in 1968, most of them encapsulated in your basic FM radio versus AM radio debate, which contained within it sub–confrontations over the superiority of album cuts versus singles, art versus commerce, and by lifestyle inference, the inevitability of the righteous, weed–eating counterculture invented at Monterey and housed in crashpads from the archetypal twin corners of bohemia—Haight and Ashbury and Bleecker and MacDougal—versus middle of the road middle America, that is, doves versus hawks, long hairs versus short hairs, hippies versus straights, and the baby boom college rebel youth versus know–nothing authority.

Complete with its own cadre of moody, slow–talking,

deep–voiced deejays quoting Dylan, the Beatles, and Kahlil Gibran, the advent of FM radio in 1966–1967, to promote and extol the extended works of the generation's poet–troubadours, was at first regarded by the white, middle class, college–age audience that was its devout constituency with all the righteous jubilation of a neo–Columbus discovering a new route to the East. As the Twist had liberated a generation from the antiquated rules of ballroom (and Bandstand) dancing, so FM radio liberated listeners from the mind–numbing box step of Top 40, the tyranny of twenty–song playlists rotating endlessly, dictated by demographics, payola, sales figures, and the fabrications of the national charts. On FM, responding to the idealistic agenda of the academic intelligensia, music reigned over calculated jingles, an enlightened sensibility over the repressed and repressive constraints of the mundane world, supported by fascist AM. On the FM dial, everyone sang all twenty–seven minutes of "The Alice's Restaurant Massacre" by Arlo Guthrie, at least once a week. On AM, they manufactured Bubblegum music for pre–teens ("Yummy, Yummy, Yummy" by the Ohio Express, "Simon Says" and "1,2,3, Red Light" by the 1910 Fruitgum Company). FM radio was reputedly programmed by whim and inspiration, a grass roots, almost–not–for–profit operation, reactive to the community, where you could flow from anti–war harangues into emotional guitar catharsis, through symphonic heavy metal into Delta blues in the same quarter hour; awake to morning ragas and nod out at four on a Tuesday afternoon to screeching electronic feedback. There were certified word poets like Leonard Cohen segueing into uncertified poetasters like Jim Morrison; there were the flaming guitars of Clapton and Bloomfield and Hendrix unchained; the confessional laments of Joni Mitchell and Lou Reed and Laura Nyro unbridled.

On AM, it was business as usual. Like television, AM

presented what it deemed palatable to the mass audience, the family audience, the short attention span common denominator. Much in the way rhythm and blues was initially bowdlerized by such a process in 1956, resulting in a product harmless enough to invite into your bedroom every night, the AM version of 1968—which has gradually become the official version—barely skimmed the surface of the musical waves crashing daily against the shoreline of complacency, mollifying the minions much like a Lyndon Johnson press briefing on the police action in Southeast Asia.

Within the AM formula, irony was nonetheless an occasional unwanted houseguest, chortling with its host over the return of the black constituency in 1967, with soul music from Memphis, sparking the first surge of activity in that town since Elvis effectively changed the color of rock & roll. In 1968, soul migrated East to Philadelphia, the land from which Dick Clark had long since absconded with his solid gold Bandstand dancers. Meanwhile, country music had its biggest year of the decade on the charts in 1968, paving the way, in 1969, for Nixon to return to the White House and Elvis Presley to return to Memphis, and number one ("Suspicious Minds"), for the first time since 1960, 1954, and 1962, respectively. Elvis scored a number three in 1969 as well, with the unconsciously ludicrous bit of social observation, "In the Ghetto"; the way he pronounced the last syllable of "ghet–toe" being more than enough proof, as if anyone needed it, that the closest Elvis had been to a ghetto since 1956 was probably when he shambled past the servant's quarters at Graceland. Of course, 1969 was also the year Diana Ross & the Supremes reached the top ten by convincing the AM constituency that they were living out of wedlock in the slums in "I'm Living in Shame."

In a year that was rent with unease and malaise,

balanced only occasionally by a president stepping down or a free concert in Golden Gate Park by the Grateful Dead and the Jefferson Airplane—except for the one that was cancelled the morning after Bobby Kennedy was murdered—AM radio would have you believe we were all blissfully singing "Judy in Disguise (with Glasses)" by John Fred and his Playboy Band, and the collected works of Gary Puckett ("Young Girl," "Lady Willpower," "Woman Woman," "Over You," and "This Girl Is a Woman Now"). Some good stuff crossed over from FM to AM, like "Sunshine of Your Love" by Eric Clapton's robust new blues/rock band, Cream, "Suzie Q." by John Fogerty's San Francisco choogling Creedence Clearwater Revival, "Dance to the Music" by Sly & the Family Stone, "Born to Be Wild" by Steppenwolf, "Piece of My Heart" by Big Brother & the Holding Company, and "Itchycoo Park" by Small Faces—but you had to listen to "Honey" by Bobby Goldsboro six times in an hour before you got to hear "Time Has Come Today" by the Chambers Brothers once.

Indicative of our generational power, in this particular confrontation, the older and hipper segment of the audience so outnumbered the younger and dumber (born after the advent of Elvis) portion, that FM succeeded in holding off the youth rebellion and pushing its more advanced agenda. In the process, the nature of rock & roll was changed (as well as its name, to rock), from an intuitive, emotional street beat, to a much more cerebral, focused, artist–driven entity, fueled, for the most part, by many of the other epic confrontations taking place in the firmament daily—the progress of these consummate struggles providing the basis for FM's sporadic, liberally biased news reports.

Beyond the obvious and more historically timeless standoffs between the young and the old and the hip and the square that rock & roll, like all cultural and political upheavals, promoted, there were also more subtle and insidious internecine battles brewing in 1968 that would split the counterculture and prove to be its undoing— between, for instance, East coast liberalism and West coast bohemianism, the folk scene spawned by Dylan and Phil Ochs to expose the shams of adult society, and the psyche- delic rock scene of San Francisco, epitomized by the Jefferson Airplane and the Grateful Dead, to expose oneself, as often as possible, to the possibilities of a life outside the adult (and even the East coast liberal) agenda.

By as early as 1967, it was clear that the West had the best agenda going, re–reinventing the blues, with a rol- licking case of reefer madness. The Grateful Dead were getting juiced on jamming "Good Morning Little School- girl" well into the night of the following day; the Jefferson Airplane's *Surrealistic Pillow*, with Grace Slick of the Great Society now in the band, redeemed RCA's investment somewhat, with the endearing optimism of "Today" and "Coming Back to Me," the high–tech ebullience of "Plas- tic Fantastic Lover" (an ode no doubt to Carol Doda); Janis Joplin's fiery debut with Big Brother & the Holding Company ("Down on Me," "Women Is Losers"), had everybody talking Bessie Smith. Back East, Dylan was in traction, the anti–Love Generation Velvet Underground were on "Heroin," the Holy Modal Rounders had "Half a Mind," and gin–soaked Tim Hardin's "If I Were a Carpen- ter," had been co–opted by Bobby Darin. For feminine companionship, we had droning Nico's celebration of Andy Warhol's downtown pop art suicidal tendencies ("Chelsea Girls," "Somewhere There's a Feather," Dylan's "I'll Keep It with Mine" and Jackson Browne's melancholy "These Days"), frowsy, blowsy Laura Nyro's histrionic Broadway funk ("Stoney End," "And When I Die," "Wedding Bell Blues," "Buy and Sell") and the quintessential 16–year–old pouting private school prodigy, Janis Fink (nee Ian) tossing "Society's Child" into our do–good faces. Obviously, we were creating the great works here, rather than frivolously tearing off our clothes. What did they have out West to compare with Tim Buckley's technicolor angst ("I Never Asked to Be Your Mountain," "Once I Was," "No Man Can Find the War"), or the enduring, front lines agitation of Phil Ochs ("Flower Lady," "Outside of a Small Circle of Friends," "Crucifixion")? The Fish Cheer? No, Country Joe and the Fish came from radicalized Berkeley (rival of San Francisco in yet another ethical confrontation). Frank Zappa's monumental *Freak Out* came from Los Angeles (which had its own intramural dispute as well with Frisco's loopy hippie culture).

In any case, by no means did San Francisco have as easy a time of it as cultural Mecca, in the wake of the Summer of Love of 1967, and the influx into the city of so many dropouts from the American Dream, as Dr. Timothy Leary ("Turn on, Tune in, Drop Out"), and Scott McKenzie ("If You're Going to San Francisco Be Sure to Wear Flowers in Your Hair") would have you believe.

"I remember one time talking to a guy at *Time* magazine, when it was just hitting and Haight Street was like a tourist attraction and people were dressed in colorful costumes like you see at the Renaissance Fair," the Airplane's Marty Balin ruminated. "I told him, 'It's great you're publicizing this and telling people about all this spirit, and everything that exists here.' He looked at me and said, 'Fastest way to kill it.' He sure was right."

Kicked off in June at the Monterey Rock & Pop Festival, the euphoria had promised to be uncontained, the acid uncontaminated by pointy–headed reality. Situated halfway between San Francisco and Los Angeles, the festival was the major pop cultural benchmark event of the period, a Rock and Soul All–Star baseball game, in which repre-

sentatives of the Eastern League (Paul Simon, Art Garfunkel, Laura Nyro), the Western League (the Mamas and
the Papas, the Byrds, the Jefferson Airplane, Big Brother &
the Holding Company), the International League (the
Who) the Interstellar League (Jimi Hendrix), the Cosmic
League (Ravi Shankar) and the Negro League (Otis
Redding) met the white middle–class Album Market—on
the playing fields of Big Sur. Outside, the war was getting
harder to avoid, with a massive draft call–up every month;
the certainty of death loomed clearer than at any time
since the Cuban Missile Crisis of 1962. In Watts, just up
the road, there was another riot going on. But in Monterey,
LSD was legal, the girls wore mini skirts, and the hippies
gave flowers to the cops. David Crosby excoriated the
Warren Report and Clive Davis opened his checkbook for
Columbia records. He signed Janis Joplin, bought out
Laura Nyro's contract from Verve/Forecast. Warner Brothers nabbed the Jimi Hendrix Experience (*Are You Experienced?* came out in August). The Who crashed the party
with *Happy Jack*, pre–empting for the moment the much–
anticipated Beatles' opus, *Sergeant Pepper's Lonely Hearts
Club Band*. And Otis Redding captivated the assemblage
("Try a Little Tenderness," "I've Been Loving You Too
Long"), enabling him six months later to die a famous man,
with a hit ("Dock of the Bay") on the charts when his light
plane went down in Lake Monoma in Wisconsin. You could
probably call the Monterey Games some sort of international dead heat. But the winner was definitely California:
the fruition of the FM version of the Rock Dream, the
Alternate Culture, the wave of the future, as would be
celebrated in the pages of its forthcoming house organ,
Rolling Stone magazine, an insulated society ruled by rock!

Factoring in seven albums that year from pop rock's
reigning aristocracy: the Monkees (3), the Mamas and the
Papas (2), and Linda (Ronstadt) and the Stone Poneys

(2)—which included Monkee Mike Nesmith's "Different Drum"—as well as some good vibrations from the Beach Boys ("Good Vibrations," "Heroes and Villains," "Vejtables"), and the mellow California quotient soars. But there were also works of redeeming social significance by the rejuvenated Byrds ("So You Wanna Be a Rock & roll Star," "Renaissance Fair," "Have You Seen Her Face"), Jim Morrison and the Doors broke through in 1967 with their poetic pretentions and sexual bravado intact in *Break on Through* ("Light My Fire," "Break on Through," the grandiloquent "The End") and *Strange Days* ("People Are Strange," "Moonlight Drive," the prodigious "Love Me Two Times," and the tragi–comically prophetic "When the Music's Over"); Country Joe and the Fish took a stance somewhere between San Francisco and Berkeley in *Electric Music for the Mind and Body* and *Feel Like I'm Fixing to Die Rag* ("Not So Sweet Martha Lorraine," "Grace," "Janis," "I Feel Like I'm Fixing to Die" and the infamous "Fish Cheer"); the Mothers of Invention followed *Freak Out* with the caustic schtick of *Absolutely Free* ("Brown Shoes Don't Make It," "Who Needs the Peace Corps," "What's the Ugliest Part of Your Body"); the Buffalo Springfield delivered two folk/rock gems, *Buffalo Springfield* and *Buffalo Springfield Again* ("For What It's Worth," "Nowadays Clancy Can't Even Sing," "Mr. Soul," "Broken Arrow," "Bluebird," and the ineffable "Expecting to Fly"), before contemplating future career moves; Moby Grape made an impact, but only as the beneficiary of a dubious marketing scheme to simultaneously release five singles from their debut album. So it's no surprise that by the end of 1967, even Phil Ochs was secretly preparing his *Tape from California*, to be released in mid–1968.

"I thought it was the Revolution," Paul Simon expressed to me, recalling how he felt about the prevailing drift of 1968. "I thought it was really going to come into effect and that Simon & Garfunkel were going to be artifacts of the New York/Eastern/ early 1960s days, which could no longer continue, because we didn't understand about things like the ecology."

It was about more than the ecology, however; it wasn't really about the ecology at all, except for the more personal ecology of feeding your head, as espoused by the Jefferson Airplane's Grace Slick in "White Rabbit." It was about the ability exhibited by certain exhibitionists in whiteface and odd uniforms on Haight Street, to live in the (albeit drug–induced) moment, in sprawling extended family–groups and rock bands, rather than the necessity folks seemed to have in the East to want to wait for some eventual perfection of the moment, isolated, with an acoustic guitar and maybe a backup second electric played by Bruce Langhorne and doleful harmonica by John Sebastian, before they could get on with their lives. In 1968, Janis Joplin's *Cheap Thrills*, with the R. Crumb cover art, immortalized some of her more amazing Monterey moments, "Piece of My Heart" and "Ball and Chain," the deeply–indebted Steve Miller sang about "The Children of the Future," and the Quicksilver Messenger Service offered the vigorous "Pride of Man" and the communal anthem, "Get Together," among their other hymnals. In New York City, Simon & Garfunkel, after honing in on urban angst in their soundtrack for *The Graduate*, chatted, in their own album, *Bookends*, with old men on park benches ("Old Friends"), sang about kids on ledges ("Save the Life of My Child"), and contemplated the very nature of the college generation hitching back and forth between reality and nothingness ("America"). Among these nervous post–graduation day dropouts was Eric Andersen, living in squalor, caught between folk and rock in *More Songs from Tin Can Alley*. Joni Mitchell's first album found her curious alter ego "Marcy," leaving town for presumably greener pastures. Her epic and unmistakable naming of the malady obsessing the chilled generation, "Urge for Going," was left off the album, but Tom Rush put it on his own *Circle Game*, along with new tunes by Jackson Browne and James Taylor. The Fugs described the mood even more succinctly in "When the Mode of the Music Changes," from *It Crawled onto My Hand, Honest*. And while music had reflected a collective euphoria, to the point of dementia, maybe, for several years, in 1968, the foundations of that euphoria were being seismically shook, within and without, politically and sexually.

"A common basis for a lot of the mistakes was that, since it was so much of a youth movement, people didn't realize that what's sexually wonderful at nineteen, may not be what you would want when you're thirty or thirty–five," Tuli Kupferberg later postulated. "Politically, the movement was never able to affiliate with the vast majority of people who were not nineteen, who had problems with work and family, education. It said this was life, when maybe it was just youth."

Though Lyndon Johnson, seemingly in response to the efforts of the protest movement, had abdicated his crown (in a 1968 shocker even more major than Pete Seeger appearing on the Smothers Brothers' TV show), making matters far worse, so had Bob Dylan—returning from the almost dead a few months earlier, in January, with *John Wesley Harding*, an album he recorded in Nashville, and which contained country tunes like "I'll Be Your Baby Tonight" and "Down Along the Cove," as if the man had finally awakened from his coma a country bumpkin! What was next? A redneck? Family man? Christian? Republican?

Instead, what it wound up making most of us followers do in 1968, was to contemplate leaving the teeming rigors of city life for the more pastoral delights of the country, more specifically, Woodstock, New York, or thereabouts, where Bob and his entourage were encamped, to glom an acre of our own, preferably on high ground, from which to view the remaining confrontations of the era with as much distance from the fray as Dylan had put between himself and the rebel ranks of protest folk and anguished folk/ rock. What was Dylan's state of mind as he watched the turmoil in the streets? The tunes he was putting together with the Band at Big Pink said it all: "Too Much of Nothing," "You Ain't Goin' Nowhere," "Nothing Was Delivered," "I Shall Be Released," "Tears of Rage," and "This Wheel's on Fire," suggesting as well as an agonized frustration over his prolonged convalescence, a pithy commentary on both the pathetic machinations of the doomed counterculture and his own diminishing place within it. From *John Wesley Harding*, enigmatic epigrams like "Dear Landlord," "I Pity the Poor Immigrant" and "All Along the Watchtower," confirmed how deeply his cynicism ran.

As a final measure of how scant Dylan's interest was in returning to his position atop the protest ranks, the following year he ambled back to Nashville to put out a pure country album (*Nashville Skyline*), with his new, Amish/ country bumpkin hat, and countrified voice, even going so far as to duet with Johnny Cash on "Girl from the North Country," a juxtaposition so inherently traitorous that it surely drove whoever was left in the sweltering city to their tarpapered rooftops in despair, to play a sort of taps on their autoharps and theramins as they gazed into the face of an extended stay in a Republican America. Which was a good thing, for had they remained indoors, they might have caught Bob guesting on the Everly Brothers summer TV show. "Lay Lady Lay," in fact, was actually written for the Everly Brothers, but they passed on the tune as being too racy.

Though Dylan's impact on the zeitgeist had up to then

been legendary—and legendarily swift—it still may be overly paranoid to blame those two Nashville tunes on *John Wesley Harding* for the wholesale country renaissance of 1968, though, in fact, the album's January release did leave room for the instantaneous reaction of his peers to surface later in the year. By August, for instance, the Band's *Music from Big Pink* ("Long Black Veil"), the Byrds' *Sweetheart of the Rodeo* ("I Am a Pilgrim," "The Christian Life") along with old Greenwich Village crony Buffy Sainte–Marie's *I'm Going to Be a Country Girl Again* all reached the charts—just a week after the rootsy rockabilly debut of Creedence Clearwater Revival ("Suzie Q.,S "I Put a Spell on You"). But, the Byrds acknowledge Gram Parsons as their primary country guru; whether or not Dylan sent Gram their way is unsubstantiated if inconsequential. Moreover, it has never been proven that Jeannie C. Riley even heard of Bob Dylan, much less that she had bought one or several of his albums by the time her future number one pop tune, "Harper Valley PTA," was released that summer; then again, had Dylan known Tom T. Hall, the song's writer, surely Bob would have hailed him as twice the poet as Smokey Robinson, or, at least, three quarters of Rod McKuen.

More likely, or, just as likely, the country onslaught led by Bobby Goldsboro ("Honey," "The Straight Life"), O.C. Smith ("Little Green Apples," "Son of Hickory Holler's Tramp"), Glen Campbell ("Wichita Lineman," "Dreams of the Everyday Housewife," "Gentle on My Mind"), Ray Stevens ("Mr. Businessman"), Roger Miller ("Little Green Apples"), Tammy Wynette ("D–I–V–O–R–C–E"), Jerry Lee Lewis ("What's Made Milwaukee Famous Made a Loser out of Me"), and Johnny Cash ("Folsom Prison Blues"), was redressing some kind of psychic imbalance created the year before by the abundance of soul music in the air, from Memphis, home of Graceland ("Soul Man" by

Sam and Dave, "Sweet Soul Music" by Arthur Conley, "The Letter" by the Box Tops, "Tramp" and "Knock on Wood" by Carla Thomas and Otis Redding, "Hip Hug Her" by Booker T. & the MG's) and Muscle Shoals, home of Rick Hall's Fame Studios ("Funky Broadway" by Wilson Pickett, "Respect," "Baby I Love You," and "Chain of Fools" by Aretha Franklin, and "Just out of Reach (of My Empty Arms)" by Percy Sledge).

In fact, while the flower–laden, drugged members of the late Otis Redding's recently discovered album market desolately slouched toward their appointed Armageddon at Grant Park in Chicago, to the tune of folk/rock, there was a virtual Final Four of black music being played out in Detroit versus Muscle Shoals versus Memphis versus Phila-delphia.

Motown surged to unaccustomed social relevance with the Temptations ("Cloud Nine") and new musical heights with Marvin Gaye ("I Heard It Through the Grapevine") and Marvin Gaye and Tammi Terrell ("You're All I Need to Get By," "Ain't Nothing Like the Real Thing" and "If I Could Build My Whole World All Around You"). Though Smokey Robinson and the Miracles failed to make the top ten with "If You Can Want," and the Supremes were reduced to nostalgically pining for the lost glory of "Yester Love," and Martha and the Vandellas frankly admitted "I Can't Dance to That Music You're Playing," both Stevie Wonder ("For Once in My Life") and the Four Tops ("Walk Away, Renee") were in fine voice, albeit covering white pop tunes made famous by Tony Bennett and the Left Banke, respectively.

Aretha Franklin, representing Muscle Shoals, had ten chart singles in 1968, including seven in the top twenty, besting 1967, when she had seven chart singles and four in the top twenty ("Chain of Fools," which peaked at number two, crossed from 1967 into 1968). But when you match

"Respect" and "Natural Woman" and "I Never Loved a Man (the Way I Love You)," of 1967 against ("Sweet Sweet Baby) Since You Been Gone," "Think," "The House That Jack Built," "I Say a Little Prayer" and "See Saw," in 1968, you can hear where quantity may not have necessarily won out over quality. Also from Muscle Shoals, Percy Sledge rebounded with "Take Time to Know Her," and Wilson Picket found a groove in "I'm a Midnight Mover" and "She's Looking Good."

Memphis, after the soul onslaught of 1966 and 1967, may have cooled a bit, with Sam and Dave's gracious "I Thank You," acknowledging the passing trend. Eddie Floyd was still cooking, however, in "Bring It on Home to Me," and Booker T. and the MGs hadn't given up the ghost of Chubby Checker ("Soul Limbo"). But Otis Redding's post–posthumous "Hard to Handle" failed to crack the top 40, and Arthur Conley was already moving onto funk, the next wrinkle in the rhythmic fabric of black music, in "Funky Street."

The chalice of soul seemed to be passing over to Philadelphia, home of the hoagie and the Liberty bell, where the Intruders ("Cowboys to Girls," "Love Is Like a Baseball Game"), the Delfonics ("La La Means I Love You," "Do the Choo Choo"), Jerry Butler ("Never Give You Up," "Only the Strong Survive"), and the Unifics ("Court of Love") were introducing the mellow stylings of record making professionals like Thom Bell, Linda Creed, Kenny Gamble, and Leon Huff to the world.

But whichever city would finally emerge with that particular crown would have to contend with some black performers who were decidedly outside the established system, and in synch with the turmoil on the streets of the alternate culture versus the empire strikes back confrontations of 1968: the rampaging experimental merger of blues, R&B, and rock (with anger, danger, sex, and high style) of Jimi Hendrix ("All Along the Watchtower," "Crosstown Traffic," "Foxy Lady," "Up from the Skies"), the multicolored funk of Sly and the Family Stone ("Dance to the Music"), the psychedelicized Chambers Brothers ("Time Has Come Today"), and the perennially elemental James Brown ("Say It Loud, I'm Black and I'm Proud").

No wonder the Beatles hardly had a chance to revel in the conceptual perfection of *Sergeant Pepper's Lonely Hearts Club Band*. Like day–glo body paint and nickel bags, the noble ideal of turning off your mind, espoused in "Strawberry Fields Forever," seemed to last no more than the time it took for the final note on "A Day in the Life" to disappear into the void. Less than a week after the Beatles, en masse, embraced the Maharishi that August, their mentor and manager, Brian Epstein, was found dead of an overdose in his London apartment. Their guiding light and father figure gone, the extended Beatle family was left in a spiritual and financial disarray from which it would never emerge. Within a year, they would disown the Guru (who had by then hooked up with the infinitely more susceptible Beach Boys), and effectively renege (like Dylan, like Elvis) on the implied cultural utopia they'd been promising us through rock & roll, backing off from actual revolutionary writing ("Revolution") in favor of artsy pop pastiche ("Rocky Raccoon," "Dear Prudence," "The Continuing Story of Bungalow Bill"), along with their more customary "we can work it out" motif ("Hey Jude," "All You Need Is Love," "Ob La Di, Ob La Da")—in increasingly dense and sophisticated works that were academic in the most ivory towerish sense of the term.

Their primary rivals, the Rolling Stones, had been caught in the mushy post–Monterey rapture as well, trying to match the Beatles' *Sgt. Pepper* with the cloying *Their Satanic Majesties Request* ("2000 Light Years from Home," "She's a Rainbow") and singles like "Dandelion" and "We

Love You," before regaining a working class rock & roll perspective in *Beggar's Banquet* ("Jumping Jack Flash," "Street Fighting Man," "No Expectations," "Salt of the Earth," and the frighteningly on–target "Sympathy for the Devil," written the day after the assassination of RFK), that was undoubtedly the reason they were able to prevail over the long haul, while the Beatles' "artistic" differences rent them apart, like the grandiose delusions of the high–minded baby boom middle class once it set foot outside the campus gates to face the billy clubs of lowbrow reality.

Anyway, it was a grotesque irony, to say the least, as well as a colossal failure of American ingenuity and wit, that outside agitators like the Beatles and the Stones, who had no real stake in the creative result, and who didn't have to live amidst the havoc they gleefully wrought, had so much influence over the downfall years of our homegrown peace movement, with a pair of songs that had rhyming titles— "Helter Skelter" and "Gimme Shelter"—symbolizing two of the most significant of the seventeen major embarrassing moments of 1969 and 1970 that sank the counterculture.

It's easy to blame that failure, as we all did then, on Richard M. Nixon. But, like the twenty–two musical confrontations of 1967 and 1968, the seventeen embarrassing moments of 1969 and 1970 that sank the counter-culture were not all his fault. It wasn't Nixon who invented Tiny Tim ("Tip Toe Through the Tulips") and David Peel ("Have a Marijuana," "The Pope Smokes Dope"). Tricky as he was, he couldn't have surmised the political gravy he'd be wallowing in when Dylan went from Nashville straight into an album of embarrassing cover tunes (*Self Portrait*) and Lennon went from the Beatles into humiliating frontal nudity on the cover of *Two Virgins*—his debut as Mr. O no! And it probably wasn't Nixon's money that bankrolled the journey of *Hair!* from off–Broadway obscurity to national cliché. On the other hand, it *could* have been Republican bankers who were behind the raising of the rents on MacDougal Street that forced Dave Van Ronk into a rock band called the Hudson Dusters that left him broke, and Phil Ochs into a gold lamé suit that left him suicidal. It was Nixon's crony Reagan who sent the reserves into Peoples' Park in Berkeley. But that's not to say the Republicans were behind every bush, although it must have appeared that way when a different rock band was busted each week: the Airplane leading the league, followed by the Stones, each of the Beatles, and even Chubby Checker! The Doors got the most image mileage out of Jim Morrison's various arrests for indecent language, behavior, and exposure. By 1970, he must have thought he was another Lenny Bruce. The FBI may have been on the Byrds' case, as well. But the Lovin' Spoonful avoided jail by turning in their supplier; they went scot–free, except in the hearts of the counter-culture.

"Nobody ever really understood exactly what happened," the Spoonful's Sebastian tried to explain. "And I think it did a lot to close up the whole good feeling behind the Spoonful, because we were quickly deserted without any kind of a listen by the majority of the rock press. In later years, [*Rolling Stone* co–founder] Ralph Gleason wrote a very good piece on the bust, which, to my mind, set things right, but it was way too late. That piece never stuck in anybody's mind—for instance, 'Oh yes, "The Vindication of the Lovin' Spoonful," by Ralph Gleason, of course . . . '"

In the midst of the unraveling of the Rock Generation, Elvis had carte blanche at the White House, fending off all inquiries counter–cultural with the mega–hit, "Suspicious Minds," while the Byrds and the Doors and the Spoonful bit the dust. Unlike–minded suspicious minds could have had a field day with that, if we hadn't been too busy burying the dead. In 1967 it was the hippie, buried in Tompkins Square Park, presided over by the Fugs. In 1968, it was the Peace Movement and all its sympathizers —Martin Luther King, Bobby Kennedy—buried on the streets of Chicago, presided over by the newly–minted Yippies of Abby Hoffman and Jerry Rubin, Rennie and Angela Davis (no relation), and the also-rans of the Democratic Party. No one awoke the morning after the election with the energy to compose any anthems, a pall that lasted through 1969, when we lost the entire year to a creative drought that had everything to do with the reactionary spirit in the White House. In New York, Norman Mailer briefly took up the chalice of injured literacy by staging a doomed campaign for mayor. In Los Angeles, a week before the Woodstock Festival, Charles Manson carved his bloody signature on the headstone of the Love Generation, humming Beatle tunes. And although no one was killed at the Woodstock Festival in August (there were three drug–related deaths and one incident of Abby Hoffman–bashing by Pete Townshend), the overzealous crowd control efforts of the Hell's Angels at the Altamont Speedway, four months later, in California, presided over by the Rolling Stones, more than made up for it. The Stones themselves had lost founding member Brian Jones twice over, six months before, when he left the band, then again a few weeks later, when he killed himself. In 1970, there were four more dead at Kent State in Ohio, shot by the National Guard and eulogized by Crosby, Stills, Nash and Young ("Ohio"). A few months later, within two weeks of each other, Jimi Hendrix and Janis Joplin died of drug over-doses, causing tipsy blues singers and raging, sky–seeking guitarists alike to lift up their bottles of Southern Comfort and their Stratocasters, respectively, in salute, and then lay them down again in pain for several years. You could have almost heard Nixon and his goon squad, Haldeman, Erlichman, Mitchell, Colson, Liddy, and Dean—their names now as emblazoned upon the consciousness of the generation as the starting lineup of the 1961 Yankees or the Chicago 7—chuckling over each new edition of *Billboard* and *Rolling Stone*.

So much for going down slow, the blues–based, left–leaning, counterculture started knuckling under in February, 1969, when Cream released *Goodbye*, Lennon exposed himself, and Tracy Nelson & Mother Earth failed to crack the top 140 with *Living with the Animals*. Creedence Clearwater Revival were more successful, with their retrogressive boogie appealing to fence–straddling moderates, though *Bayou Country* did contain the fairly plangent "Bad Moon Rising." But killing off even the ghost of the blues for second generation purists was the appearance of Jimmy Page's new Yardbirds configuration, Led Zeppelin ("Dazed and Confused"), a shrill guitar blast at the pristine parameters of our borrowed heritage. Where Eric Clapton's Cream was exhilirating, and Jeff Beck's excursions with Rod Stewart illuminating, and Jimi Hendrix's Experience mind–altering (indebted, all, to the Yardbirds), Robert Plant's panoply of groans, moans, and yelps seemed adolescent exploitation, pure and simple, the sexual growl of the blues removed from the pain, a triumph of form hardly redeemed by Page's extended guitar shenanigans. Had they appeared in 1967, a unified hip front might have been aligned to oust these blowsy pretenders, on behalf of the Paul Butterfield Blues Band, if no one else. But this being the doldrums of 1969, the best we could muster was the whiter than white (albino) Texas bluesman Johnny Winter, who released four albums on three different labels, in eight months. But it was not enough to stem the tide of a younger generation fighting for their own (obviously inferior) handle on the blues, one which would overrun the succeeding decade—much to the consternation of those baby boomers who considered themselves sole proprietors of the form, to whom anyone younger should have had to come to for signatures in order to rent it out. This new low point in the history of the blues would be called heavy metal, and it would not only dominate, but pervert the sensibility of succeeding rock audiences for the next twenty years.

By the summer of 1969, a kind of album–oriented musical schizophrenia reigned: heavy metal sex and violence by the MC–5 (*Kick out the Jams*), Blue Cheer (*Blue Cheer*), Alice Cooper (*Pretties for You*), Deep Purple (*The Book of Taleisyn*), Grand Funk Railroad (*Grand Funk Railroad*), and *Led Zeppelin II*, versus passive introspection by Tim Buckley (*Happy/Sad*), Leonard Cohen (*Songs from a Room*), Bob Dylan (*Nashville Skyline*), Joni Mitchell (*Clouds*), Neil Young (*Everybody Knows This Is Nowhere*), The Flying Burrito Brothers (*The Gilded Palace of Sin*), Arlo Guthrie (*Running down the Road*), and Phil Ochs (*Rehearsals for Retirement*). Only the Who played to both sides of this incipient working class versus middle class confrontation with the angry rock opera *Tommy!*, about as abject an example of how malleable thus meaningless the term rock had already become—in the space of the two short years we of the post–collegiate FM crowd had hold of it!

To celebrate the bitter passing of the rock era, the baby boom album market decided to hold a party. And where better than Woodstock, symbolic home of Bob Dylan, our creative heart and soul, motivator, energizer, political avatar, caustic poet laureate, who had effectively cast his lot with Elvis on the sidelines, rendering the fact that the event didn't actually take place at Woodstock, as pundits are so fond of noting, ironically moot. Though not on the bill, Dylan was a much–rumored surprise guest; in retrospect, his no–show was entirely consistent with his flagging relevance as a generational voice. Instead, the chalice was passed to someone more worthy of that mantle, Wavy Gravy, the former standup comic, Hugh Romney, who brought being stoned to the level of performance art, and who may or may not have been credited with delivering the famous eulogy for the Love Generation heard at Woodstock sometime after the fifteenth hour: "From now on, this is a free concert!"

If this was the memorial by which our lifeblood, the totality of our body of social and musical thought, the magnitude of our bohemian promise, the depth of our generational power and potential will be forever measured, no wonder the 1960s has gotten such a bad rap in succeeding decades. John Sebastian, obviously happy to be there, on a prodigious acid trip, seemed blissfully oblivious to what happened in Chicago a year before, as if he didn't know the dream was already over, whatever the dream may have been (and that he himself wouldn't have another hit on the charts until 1976). But Sebastian's presence was hardly the shining lowlight of the festivities. For that dubious honor, there was something like a six way tie between the crowds, the elements, the drugs, Bert Sommer, Melanie, and Sha Na Na! In another withering irony, what has come to be thought of as Woodstock's true signal moment, Jimi Hendrix's typically incendiary set, came way after the damage was done, on the final morning, with almost everyone already gone.

Perhaps the only musician to truly benefit from the proceedings was Richie Havens, who must have made a lot of friends with his protracted opening set, waiting for the rest of the acts to arrive. It would be these loyal friends with their Woodstock memories of youth and naked long–haired men and women dancing in the mud and the rain, who would wind up assuring Richie's future, once his negligible chart career fizzled, with a scad of commercial voice–overs, as if his voice, his voice alone, deep and wide and limitless as a Grand Canyon of potential, selling us coffee and train rides and long distance phone calls, could sell us on the notion that we were different after all, that our struggles against the grain had amounted to something heroic.

There was nothing heroic, however, about our ultimate unraveling as a cultural force, in the months between Woodstock and Altamont, Altamont and Kent State, Kent State and the launching, at the end of 1970, of the first abortive Jefferson Starship, which, only a year earlier, as the Jefferson Airplane, were still advising in *Volunteers of America*, those who were not part of the solution to be counted "Up against the wall." The final months of our reign were marked by similar, if polar opposite, entreaties. "Get Together" finally saw its time arrive, by the Youngbloods, imploring people to "love one another, right now." In *Abbey Road*, the Beatles offered the tired "Come together over me"; capping off their musical wizardry with the lulling, almost tearful "In the end, the love you take, is equal to the love you make." At the same time, John and Yoko were kvelling "Give peace a chance," while Phil Ochs was declaring that "the war is over." But not to revisionist thinkers like Creedence Clearwater Revival, who instead noted "It looks like a bad moon on the rise." As melodramatic as Laura Nyro was in "Save the Country," from *New York Tendaberry*, the Grateful Dead were as surprisingly clear–eyed in "Casey Jones," from *Workingman's Dead* and "Truckin'" from *American Beauty*. While John Lennon primally howled "Mother" and "Cold Turkey," Dennis Hopper and Peter Fonda were getting shot in the back in *Easy Rider*, with a title tune by Dylan, sung by Roger McGuinn, about as apt a pairing for a swan song of an era as you could ever hope for. It was about this time you might have heard Merle Haggard singing "Okie from Muskogee" on their graves. If not, it would

have been Mick Jagger in *Performance*, crooning the morbid "Memo from Turner." The Rolling Stones countered,
as was their wont, the Beatles' genteel precocity with
daggers to the heart of the counterculture in *Let It Bleed*:
"Love in Vain," "Midnight Rambler" ("I'll stick my knife
right down your throat"), "Gimme Shelter" ("Love is but a
shot away") and "You Can't Always Get What You Want"
("But sometimes you get what you need").

And, in truth, while the Beatles were actively disinte-
grating ("I Me Mine"), and passively copping out, both as a
group ("Hey Jude," "Let It Be") and individually (Paul
and Ringo's irrelevant solo albums, George's fatalistic *All
Things Must Past*, John's sarcastic "Instant Karma"), it was
the Rolling Stones after all, our streetwise and pockmarked
older brothers, who sat the generation down for a much
needed talking to. School days were over, they were saying,
handholding communal ideologies and love–ins a thing of
the past (they helped make them a thing of the past). Like
it or not, we were hitting our middle–twenties still in
tie–dyed regalia, stunted adolescents lost in loopy rheto-
ric, afraid to grow up ("Sometimes you get what you
need"). What we needed but didn't want was the rude slap
in the face they gave us.

Nineteen seventy was filled with rude awakenings. The
Temptations summed it up in "Ball of Confusion." Les
McCann's jazzy "Compared to What," was even more
direct. Simon & Garfunkel offered us the gospel–inflected
placebo, "Bridge over Troubled Water," but they themselves were in the drink, at the height of their success,
unable to stand each other, much like the principals in
some of our other more mythic communes: John Lennon
and Paul McCartney, Marty Balin and Grace Slick (Roger
McGuinn and David Crosby, Janis Joplin and Big Brother).
Even the generation's righteous engine for social change,
Phil Ochs, ran out of steam, releasing the tongue in cheek

Greatest Hits in the face of widening gulfs between liberals and radicals, democrats and republicans, blacks and whites, men and women, the old and the young, and especially baby boom middle class draft dodgers who had all the options and the baby boom working class who bore the brunt of the hard choices, as well as the bullets.

Rather than face these rifts, and attempt to do something about them, Bob Dylan showed us a grotesque portrait of himself in *Self Portrait*, that may have been his final mocking gesture to the sheep who'd made him rich. Thus slapped again, even harder, many were driven, as was Bob himself, to the comfort of religion, a retreat past country, more East than Woodstock. The Byrds sang "Jesus Is Just All Right," the Beatles invoked Mother Mary, Norman Greenbaum hit the top of the charts with "Spirit in the Sky," and lots of white kids, in the mode of Lennon's "Instant Karma," followed the first guru they could find, into extended family groups, so they could shut out the encroaching world and sing "God, Love and Rock & Roll" by Teagarden and Van Winkle, and "My Sweet Lord" by George Harrison, indefinitely. Mel Lymon apparently took the whole Kweskin Jug Band with him when he decided he was God. And he wasn't the only one. Everyone, it seemed, was God, except Peter Green, who left Fleetwood Mac to become a disciple of the Children of God, and Eric Clapton, who'd already been God once, and was now out on the road with Delaney and Bonnie, living on "Blues Power."

But the blues couldn't save us from ourselves this time, thrill us, ennoble us, bring us together, not even Hendrix and his Band of Gypsies, not even "Layla." Certainly not Pink Floyd's founding drug casualty, Syd Barrett. Though Jimmy Page showed honorable signs of maturing in Led Zeppelin's third album, Zep's marauding legacy was already on its way to being irrevocably mis–applied by a new generation even further removed from his influences, using Page as the influence, his rock & roll devil, not his bluesy angel (in particular Black Sabbath, which spawned the ultimate rock miscreant, John 'Ozzy' Osbourne). Neither could we hide behind our love of black music in general, the Motown soundtrack of our coming of age. Three albums by the Jackson Five were one thing (wasn't that Michael cute?), but now that the Civil Rights Movement had officially flopped, all pretense that integration on the charts had anything to do with real life gave way to the Black Panthers (John Sinclair's White Panthers, too), and further polarization, the hard funk of Funkadelic, the hard line of Gil Scott–Heron and the Last Poets.

Maybe even the Sexual Revolution, surely our one redeeming legacy—at least as far as men were concerned —would soon be revealed as just another drug–induced fantasy. Yes, Grace Slick had sung "Triad," about living together with two men as a threesome, but the song was written by David Crosby, and its application, in crashpads from Berkeley to Brooklyn, found its currency in the original version. Janis Joplin's experience was more typical, if less cosmic ("Women Is Losers," "Down on Me," "Ball and Chain," "Piece of My Heart," etc.). Tracy Nelson's psyche was equally fragile ("Down So Low," "I Need Your Love So Bad"). Linda Ronstadt had graduated from the semi–depressed *Stone Poneys* to a solo career (*Hand Sewn . . . Home Grown,* and *Silk Purse*) that left her stranded, a voice without a song. Laura Nyro, in *Christmas and the Beads of Sweat*, became increasingly overwrought and despondent ("Been on a Train"). Only Joni Mitchell, having moved to Laurel Canyon, seemed to survive the decade with ego intact ("Both Sides Now," "Big Yellow Taxi"), sadder but wiser after reportedly brushing off the entire rock star community, from James Taylor to David Crosby. So Gale "We'll Sing in the Sunshine" Garnett was

a one–hit fluke, Maria Muldaur was in a cult, Leonard
Cohen's Suzanne was in therapy eight days a week, and
Ray Davies' "Lola" was very much in need of the same.
But the Women's Movement was just around the corner—
with Helen Reddy gargling in the wings.

Prescient as ever, Bob Dylan re–emerged just at this
time, from his orgy of self and audience loathing, a married
man, with, remarkably, five kids, showing the way to
connubial bliss in *New Morning* ("Sign in the Window,"
"Time Passes Slowly"). Yet there was something melancholy in his tone ("that must be what it's all about"), as if
he were still trying to convince himself. But after our two
rowdiest sex objects, Janis and Jimi, had paid the ultimate
price for their willful defiance of the norm, who wouldn't
be thinking about settling down? Only Jim Morrison was
still out there, dropping his pants. David "Why can't we go
on as three" Crosby wrote the first, and perhaps only
anthem for this new domesticity, "Our House," but he was
living out of wedlock at the time. More appropriate to the
oncoming return to family values were the newlyweds,
Paul and Linda McCartney. He even put her in the band,
though as a musician she was only an average photographer. The brother and sister act, the Carpenters, were even
more soothingly complacent ("We've Only Just Begun").
John and Yoko Ono–Lennon (Plastic Ono Band) weren't
beyond salvaging either. Sure they were still into love and
peace and rock & roll, but at least she was getting him to
reaffirm his roots in "Working Class Hero" and plunge to
the very core of family feelings in "Mother."

If marriage was the way, though, weren't labor pains
sure to follow? Meaning steady work, and children too,
maybe. A nine to five reality, previously anathema to the
Feed Your Head generation. At work, unless you were
lucky enough to have a mailroom job, you probably
wouldn't be able to listen to the radio as much as you were

accustomed to in the 1960s. That heartline cut, the music itself might cease to matter as much, supplanted by concerns more pressing than the AM–FM great radio debate. Of course, safe in family units, twos and threes and fours instead of massive demographic blocks attempting to raise (or was it raze) the mass sensibility (or was it the Pentagon) by the force of our collective will, no music would be able to muster a similar generational force again. Though, when a song like "Ohio" by Crosby, Stills, Nash & Young, not only got airplay, but became a national hit within months of the shootings at Kent State, you could get caught short for a second, thinking maybe the charts and the radio might not be totally irrelevant after all. The silent majority might not be totally conservative either. There could be hippies in three–piece suits living down the hall. But then the Who ("Won't Get Fooled Again") reminded you not to be so gullible. Married now, with a steady job, maybe a kid on the way, it was far safer to assume that AM radio was the Voice of America, Nixon America. FM radio was the same, but different, some demented commune of guitar soloists repeating the same tired riffs.

Finally, the Beatles, in their separate new family units, citing business disputes, brought us back to where we once belonged, in "The Long and Winding Road," a Phil Spector production that left us on the doorstep of 1959! No doubt about it, whether you called it rock & roll or rock, it was surely on its deathbed now. Maybe a new generation, born in the late 1950s, entering high school, would revive it, do it better, take it further. At the end of 1970, after all the hype, was this what we'd come to?

If that were true, then Stevie Wonder was more of a poet than Smokey Robinson or Bob Dylan, when he summed it up in his top ten smash of the time: "Heaven Help Us All."

Six

The Sexual Evolution

(1971–1974)

To the tunes of the Osmond family, the Carpenter family, the Gibb family (otherwise known as the Bee Gees), the Turner family—Ike and Tina—the Bono family—Sonny and Cher—the Knight family—Gladys and her cousins, the Pips—the Staple family, the Lennon family, the McCartney family, the Bramlett family—Delaney and Bonnie—the Partridge Family, the Jackson family—Michael, Marlon, Jermaine, Tito, etc.—Sly and the Stone family, and the Cornelius Brothers and Sister Rose, the men and women of the baby boom sat down in 1971, not often together, but usually within shouting distance, to contemplate the changing nature of the relationship between the sexes, and, if there was any time or energy left over, whether or not we had blown our role as cultural avatars, as well as our last best chance for a turned-on, liberal, peaceful, communal, egalitarian society in the image of rock & roll.

Impeding the process somewhat, the traditional image these young men brought to the bargaining table had taken quite a beating in the previous decade. Whether we were

141

closing down an administration building or protesting Nixon's beady–eyed grin or intent on spending the next ten years as we'd spent the last, flaked out beneath a stereo set, as role models for the 1970s, we were a quirky bunch of semi–neurotic draft–dodging dropouts, stunted adolescents with painted faces and ponytails, who not only followed leaders and failed to watch the parking meters, but had all the pretentions of poets, or at least rock stars, or at the very least, political pundits—weathermen, white panthers, Hare Krishnas—joining cults and spouting slogans and changing our names from Jim McGuinn to Roger because "some guy in Indonesia picked it out of the air. It had something to do with vibrations."

Alienated from the system that had roundly defeated those of us bearing the banner of the Alternate Culture, the FM culture, the radical hippie left, in all the important points, we were also cut off from our other half, that portion of the male generation our own age that we'd openly reviled, who were even then still in the process of being emasculated in Vietnam, and who in turn most likely regarded us with more of a logical rage than any supposed enemy in red pajamas.

No wonder, coming up for air in 1971, a lot of men in their twenties were suffering from an acute case of the Emotional Bends: Randy Newman ("Maybe I'm Doing It Wrong"), Leonard Cohen ("Sisters of Mercy"), John Prine ("Illegal Smile"), John Lennon ("Crippled Inside"), Bob Dylan ("Watching the River Flow"), Al Green ("Take Me to the River"), Brewer and Shipley ("One Toke over the Line"), Neil Young ("Helpless"), Buddy Miles ("Them Changes"), Sly Stone ("Runnin' Away"), David Crosby ("If I Could Only Remember My Name"), Rod Stewart ("How Can We Hang on to a Dream"), the New Riders of the Purple Sage ("I Don't Need No Doctor"), Cat Stevens ("Wild World"), Crazy Horse ("Gone Dead Train"), Neil

Diamond ("I Am . . . I Said"), Billy Joel ("The Ballad of the Angry Young Man"), Loudon Wainwright ("Careful, There's a Baby in the House"). Steven Stills, who proffered the typically unselective 1960's attitude toward monogamy and morality, in "Love the One You're With" and "Change Partners," nevertheless pre–figured the current Men's Movement by some twenty years in "We Are Not Helpless (We Are Men)." Closer to the emerging feminist zeitgeist of the period were liberated fellows like James Taylor ("You've Got a Friend"), John Denver ("Friends with You"), Bill Withers ("Lean on Me"), Paul McCartney ("Oh Woman Oh Why"), and Peter Yarrow ("The Wedding Song—There Is Love"), who would each undoubtedly do the dishes and change the diapers on their girlfriends' cat, Scheherezade.

Like the lonely longhairs wandering the neighborhood less than a decade back, these trendsetting sensitive and reflective males predictably drew unfriendly fire from their rougher peers on either side of the Vietnam dividing line, who championed the male supremacy of the Doors ("Love Her Madly"), Led Zeppelin ("Whole Lotta Love"), James Brown ("Hot Pants"), the Holy Modal Rounders ("Boobs a Lot"), the Rolling Stones ("Brown Sugar"), the J. Geils Band ("First I Look at the Purse"), and Alice Cooper ("Eighteen"). For many of them, still plotting revolution under a poster of Che Guevara, there were more marches to be held, new and zestier epithets to be hurled, headlines to be grabbed—and women were needed to make the sandwiches. Country Joe's latest album was called *War War War*. John Lennon was singing "Power to the People" and Graham Nash "Military Madness." Marvin Gaye was particularly concerned ("What's Goin' On," "Mercy Mercy Me (the Ecology)," and "Inner City Blues"). But in more and more cases such social statements were beginning to seem like evasions of the central male/

female issue: how can men expect to change the world until they change the way they relate to women?

In 1971, in response to a decade of retrogressive male behavior, and an immediate future of crippled psyches, women artists stepped to the center stage, placing more hits at the upper echelons of the record charts than in 1969 and 1970 combined—more, in fact, than at any time since 1963. Janis Joplin's posthumous *Pearl* set the feisty tone for this second phase of the Sexual Evolution ("Mercedes Benz," "Me and Bobby McGee")—one that would have many men, by year's end, wearing women's clothes and putting on makeup in preparation for a night out with the boys.

Barbra Streisand entered the rock arena in 1971, with Laura Nyro's "Stoney End," a perfect marriage of Brooklyn histrionics and Bronx angst, meeting on the D train. Laura herself remained in the station, singing do–wop with the members of Labelle ("The Wind," "Up on the Roof," "I Met Him on a Sunday"). Diana Ross continued her solo career, coming off the affirmative number one, "Ain't No Mountain High Enough," with "Remember Me." Tina Turner strutted through a nice and rough rendition of "Proud Mary," while Aretha Franklin did her one better, gospelizing "Bridge over Troubled Water" and "Spanish Harlem." Joan Baez achieved something approaching funkiness in "The Night They Drove Old Dixie Down." Bonnie Raitt's debut album featured what would become her signature tribute to her blues forbears, Sippie Wallace's "Woman Be Wise." Tracy Nelson continued her own soulful, if commercially unsuccessful, journey toward her blues roots, in "Soul of Sadness."

In Linda Ronstadt's countrified "Long Long Time," Karen Carpenter's coy "For All We Know," the handscrabble realism of "I Never Promised You a Rose Garden" by Lynn Andersen, and the cultured ambivalence

of Carly Simon's "That's the Way I Always Heard It Should
Be," the ambiguous parameters of the new woman were
being implicitly drawn. There were no limits. You could be
in rowdy rock bands, like Joy of Cooking ("Brownsville")
and Fanny ("Charity Ball"). You could talk back to sexist
dogs, like Jean Knight did in "Mr. Big Stuff," or stand up
for your sisters, like Laura Lee did in "Women's Love
Rights," or revert to blissful childhood, like Melanie did in
"Brand New Key." You could wreak vengeance on past
loves, like Joni Mitchell in "The Last Time I Saw Richard,"
or dominate your husband every week on network TV, like
Cher ("All I Ever Need Is You"). Or have a fling with the
Lord, Jesus Christ, himself, like Yvonne Elliman ("I Don't
Know How to Love Him"). If all else failed, you could
advertise, like Honey Cone did, in "Want Ads," or get up
on a soapbox and spout pure propaganda, like Helen
Reddy did in "I Am Woman."

Heading this resplendent breakthrough of free choice
was Carole King, whose album, *Tapestry*, would define her
as the perfect mellow middle ground alternative for wom-
en and men to adopt as their feminine prototype for the
near future. Neither so fearsomely intellectual as Joni
Mitchell, nor so cloyingly bubbleheaded as Melanie; nowhere near as stridently political as Baez, as emotionally
overpowering as Tracy Nelson or Aretha, as threateningly
nubile as Ronstadt, as haughtily unattainable as Diana Ross
or Carly Simon, King had transported her Brooklyn ethos,
accent, stoop, and candystore to the land of perpetual sun
and smog, adapting to the geographical dislocations ("So
Far Away"), personal upheavals ("It's Too Late"), and
seismic changes ("I Feel the Earth Move"), such a shift is
naturally heir to; among the starlets and harlots and retired
surfdolls of L.A., her voice was a nasal whine of fresh air.
In fact, if Bob Dylan hadn't been up to his eyebrows in
diapers out in a cabin in Utah at the time, or else too busy

accepting his honorary degree at Princeton and consorting with Nashville cats, he almost certainly would have dubbed her the greatest rock & roll poetess since Judith Viorst.

With the Sexual Revolution tilting toward the female, and the political pendulum veering toward the right, and the Fillmores on both coasts closing down, men and women, through that painful year of 1971, increasingly found themselves meeting, when they met at all, for emotional sustenance and counseling, at a certain woodsy crossroads of folk and blues, country and middle of the road pop, where R&R stood for Rest and Rehabilitation, in a place I call the Middle of the Dirt Road—the greening of pop, the maturing of folk, the ripening of rock—a sound which the baby boom middle class would eventually salvage as their own, effectively making it the most popular sound of the period, if not the entire decade.

Middle of the Dirt Road, as propounded by its many varied adherents, was an inner–directed search for meaning amid the disillusionments of age and the Age; with mainstream rock mired in classical overkill (Yes, ELP, Jethro Tull) and kiddie mysticism (Black Sabbath, Deep Purple, T. Rex), and juvenile noise (Grand Funk Railroad, Black Oak Arkansas), with black music getting angry ("Maggot Brain" by Funkadelic, Sly Stone's "Thank You for Talkin' to Me Africa," Melvin Van Peebles's "Tenth and Greenwich," from the musical, *Sweet Sweetback's Baddass Song*, and the score to *Shaft* by Isaac Hayes), and country music getting smug ("When You're Hot, You're Hot" by Jerry Reed, the entire Kris Kristofferson catalogue, Elvis's open door at Nixon's White House), it was a protective reaction as much as a lifestyle. Looming up ahead as real generational possibilities were Perry Como, Andy Williams, and Tom Jones, the stultified alternative our parents had predicted for us, all taking advantage of our momentary stasis to have comeback years in 1971, promenading such exemplary much–younger ladies as the docile Olivia Newton–John, the acquiescent Karen Carpenter, the increasingly glitzy Cher, the primarily showbiz Streisand, and the second coming of Petula Clark, Helen Reddy.

A life of clean fingernails, diet soda, and ballroom dancing, defanged, unfettered domesticity, and the spectre of Wayne Newton, running, not walking, to a Las Vegas recording studio, informed, as much as anything, the imperative that caused our recumbent emotional Geiger–counters, the musicians encamped at the front lines in the Middle of the Dirt Road, to send us back their cryptic messages of sadness, experience, and retrenchment. To which the AM radio mainstream responded with the insipid overreaction, "Joy to the World" by Three Dog Night—as if a word of truth would send us all into therapy, some religious cult, the Republican party, IBM, or the Green Berets. But, for the most part, even the hits were doleful, rueful, and mournful. Richie Havens's "Here Comes the Sun," for instance, in this context, is almost unbearably melancholy, and Jonathan Edwards's "Sunshine," as gloomy as a dirge by Strauss. The somber tone of our period of recovery and reconciliation was captured perfectly by Elton John's "Your Song" and Rod Stewart's wistful "Maggie May," a reminiscence of first love that gains added power for its evocation of our time of unbridled lust and innocence that would probably never come again.

Contemplating our dreamladen, frustrated past, Laura Nyro released a whole album of her subway love songs; contemplating the anxious present, the Jefferson Airplane decided to break up in "Third Week at the Chelsea"; contemplating his hassled, impotent future, Jim Morrison fled to Paris, where he was found, huddled in a bathtub like Marat; contemplating its dwindling hold on the marketplace, Motown Records left Detroit for Los Angeles; contemplating his legacy, John Lennon lashed out at his former partner in "How Do You Sleep," lashed out at the world in "Gimme Some Truth," and offered his program for salvation in "Imagine." Contemplating his naval, Cat Stevens retreated further into the void in "Into White." Bob Dylan and the Grateful Dead both offered rare contemplations on their own voluminous legacies, in "When I Paint My Masterpiece" and "Truckin'," respectively. The previously dreaded Led Zeppelin did Bob Dylan one better, actually producing their masterpiece, in 1971, when "Stairway to Heaven" was released on their fourth album, a massive, murky, droning, dislocated, moody paradox of pretentious Elizabethan heavy metal, which has since inexplicably become revered for its musical majesty. However, it is as revealing as anything produced in the seventies, of the schizoid polarities loose in a generational psyche once thought solidly of an anarchic piece.

By the end of the year, the collective frame of mind was even ready to receive Don McLean's jigsaw epic, "American Pie," which may or may not have been a symbolic eulogy over the ghost of rock & roll or a retrospective celebration of its nine lives, but was definitely less about the day the music died, than it was about the *year* the music died, 1972, when American–made rock & roll virtually vanished from the landscape and the airwaves, while Nixon and his trusty squire, Spiro, continued their reconstruction project begun in 1969, all but unimpeded by the voices of the baby boom constituency.

Collected in the Middle of the Dirt Road, we remained silently pacified by the mid–tempo plaints of Jackson Browne ("Song for Adam"), the Eagles ("Take It Easy"), John Prine ("Donald and Lydia"), Jim Croce ("You Don't Mess Around with Jim"), Eric Andersen ("Is It Really Love at All"), Danny O'Keefe ("Good Time Charlie's Got the

Blues"), Harry Chapin ("Taxi"), Neil Young ("Old Man"), Bonnie Raitt singing John Prine ("Angel from Montgomery"), Arlo Guthrie singing Steve Goodman ("The City of New Orleans"), Paul Simon ("Peace Like a River"), John and Yoko's then politically incorrect "Woman Is the Nigger of the World," Randy Newman's uproariously cynical "Political Science," Ellen McIlwaine ("Honky Tonk Angel"), the Nitty Gritty Dirt Band singing Jerry Jeff Walker ("Mr. Bojangles"), and the entire Taylor family—Alex, Kate, Livingston, James, and Taylor–to–be, Carly Simon ("Anticipation")—a dangerously large percentage of Woodstock nationals, effectively rendering ourselves moot, mute, and utterly beside the point.

Capitalizing on the atmosphere created by Don McLean's glorification of the Chevy, the levee, and especially, our checkered middle class rock & roll history, epitomized by Buddy Holly's passing, which had once so energized and ennobled the Beatles, our own legendary baby boom advance guard was further depleted, as 1972 inched toward Nixon's coronation, by a killing wave of nostalgia that sapped whatever political strength George McGovern's eager legions of mellow pop stars might have otherwise mustered. Then again, after seeing Dion return a Christian, in *Sanctuary*, and former Deep Purple frontman, Ian Gillan, star in Andrew Lloyd–Webber's *Jesus Christ, Superstar*, and George Harrison and Bob Dylan, after abandoning their own kind halfway up the Big Rock Candy Mountain, try to enlist support for some unknown starving orphans in a place we all knew didn't really exist, called Bangladesh, a kind of measured irrationality might have been the only proper response to any further indignities of the soul and the memory.

But that was not the case. As the year progressed, we had to witness not one, but two, teeny superstars so bereft of their own creative energy that they deemed it necessary to ravage our fragile equilibrium with squeaky renditions of classic tunes ("Rockin' Robin" by Michael Jackson, and Paul Anka's "Puppy Love" by Donnie Osmond). Maybe these weren't the absolute nonpariel mementos hindsight made them out to be, but once the psychic door was flung open, all sorts of riffraff could traipse in, tracking mud and bubblegum on the vinyl carpets of our pristine heritage.

But, actually, aside from the Partridge Family's innocuous remake of Neil Sedaka's "Breaking up Is Hard to Do," Don McLean's mandate for inflated nostalgia was taken up less by a second generation, than by the first. Having more or less patiently waited out America's infatuation with the Beatles, and its subsequent leftward swing to the spontaneous street beat of the blues, buoyed no doubt more by Elvis's return to Nixon's airwaves than McLean's cryptic poetry, guys like Dion and Jerry Lee Lewis, Paul Anka himself, Rick Nelson ("Garden Party") and Chuck Berry ("My Ding–a–Ling") felt safe enough to entertain delusions of relevance to our tear–gas ravaged sensibilities. Before the spring was out, the off–Broadway musical *Grease* would commence its ascension toward a nationally institutionalized rendering of a universal Fifties Experience ("Summer Nights," "Beauty School Dropout") that was far worse than *Bye Bye Birdie.* In its mindless celebration of innocent chrome and crinolines, the tragicomic victory of Bobby Rydell over do–wop, it negated the essence of the generation's shared heritage, the magnificent wonder of Elvis, the existential truths only to be found Up on the Roof or Under the Boardwalk, winking as it did so, as if to imply that the years that followed were basically a frat house joke gone awry. As comfortable an excuse as anyone had yet come up with for 1968, the success of Grease led quickly to *American Graffitti* in the movies, and "Happy Days" on television.

Surely, however, the fact that "Burning Love" by Elvis

Presley was among the three—count 'em—hardest white American rock & roll songs to hit the top ten that year ("School's Out" by Alice Cooper and "Go All the Way" by the Raspberries virtually completing America's rock & roll statement for 1972) led some to conclude that between Middle of the Dirt Road (America, the Eagles, Neil Young, Neil Diamond, Seals and Crofts, the New Seekers, Robert John, Carole King) and—with the exception of the Temptations' "Papa Was a Rolling Stone" and Curtis Mayfield's "Freddy's Dead" and "Superfly"—its black counterpart Philly soul (the Chi–Lites, the Stylistics, the O'Jays, Billy Paul, Harold Melvin & the Bluenotes, the Spinners, the Dramatics, Luther Ingram), not only as a generation, but as a country, our will to move and be moved had been systematically and entirely supressed—as further evidenced that November by the Nixon landslide.

Torn apart, creatively exhausted, mired in a muddle of sexual ambivalence, as if in answer to an arrested generation's cry for a shove in some direction, even if down a well of moral ambiguity, some men, following a seemingly au–natural progression, much like the rumored straight line from a mere whiff of reefer to the hard stuff, went from letting their hair grow past their shoulders, and adopting the loose fitting thong and burlap and dayglow chic of the sixties, to cutting out of the male/female nexus entirely—in favor of a lifestyle devoid of any traditional family responsibilities—dressed like Ziggy Stardust and ready for "Ch–Ch–Ch–Ch–Changes."

Alice Cooper, the first male rocker to adopt a woman's name, wore makeup. Roxy Music's debut album featured a drag queen on the cover, implying perverse pleasures inside. *The Slider* was Marc Bolan's bid for similar attention in T–Rex. David Bowie released three albums in 1972, two in November, *Space Oddity* and *The Man Who Sold the World*, the same month as Mott the Hoople's anthemic "All the Young Dudes" signalled the arrival of this dangerous new alternative mode of behaviorism, and the Belle of the Baths, Bette Midler, put her unabashedly campy gay cabaret act on vinyl in *The Divine Miss M*, with Barry Manilow at the keyboards. Lou Reed put the power of his devious presence firmly on the side of the New Man, in *Transformer* ("Vicious"), which appeared the next month, at the same time as strong statements from Joni Mitchell ("The Blonde in the Bleachers") and Carly Simon ("You're So Vain"). For women like Joni and Carly, and legions of others, the number one song in the country was "I Am Woman" by Helen Reddy. But also on the charts was a song that could be considered the rousing male reaction to such strident feminism, Slade's "Mama, We'er All Crazee Now." Finally, presaging 1973's frontal assault on the libido and the imagination of the male generation, we were faced with the pouty presence of David Johansen in the updated bad boy/girl posturing of the New York Dolls ("Personality Crisis")—which would lead, by the end of that year, to the full flowering of this demented theatricality, in the painted faces of Kiss ("Kissing Time").

A slightly more intellectual and less personally unsettling response to the dilemma was conjured by another group of disenfranchised men (and a few highly motivated women), who had grown up believing not only in the power of rock & roll to set them free, but to provide for their old age as well. Having failed to achieve either of those ends in coffee houses or concert halls, college newspapers or radio stations, or fledgling rock bands during the 1960s, they now, with the desperate ingenuity of worldclass cribsheet and "classics illustrated" connoisseurs, sought to redress this psychic and financial imbalance by writing about the topic. Inaugurated as an artform by the gushing effervescense of San Francisco's *Rolling Stone*, trade journal of the counterculture, in 1967, and practiced with regularity by dilettantes and pragmatists in such elitist journals as the *Village Voice*, in New York, by the time of its popular surge in 1972, becoming a Rock Critic, as a profession or a calling, rivaled Independent Filmmaker, Spiritual Leader, and House Husband as the white middle class alternative to getting honest work.

Not as revered as the Advice to the Lovelorn Columnist, the Movie, TV/Radio or (certainly) Drama Critic, the Rock Critic of 1972 was motivated far more by passionate partisanship than easy cash (at $125 a week, you'd better be in love with the job). With the New Journalism of Tom Wolfe and Hunter Thompson as its Beatles, the Black Humor of Heller and Pynchon its Dylan, and a pent–up over–intellectualism inspired by the dozen or so years most of its practictioners had spent idling in college, Rock Criticism's truest mandate sprang from the desire not only to defend one's creative turf from the encroaching (younger) philistines, and to define it for the ages, but, literally, to assume responsibility for its survival.

Much in the way it took an Elvis Presley to crystallize the nascent polarities at play in the atmosphere of the early 1950s, coalescing our angels and devils into one seductive, toxic brew (for a year or so, anyway), Rock Criticism came into its own in 1972 as a means of affecting change, wielding power, getting published, or obtaining a better paying job in the record business, largely through the appearance on the horizon, as if in a simultaneous mass vision, of a man who magically embodied all the as yet unexpressed, unsung, and certainly unwritten hopes and dreams of this particular throng of white middle class baby boom wordaholics weaned on Norman Mailer and Wolfman Jack and baptised at the feet of Bill (not Billy) Graham. While *Jesus Christ, Superstar* gave some people (probably) a religious experience in 1972, it was nothing compared to the epiphanies the Rock Critic generation experienced as one when Bruce Springsteen's *Greetings from Asbury Park* was released, modestly, unceremoniously, seemingly at random, but just as definitely ushering in the Golden Age of Rock Criticism (for a year or so, anyway).

According to the instant consensus of the rock critical community, from the dryest of trade journals to the wettest fanzine, Springsteen could well have been the white Otis Redding, a working class guy like Elvis, who sang like Jay (of Jay and the Americans—either one of them), and played a guitar like Steve (Cropper, the Steve in Sam & Dave's famous exhortation, "Play it, Steve," from "Soul Man"). Spewing amphetamine lyrics that scanned like Dylan and romanticized the eastern Under the Boardwalk ethos of blood, sweat, and urban lust like Spector in his heyday, and with a big black saxophone guy in the band, like Gene Barge, the mythical Daddy G from "Quarter to Three" by Gary U.S. Bonds, named Clarence, all Springsteen lacked for sheer rock & roll perfection were the castanets! At the same time as his love stories ("Spirit in the Night," "For You") and his growing up stories ("Growing Up") brought back Dion & the Belmonts and the Ronettes, his sense of urgency and emergency could make you think of Kerouac all over again, Mailer and Ginsberg at the barricades. Then again, his war stories ("Lost in the Flood") and his street stories ("The Angel") were honest and driving enough to win back the blue collar rock audience that had lost faith with the anti–war, hippie agenda of free love and racial equality of the 1960s. In one man, we could see this hoped for unification with our brothers, this end to our long civil war; with the energy of the innocent, we sought to communicate the revelation of this beatific new arrival.

Of course, the album was a colossal flop.

But that didn't mean the cause of literacy, rebel energy,

the new togetherness, the resurgence of hard–edged rock, a Critic–inspired general creative renewal, and the eventual Second Coming wouldn't happen. And that it wouldn't bring with it all the social and emotional and artistic and political gravy that had been siphoned off our plates by accident and assassination and other dubious acts of human nature in forty–eight of the fifty states.

In fact, it must have been rock & roll on the radio in the cityroom of the *Washington Post* when the first inklings of Watergate started beating through the static like the Clovers at the far end of the AM dial, presenting to the losers now a challenge impossibly beautiful and dangerous and uncontrollable. With Woodward and Bernstein as Alan Freed and Deep Throat as R&B, this new sound of redemption swept across 1973, uniting a generation around the radio with a sense of purpose missing since 1968, when last we coalesced around the FM band to unseat a sitting President.

It would be overly self–congratulatory, of course, to attribute rock criticism alone for this refreshing turnaround, not only in music, but in life as well. But, why not? Otherwise, you'd have to chalk it up to antiquated notions of checks and balances, the mills of the gods, the inevitability of justice, old–fashioned hard work, when you know there were chips being called in on this one, ancient vendettas, memories of the Checkers speech, Haiphong, Agnew, Trisha, Julie, a Black Humor heyday of retribution. So you might as well credit Lester and Dave, Meltzer, Goldstein and the Dean, and all the other noble scribes responsible for a year in which Chicago columnist Bob Greene made the best seller lists with *Billion Dollar Baby*, his book about traveling around the country as Santa Claus in Alice Cooper's backup band, and the cover of *Rolling Stone* made the top of the record charts.

Actually, that ditty by Dr. Hook, written by *Playboy*

cartoonist/songwriter, Shel Silverstein ("Blue Eyes," Johnny Cash's "A Boy Named Sue," Loretta Lynn's "One's on the Way"), was one of the least literary songs of 1973. This was a year when songwriter Alex Harvey's "Delta Dawn," as interpreted by Bette Midler, and popularized by Helen Reddy, evoked Flannery O'Connor, and Lou Reed evoked Nelson Algren ("Walk on the Wild Side") and admitted Pynchon fans, Steely Dan ("Reeling in the Years"), evoked Black Humor, their name inspired by William Burroughs, the man from whom the term Heavy Metal was purportedly taken. Which brings us to Blue Oyster Cult, the purported heavy metal band that sang the songs of the sagacious critic, R. Meltzer himself. Then there was Iggy Pop, who could have been Celine, writhing in the grip of *Raw Power* ("I Want to be Your Dog"). Peter Townshend wrote another rock opera for the Who, in the mode of a British Angry Young Man (*Quadrophenia*). Neil Young, who announced the ending of the war in Vietnam, during a concert at Madison Square Garden in January, did a film (*Journey Through the Past*). The folks at the *National Lampoon* did a Black Humor musical, *Lemmings*, introducing to the survivors of "Woodchuck nation" future *Saturday Night Live* stalwarts Chevy Chase, Garrett Morris, and John Belushi; Elliot Murphy ("How's the Family") briefly attempted to be F. Scott Fitzgerald. John Prine ("Christmas in Prison"), Jackson Browne ("For Everyman"), and Paul Simon ("American Tune") were short story stylists in pop song form. Bob Dylan, having fed the hungry, now emerged with a protest song ("George Jackson"). A New Journalist, Pete Hamill, would write the liner notes to Dylan's 1975 album. At the same time as Patti Smith, the dark–haired poet–type, was prowling around the East Village, quoting Rimbaud and the Shangri–Las, Tom Waits was out West, quoting Ferlinghetti and the Coasters. By the end of the year, Springsteen's second effusive effort, *The*

Wild, the Innocent, and the E-Street Shuffle ("Wild Billy's Circus Story"), was inspiring similar effusions from the dozens of rock critics who had discovered him in the selfsame Max's Kansas City where Andy Warhol's effete corps were still claiming to represent the hip elite—and who continued to regard him as personally responsible for their own creative renaissance, to say nothing of their sustained livelihood.

The new recovery of our lost bohemian spirit was even being felt deep in the reactionary loins of country music, where an about–to–be–divorced Elvis Presley appeared, live from Hawaii, a rocker reborn, and Nashville's grey–haired rookie, Charlie Rich ("The Most Beautiful Girl in the World," "Behind Closed Doors"), had his long–awaited commercial breakthrough. Tracy Nelson moved to Tennessee, to get closer to the earth, if not Mother Earth, and Donna Fargo, Dottie West, Linda Ronstadt, Anne Murray, Brenda Lee, Lynn Anderson, and Tanya Tucker all had chart successes. The implications of this slight soul–awakening of country music— previously a bastion for tales of homespun repression—would prove to be nearly as significant as the rise of rock journalism, in affecting a change in the mood of the nation.

Closer than Tennessee to this spiritual center in 1973, was Georgia, with two titles at the top of the charts, songwriter Bobby Russell's Faulknerian (or at least Bobbi Gentrian) "The Night the Lights Went out in Georgia" by Vicki Lawrence, and Gladys Knight & the Pips' "Midnight Train to Georgia." Charlie Daniels, who would later come down to Georgia to meet the Devil, got the devil scared out of him by some rednecks in a truckstop in "Uneasy Rider." Elsewhere, all through the South, rocking rebels were suddenly arising to reclaim their manhood in memory of the dear departed Duane Allman: "Rambling Man" by the Allman Brothers, "Smokin' in the Boy's Room" by Brownsville Station, "Frankenstein" by the Edgar Winter Group. Jim Croce's good old boy portrait of southern machismo, "Bad Bad Leroy Brown," was by far a manlier alternative to the weeping Don McLean–sensitivity Roberta Flack was extolling in "Killing Me Softly with His Song." Over in the Middle of the Dirt Road, where Loudon Wainwright's "Dead Skunk" was found "stinking to high heaven," evidence of the deliverance of the male ego from its premature burial ground (as symbolized in the film, *Deliverance*) was striking—if not as immediately compelling as the Gospel–inspired lunar escapism propounded by Pink Floyd in what would become their forever–best selling album, *Dark Side of the Moon.* Elsewhere, however, we were getting ready to abandon our citified cynicism ("Kodachrome" by Paul Simon, "Reeling in the Years" by Steely Dan). A return to childhood innocence beckoned ("Your Mama Don't Dance" by Loggins & Messina, "Diamond Girl" by Seals and Crofts, and "Rosalita," by Bruce Springsteen). A merger with our country cousins in the Middle of the Dirt Road seemed not only accessible and desirable, but cool, rebellious, chic ("Outlaw Man" and "Desperado" by the Eagles, "Knocking on Heaven's Door" by Bob Dylan, "China Grove" by the Doobie Brothers, "Redneck Friend" by Jackson Browne). Moreover, we were not prepared to concede that all our attempts to achieve racial harmony were summarily doomed ("The World Is a Ghetto" by War). By early the next year, the combination of middle class muscle and backwoods backbone had Nixon and his bungling Purple Gang kneeling in prayer at regular intervals in the oval office. At around this time, the about–to–be–divorced Bob Dylan was seen, socializing with the lust–in–his–heart governor of the great state of Georgia, Jimmy Carter.

Opening his comeback tour with the rousing song to his fans, his wife, his detractors, the New Left, the Old Right,

the critics, the folkies, the cynics, as well as the members
of his own backup band, the Band, and perhaps, even, his
new–found country audience, "Most Likely You Go Your
Way (and I'll Go Mine)," Dylan mangled his old standards
with a vengeance that brought standing ovations, tapping
into the grassroots closet unrest of the multitudes as he
hadn't since 1966. Burning his rock & roll bridges as
surely behind him as he had his folk roots, Dylan's
subsequent journey to the unexpected forefront of the
political future brought a slew of strange backwoods
bedfellows curled up in his coattails. Tom T. Hall had his
biggest pop hit, "I Love." Post–hippie crooner Jimmy
Buffett had his first, "Come Monday." The dour trouba-
dour Hoyt Axton had his one and only, "When the
Morning Comes." Dolly Parton, the ultimate truckstop
waitress, crossed over with "Jolene." Linda Ronstadt was
purity personified, in the country chestnut, "Silver
Threads and Golden Needles." Even Mac Davis, on his
way to Vegas, had a tantalyzing, if patently insincere,
second thought, in "Stop and Smell the Roses." More
ironic was Randy Newman, on his way to a date with the
Atlanta symphony orchestra, who stopped and delved into
his roots, in "Louisiana 1927," from his album about Huey
Long, *Good Old Boys*. John Denver's country conversion
was complete, if overly optimistic, in "Sunshine on My
Shoulders." But Tanya Tucker's awakening vixenhood was
anything but saccharine, in "Would You Lay with Me (in a
Field of Stone)," written by the ex–con, David Allen Coe.
And our own dreamy Greenwich Village cum Cambridge,
Mass bohemian, Maria Muldaur's monumental breakthrough with the upstate New York rhythms of "Midnight
at the Oasis," was as sweet as it was funky. Everywhere,
the message from the country was equally inevitable, in
the works of Gregg Allman ("Midnight Rider"), the
Allman Brothers ("Jessica"), ZZ Top ("La Grange"),

Lynyrd Skynyrd ("Sweet Home, Alabama,") and Rick Derringer ("Rock & Roll Hoochie Coo").

Having just three years before observed his thirtieth birthday at the Wailing Wall, Dylan, however, like many a reformed hippie turned rural hermit, was approaching a spiritual crossroads in 1974, that would lead him, divorced and hungry, to a Christianity phase that once again all but demolished his grip on the mortal energy of his constituency, most of whom were at the time finally regaining a sense of the pleasures of their own flesh not felt since 1966. In the cities, especially, a generation of repressed and dominated, politically decimated, castrated and frustrated young men in the image of David Bowie threw off their chains of intimidation, literally threw off their old clothes, and stepped into sleek new outfits—but not before streaking the neighborhood clad only in a pair of high–top US Keds. Country satirist Ray Stevens noted their abundance in "The Streak," but not their significance. Once dressed, or cross–dressed, as the case may have been, they lit up the urban nightlife as it hadn't been lit for years, to the blatant throb of rhythm and blues.

Not since Annie had her baby in 1956, had the city rhythm been so blue. Parliament gave us "Up for the Down Stroke," the Ohio Players "Skin Tight," B.T. Express "Do It Till You're Satisfied," George McCrae "Rock Your Baby," and Barry White "Can't Get Enough of Your Love, Babe," his voice an invitation that would have made even Johnny Mathis blush. In Germany, Donna Summer was preparing her simulated sexual response. It would launch a Disco age to rival the heyday of Chubby Checker and Annie's daddy, Hank Ballard. Buoyed by the comeback of the backbeat, the sounds of the city were direct and strong; ("For the Love of Money" by the O'Jays, "Love Don't Love Nobody" by the Spinners), cerebral as well as sensual

("What Is Hip?" by Tower of Power), positively ebullient ("You Make Me Feel Brand New" by the Stylistics); Stevie Wonder's "Living for the City" would be the first city anthem. And it was to tunes like "Dancing Machine" by the Jackson 5, "Jungle Boogie" by Kool and the Gang, "Boogie Down" by Eddie Kendricks, "Rock the Boat" by the Hues Corporation, and the revived "Locomotion" by Grand Funk Railroad, that nascent hoofers black and white gladly danced on Dickie Nixon's political grave.

Undoubtedly symbolic of our increased receptivity and red blood cell count, 1974 was a year in which the individual Beatles were responsible, collectively, for nine tunes that made the top twenty, their best showing since they arrived here in 1964 (when they had 15), and almost perfectly reflective of their own schizophrenic 1970s directions: Paul showing his wings as a rock & roller ("Helen Wheels," "Jet," "Band on the Run," "Junior's Farm"), John bitterly fighting with his demons, his memories, and Yoko, as well as the government's best efforts to get him deported ("Whatever Gets You Through the Night"), George suitably mystical and obscure ("Dark Horse") and Ringo, relentlessly retrogressive ("You're Sixteen," "Oh My My" and "Only You"). But, as usual, it was the Rolling Stones who tried to put a lid on our expectations, with "It's Only Rock & Roll (But I Like It)," summing up, with that compulsive parenthesis, the extent of our ambivalence.

For, if it was all indeed "only rock & roll" (echoing Dylan's long ago "life and life only"), some sideshow we could boogie to uptown at the Disco or in the Middle of the Dirt Road to an endless guitar serenade, no more meaningful than a night on the town, great sex, and a President given the boot, then we might as well have been back in 1968. So, while the country's midsection did the bump and grind, at the edges our morose thinkers sat this one out, attempting to take stock of what had changed and what had remained the same.

Closer to thirty now than twenty ourselves, as a self–contained baby boom blip in 1974, enough of our confidence in the system had been restored by the ending of the war and the resignation in disgrace of our prime tormentor to express our outrage at all he'd stolen from us, in song, in dance, in style again. But we were, nevertheless, still paying the price of our outlaw past in the wages of confusion. Many men had yet to buy a suit; it would be years before they'd have the spare change (to say nothing of the conventional desire, let alone the marketable skills), necessary to obtain a conventional mortgage. Many women had yet to have a baby; it would take years of group therapy (to say nothing of hours trying to expunge from their frontal lobes the melodies of such baby–centric propaganda as Paul Anka's singularly patronizing "You're Having My Baby" and Seals & Crofts' more insidious "Unborn Child") before they would decide if they even wanted to. Jackson Browne was obsessed by the magnitude of the innocence we'd lost ("Before the Deluge"); Lou Reed was almost criminally bitter about the waste of life and promise ("Kill Your Sons"), Leonard Cohen took it a bit more personally ("Take This Longing"); and Bob Dylan was still in emotional hiding ("Shelter from the Storm"). Both men and women were deep into a kind of spiritual rootlessness ("Free Man in Paris" by Joni Mitchell, "Please Come to Boston" by Dave Loggins, "Must of Got Lost" by the J. Geils Band). Some decided to deny it ("Haven't Got Time for the Pain" by Carly Simon), avoid it ("Carefree Highway" by Gordon Lightfoot), act it out ("Rebel Rebel" by Davie Bowie), romanticize it ("Seasons in the Sun" written by Rod McKuen, "The Way We Were" sung by Barbra Streisand), wallow in it ("You and Me Against the World" by Helen Reddy), plunge themselves into catch–up ball ("Cat's in the Cradle" by Harry Chapin), or follow the pious example of the recently deposed ex–president ("The Lord's Prayer" by Sister Janet Mead).

The generally confused state of our psyche (Middle of the Dirt Road), where the compulsive need for freedom (Southern Rock) had been perverted into an omnipresent fear of any kind of commitment (Disco), was nowhere better epitomized than by the record charts, in which an unprecedented thirty–five different songs made it to number one, only four of them remaining there for more than two weeks, and an amazing twenty–one lasting but a single week apiece. The choices, once so obvious and dramatic, between AM conservatism and FM rebellion, the hip righteousness of the alternate culture and the uptight fascism of the straight world, the nobility of the black cause verses the slave–trading mentality of the white majority, the dominant male role, the submissive female role, and the rock role in electing the next president, were all up for constant inner re–evaluation. FM radio was increasingly bathing itself in meandering sludge: Yes, Procol Harum, Jethro Tull, Deep Purple. AM radio, meanwhile, gave us "I Shot the Sheriff" by Eric Clapton, "Raised on Robbery" by Joni Mitchell, and, especially, "Rikki, Don't Lose That Number" by Steely Dan. The alternate culture was living underground, subsisting on a diet of yellowed, macrobiotic headlines about the Symbionese liberation of Patti Hearst, while the so–called straight world showed signs of breaking from their Monday through Friday chains, in gold chains down to their navals, at strobe–lit Odyssey 2000s all across the country. The new economic reality of layoffs and gas lines was in the process of rendering moot much of the sixties sloganeering about equal rights for blacks; the race struggle was now a class struggle. Sexually, the celebrated reversals going on between John and Yoko, Dylan and Sara, Elvis and Priscilla, Ike and Tina, and Sonny and Cher, were mirrored in the unsettled mid–life of the populace, dividing with the skill and speed of paramecia, and celebrating at the disco their second teenage, even while the televised version of their impossibly halcyonic first, "Happy Days," was prompting more than a few of them to leave any further soul–searching explorations and political triumphs to kids born after Elvis hit the charts ("Oh Very Young" by Cat Stevens, "Forever Young" by Bob Dylan). A few kids took them up on it; in 1974, the Ramones quit their day jobs in Queens, New York, to pursue their simple dream of resurrecting mindless rock & roll out of the obtuse confusions we'd made of rock, at CBGB's on New York's Lower East Side.

Probably the only group not confused about the meaning of the music and their place within it was the amalgamated society of rock critics, who were still, to a man (and the occasional woman), united around their mythic quest on behalf of their working class hero, Bruce Springsteen, which was quite consuming enough to obliterate all else, failing marriages, the noisy death rattle of corpulent corporate FM, unrelenting class, race, and sexual warfare. With his first two albums having stiffed, Springsteen was barely clinging to life in 1974, on the legacy of his live shows, the grassroots support of his fervent denim army, visionary as the crewcut Elvisites of the South in 1954, yet dewy–eyed as the screeching Beatlemaniacs of 1964 America. Despite rumors of dirty pool at the label, some predictable weird stuff with his manager, once onstage, Springsteen, not yet "The Boss," but certainly the hardest working white man in show business, was just about the only rock act capable of making a grown man cry, dance, see God—to say nothing of the future of rock & roll. Who needed Disco, the Peace Corps, love forever, or eternal youth? Springsteen was our commitment, our lasting relationship; to some he was even more, as I detailed at the time, in my now prophetic essay, written in 1975, but suppressed until its eventual publication in 1978. Solely in the interests of historical completeness, I reprint it now in its entirety.

Proceedings of Discovery

We rock pundits, critics and reviewers, Rockwells of good taste, Cristgau's of moral fervor, are in reality no better than the average slob on the street, nose pressed up against the windowpanes of status. We have our own highly defined Continental League where we vie in the standings for points, key by–lines, new discoveries, lead blurbs. Each of us reads the daily papers to keep tabs on the opposition. Each scans the monthlies nervously, afraid of missing a shift in the national musical mood. The competition is fierce and deadly. At times sly and subtle, it is often hidden in the guise of camaraderie.

Let me take you back to the summer of 1974, to the Bottom Line, New York's famed hot spot and hangout, where the group known as Kansas was being showcased before the press and trade over cocktails, convivial chatter, and free food. I arrived early, nodding and smiling at familiar faces as I moved toward the free food. Halfway there I spotted a face too familiar to ignore: Bruce Springsteen, then as yet a budding superstar, still a year away from the hoopla and simultaneous covers of *Time* and *Newsweek* which are now media legend.

Springsteen and I went all the way back to 1973. I was, in fact, one of the prime contenders for the title of "The Man Who Discovered Bruce Springsteen," along with three or four other prominent journalists, each convinced his case was at least as good as mine.

Originally published in 1978 in the Gannett Suburban Newspapers. Reprinted by permission.

"Hey, Bruce!" we said to each other, almost in unison, as I slid into the last vacant seat at his table, next to him and across from his manager, a photographer, and the photographer's girlfriend from Ohio. Taking this seat, I was aware of my honored status. Not every pundit was invited to sit at the arm of a budding superstar—and I was at his arm; his mouth was less than a foot from my ear. I was in position, through judicious disarming tactics, to elicit virtually a column's worth of spicy quotes, perhaps to scoop the entire music press on some unsavory scandal heretofore unknown even to avid Springsteenophobes. If I maneuvered it right, perhaps I could get the photog to snap one of me and Springsteen together, which I could paste into my scrapbook, alongside the one of myself and Martin Mull. I even saw the caption: Bruce and Bruce—Two Rising Stars!

At which point, who should saunter by, but another contender for "The Man Who Discovered Bruce Springsteen" title (in the post–Watergate tradition of morality and candor, I shall refer to him as Deep Craw). Now, the history of my rivalry with Deep Craw, for the B.S. trophy (the Bruce Springsteen trophy, that is) was already probably legend in the industry. Although I was one of the first of the press to view the Asbury Park kid when he opened for David Bromberg one dismal January evening in 1973, at Paul's Mall in Boston, Deep Craw ran a cover story on the boy wonder in his magazine a full month before my ecstatic review hit the stands.

During the long lull before Bruce's second album, Deep Craw could be heard on the street, claiming to have written the liner notes for it. But when said album appeared, no liner notes could be found. (God, was I relieved!) Instead, it was I who came up with the plum, a review of the album in Section Two of the Sunday *New York Times*, which offered written notice to the world that I (as well as, of course, Springsteen) had arrived.

Then, the capperoo. When *Rolling Stone* ran the Springsteen ad, there was my name under the huge lead blurb—associated in one shot not only with Springsteen and

The *New York Times*, but *Rolling Stone* as well. Below it, definitely in second place, came Deep Craw's quote (hardly the equivalent of liner notes), no less ecstatic, no less huge, but obviously outgunned. Perhaps Deep Craw had been there first, but clearly, I was the one to watch.

At the Bottom Line, Deep Craw could not squeeze in next to Bruce, so had to settle for a seat way at the far end of the table, sandwiched between the photographer and his girl-friend from Ohio. I chuckled as I leaned over and whispered a joke for Springsteen's private benefit.

At which point, Don Kirshner appeared on the horizon. Kirshner was the indomitable impressario who had signed Kansas to his label. He and I went part of the way back. So I had to momentarily leave the table, to score a point with Donnie. When I returned, I found that Deep Craw had swiped my seat next to Springsteen! Blinded by rage and yet too cool to make a pathetic scene, I stumbled into Deep Craw's old seat, from which obscure vantage point I endured Kansas's endless set—chagrined, dumbfounded, alone.

Suddenly, when the set ended, the [then]–president of Columbia Records, [the late] Goddard Leiberson, spied Springsteen, and joined the table in a hail of hearty greetings. Room was somehow made for the prez to sit down—between Bruce and Deep Craw—while I was edged even further out of the action, forced to mutely watch as the table rapidly became the focal point of the entire Bottom Line, with photogs circling, groupies gaping, and Leiberson, Spring-steen, and Deep Craw sharing racy stories and secret hand-shakes. (Needless to say, it should have been *me* in that seat, getting my mug in the trades, nuzzling up to the chief exec and the superstar!)

Ever since then, a certain Deep Craw has been going around town thinking he had the last laugh on me. Well, if he's reading this (and I know he is), I'd just like to mention that I have recently had lunch with a very high source at Columbia Records, who confirmed to me, exclusively, that the new Springsteen album will be out imminently. Although I have yet to hear the LP, I would like to go on record right now as having this to say about it: "I have seen Bruce Springsteen's future, and his middle name is rock & roll."

Eat your hearts out, all you runners up.

By the end of 1974, urged on by those of us who persisted in writing about our musical legacy in the kind of exalted terms usually reserved for Hollywood movies and Broadway plays, a creaky bunch of twenty–something boys and girls had reclaimed the turf, dancing up a storm in each other's clothes, and in general experiencing the second adolescence of an artform and a generation desperately trying to measure up to its blurbs.

Seven

Elvis Has Left the Building

(1975–1978)

First there was "Donna," the chaste, hoop–skirted, pom pom girl who broke Richie Valens's greasy heart in 1957. Then there was "Donna the Primadonna," something of a cycle slut in pedalpushers, who gave Dion a royal case of blue balls in 1963. She was followed shortly thereafter by "Dona Dona," the vaguely Mexican folksong, as interpreted by Joan Baez, that defined the pristine purity of our baby boom sixties social agenda by refusing to even submit to literal translation. But, in 1976, they were jettisoned, one and all, by Donna in the flesh, Donna Summer, the embodiment of the smouldering 1960s come to life, a Promethean virtuoso of sex, lust, rhythm, dirty secrets, dirty words, foreign intrigue—part Amazon, part Mississippi, discovered along the banks of the Rhine, where children routinely grow up to be Ursula Andress or Elke Sommer or Britt Eckland or any others of the sort only someone like Rod Stewart could be man enough to de-flower.

Just a myth at first, a whisper in the dark of the nightlife an ocean away, growing louder as the soundwaves trav-

169

ersed countries, continents, the legend growing exponentially along with the sound, this rapacious insatiable sexual
Godzilla of a woman, capable of lip–synching multiple
orgasms in a single take, devouring Helen Reddy, Bette
Midler, Yoko Ono, Carly Simon *and* James Taylor,
creampuffy Olivia Newton–John, stringbeany Cher, and
everyone else who dared cross vocal chords or coital
soundtrack arrangements with her, Donna blasted past
myth into pure sound, until it became impossible to
separate the myth from the sound from the whispers in the
dark, from the dark itself, the vast nightlife of hidden
Europe, especially Germany, the capitol of decadence,
where Marlene once reigned on a backwards chair, and
later the Beatles subsisted on Lowenbrau, hookers, and
advice from Brenda Lee. Donna didn't invent Disco, she
just swept over it like a monsoon, and claimed the remains
in her own name. So totally, in fact, did she become the
one and only symbol of Disco, that she would eventually
affix her name to the opening syllable of the next Disco–
era's aspiring goddess, thus becoming a part of the Madonna era as well.

In 1975, as yet unaware of the impending Donna
takeover of our bodies and minds, our notions of primal
ecstacy, we were still a generation of mere boys and girls,
even though some of us were approaching "the big three–
oh" (which would later pale in comparison to every
succeeding biological digit). Our recent history replete
with legendary communal orgies of incense, reefer, guitars, and silicone body parts, you'd think we'd have been
more than a match for this giant looming shadow of sexual
liberation overtaking Europe in the form of a great throbbing bassline heartbeat, pulse of the libido itself. But over
here, K.C. & the Sunshine Band ("Get down Tonight,"
"That's the Way I Like It") was a pitiful substitute for the
real thing, near–beer, a frat house lift of smarmy "Louie

Louie" in patent leather, or the Beach Boys on reds—well
–mannered, safe in comparison, like the Sunshine State, a
daylight–orange fiesta holiday with the family in the VW
van. And Disco Tex and the Sex–o–lettes ("Get Dancin',"
"I Wanna Dance Wit' Choo"), featuring the relentlessly
starstruck Monti Rock III (as if there were actually a I and a
II), was a joke on a joke—Sylvester's ubiquitous cousin,
Tiny Tim's nutsy uncle. Neither was Andrea True ("More
More More") anything more than a paltry falsehood, as
much a heavy–breathing phony as her previous porno-
graphic tinsel legacy, the bump and the grind as real to her
under the swirling strobes as it ever was before the 16mm
underground cameras—that is, totally unreal, a calculated
sham, adolescent con, titilating ruse, theatrical hustle.
Measured against these harbingers of a bogus future of
drum machines and mechanical sex, our finally requited
letch in 1975, for funky Maria Muldaur, should have been
treasured as a freewheeling, Whole Earth, last chance
anti–Disco statement of the direst magnitude. But even
though her nostalgic version of her one–time classic, "I'm
a Woman," miraculously cracked the top twenty, Maria's
sandaled waif proved much too coy and fragile for the
coming moral slide. Like many of us dewy–eyed former
free lovers, Maria could only stare and giggle at what was
going on Behind the Green Door, at the X–rated movie
house or the discotheque, while less self–consciously hip
participants were beginning to merge with the action.
    Truth is, our flailing ministrations at the feet of the
Grateful Dead, and other such cosmic boogie bands on
acid to the contrary, grueling, exhilirating, or humiliating
as they may have been, despite the recent rise of Disco, we
baby boom minions were not as a group naturally taken to
public physical displays involving moving in rhythm (i.e.,
dancing). It is not by accident that in the everyday lingo of
the working musician, the stiff early rhythms of rehearsal,

before a piece of music is fully absorbed into the blood-stream of the band are called "white." Moving less in a straight line than in the herky–jerk saunter of the eternally repressed, from the loping constraints of the Lindy to the undulating anarchy of the Twist, through group grope and free fall into Frug and funk into stupor, we saw the discotheque as a distant castle of horrors, rather than a Funhouse, with rooms full of wavy mirror–covered walls, into which you could step like Alice into a Wonderland of surreal escapism.

To a man in those days, we much preferred thinking about it over doing it. Entering 1975, we were still too laden with doubt, guilt, acid flashbacks, too absorbed in self–examination to commit to anything beyond momentary distractions. The period between January 18th and April 12th, in fact, saw twelve consecutive songs fail to hold the number one spot for more than a week; sandwiching these fleeting whims of passionate evasion were a couple of tunes by the virtual Godfather of sexual and emotional ambivalence, Elton John ("Lucy in the Sky with Diamonds" and "Philadelphia Freedom"). Within this period, such other paragons of the male image as Barry Manilow ("Mandy"), and the comeback falsetto twins, Neil Sedaka ("Laughter in the Rain") and Frankie Valli ("My Eyes Adored You") set the mealy, mewling tone. We were meanwhile roundly chastised by Linda Ronstadt ("You're No Good") and Olivia Newton–John ("Have You Never Been Mellow"). Surely, the Eagles were as mellow and acquiescent as they'd ever been in "Best of My Love." The Average White Band's "Pick up the Pieces" was at least representative of a more realistic frame of mind than the Doobie Brothers' mystic naturalism, in "Black Water." Even submissive Karen Carpenter was more demanding than ever in "Please Mr. Postman." Only among blacks did there seem to be any kind of sexually rhythmic accord

("Lady Marmelade" by Labelle, "Fire" by the Ohio Players), the mundane workaday ending up at night approaching the sublime ("Lovin' You" by Minnie Riperton).

Rather than set foot anywhere near the disco, as recalcitrant aging roustabouts, many of us preferred to take our communion standing in place, among our grungy, white, dungaree–clad brothers, boogieing at hockey rinks like Cobo Hall in Detroit, the Spectrum in Philadelphia, the Forum in L.A., and Madison Square Garden in New York City, to outsized, mega–decibel anthems of chauvinist solidarity in the Age of Women's Lib: "Free Bird" by Lynyrd Skynyrd, "Rock & Roll All Night" by Kiss, "Sweet Emotion" by Aerosmith, "Killer Queen" by Queen, "Song for America" by Kansas, "Tush" by ZZ Top, and "Trampled under Foot" by Led Zeppelin—the sexist granddaddy of them all, with all six of their albums on the charts at the same time!

More solitary sorts, introverts, cowards, married people, their night lives confined to the limited scope of their imaginations, found solace in the jazz–tinged wistfulness of Steely Dan's "Bad Sneakers," Joni Mitchell's folky ecology, "Big Yellow Taxi," Gil Scott–Heron's urgent "Johannesburg," Phoebe Snow's winsome "Poetry Man," Loudon Wainwright's wounded "Whatever Happened to Us," Janis Ian's self–pitying "At Seventeen," and Bob Dylan's cathartic "Idiot Wind."

Still others on the hip frontier disdained both "The Hustle" by Van McCoy, destined to move Disco another giant step closer to its ultimate dominion, and the more generalized but equally pervasive Hustle of Corporate Rock's "numb the lower classes into submission" agenda, for a decidedly Middle of the Dirt Road alternative, going from Elton John's *Captain Fantastic and the Red Dirt Cowboy*, which debuted on the album charts at number one in June, to the much–bootlegged post–accident retro

—nostalgia of Bob Dylan and the Band, from 1967, *The Basement Tapes*, released the following month. And then we tossed them both aside, to take in the opening of Robert Altman's eloquent evisceration of country folk, *Nashville* ("It Don't Worry Me" by Barbara Harris, "I'm Easy" by Keith Carradine; Glen Campbell's "Rhinestone Cowboy" was not in the movie, but Glen was, and the tune was number one by September), that would succeed where rock journalism couldn't in showing the mindset that would elect our first president from the deep South since the Civil War, the following year—to the tunes of the Allman Brothers and Marshall Tucker.

Rock journalists were nevertheless keeping busy collecting the assorted rewards accruing from our fleeting heyday. With Robert Plant's car accident in August, 1975 effectively removing Led Zeppelin from the frontal lobe of the hard rock constituency for almost two years—thus eliminating a major obstacle in making possible the pristine atmosphere for the kind of intelligent discourse upon which the form thrived, if not depended—critics were free to do their work without worrying over Zep breaking any more album sales or attendance records. It was undoubtedly pressure from this vastly demeaned branch of the press that helped John Lennon at last defeat the Nixonian forces of repression who were out to toss him from his roost at the Dakota apartments in Manhattan, when he secured his vaunted green card in October (for which, in return, he repaid us with nearly five years of silence).

In the same month, not only did a rock journalist accomplish the equivalent of the sportswriter's dream of managing a ballclub, by producing Bruce Springsteen's commercial–breakthrough third LP, *Born to Run* (blasting into smithereens, I have to admit, my own until–then significant achievement as the Blurb King; at least the producer—and soon to be new manager—was the quota-

ble Jon Landau, and not the aforementioned Deep Craw),
but his compadres in cold type were virtually standing
inside each other's shorts to get the Springsteen story out
first (first! the story was already two years old), like
fedora–clad, cigar–chomping, Depression–era deadline
hounds, racing with shoelaces tied together, to the single
red telephone in the next room, and getting squashed
together in the doorway like the Three Stooges on the way
to a love–in. *Time* and *Newsweek* wound up in a simultaneous deadline dead heat, with Springsteen's grizzled mug
—and within it, the welled–up, glistening visage of rock
journalism itself ("Jungleland," "Backstreets," "Thunder
Road")—in an unheard of double headline mirror image
of national magnitude (talk about your slow news weeks!).

Lost in the hoopla was the at least just as heartening
launch of Bob Dylan's Rolling Thunder Tour in Plymouth,
MA, with his old mentor, Rambling Jack Elliot, his old
squeeze, Joannie (whose "Diamonds and Rust" would
easily be her most emotionally revealing statement ever, as
if anyone cared), and his old stalwart cronies, Roger (no
longer Jim) McGuinn and the irrepressible if superfluous
Bobby Neuwirth. Actually, it may have been more heartening, since Springsteen would soon fire his manager and not
have another record out for three years; although *Born to
Run*, as an album, made the top five, "Born to Run," as a
single, failed to make the top twenty, while Dylan's tour
would culminate in December at Madison Square Garden
in a rousing benefit for the jailed boxer Rubin "Hurricane"
Carter (no relation to Jimmy) that would eventually result
in his (Rubin's) murder conviction being overturned!

Delirious with the promise of not only Springsteen but
Dylan out on the road at the same time, baby boom
originals nearly had no room left in their sleeveless hearts
to celebrate the reunion of Simon & Garfunkel on the
single "My Little Town" (contained in both Paul's *Still*

Crazy After All These Years and Artie's *Breakaway*), which
they performed live on network TV, arm in arm, as I recall,
shyly glancing at each other in embarassment, suspicion
and guilt, on the second installment of a strangely deviant
little afterhours variety show called "Saturday Night
Live," presided over by the renegades from *Lemmings* and
the *National Lampoon*, the Not–Ready–For–Prime–Time
Players, Ackroyd, Belushi, Radner, Chase et al. Switching
off the TV, similar delight could be found in turning on the
radio and discovering that Marty Balin was back with the
Airplane—they called themselves the Starship now—in
fact, the tune he collaborated on, "Miracles," was number
three in the country! Surely, the triumphant momentum of
our sophisticated generational sensibilities would at last
carry the new Bonnie Raitt record to a deserving prominence ("My First Night Alone Without You," "Good
Enough," "Run Like a Thief"). But if not, we could take
solace in the beatnik poetry of tyros like Patti Smith
("Land") and Tom Waits (*Nighthawks at the Diner*), and
veterans like Joni Mitchell ("Don't Interrupt the Sorrow").
Further tribute to our raising of the aesthetic standard
could be found in the presence in 1975 of the words of a
real novelist on the singles charts (Kurt Vonnegut's "Nice,
Nice, Very Nice," by Ambrosia), the first such offering
since Thomas Pynchon's "The Eyes of a New York Woman" from V, was covered by rock critic Robert Palmer's
band, Insect Trust, on their instant cut–out album of 1970,
Hoboken Saturday Night.

Stoked by this return to literacy, pumped, celebrating a
massive generational recovery in grand multi–media style,
with TV getting subversive, novelists and poets on the
record charts, Dylan writing protest songs, country music
in the movies, *A Chorus Line* on Broadway and *The Rocky
Horror Picture Show* somewhere off it, we were a bit
distracted or perhaps overconfident, certainly deaf–eared

and sluggish of limb and loin when the sultry voice of Donna Summer slipped by night across the water, across the borders of the subliminal, riding like Godiva astride "Love to Love You Baby," into the tiny rural hamlets and outbacks of the American dreamscape that form our first line of defense in the hit–making process. Already having set the European night on fire, where the men are so much more secure, this nearly five–minute musical sexual marathon, of which at least 85 percent was pure orgasm, in multiples a mere mortal American white man could never hope to provide his increasingly and incessantly demanding mate, was initially deemed simpatico by the devotees of a super hip underground circuit of all–night, white–hot, gay dance clubs, in trendy locales from Sausalito to Key West to Fire Island, where Disco was a way of life long before it became a lifestyle. More unsettling to parents of the status quo than a soiree in the bad neighborhoods of the fifties, more threatening than tripping across the borderlines of Commie–symp hippiedom of the sixties, the gay lifestyle, as propounded by Disco in general, and specifically, by "Love to Love You Baby," its national anthem, exceeded either of those two preceeding decades' prevailing guise of rebellion disguised as hedonism, and vice disguised as verse, by offering the promise not just of perversion and rebellion, true love, and free love, as in rock epochs past, but sexual love, and more than that, endless love, or, failing that, endless sex, the penultimate passion, with a dress code designed to weed out the smarmy and reward the suave.

As it was in the 1960s, once again the square anathema was the "straight" world. In the Disco Society of the 1970s, however, the "straight" world was no longer defined merely as being comprised of those who had never puffed a reefer at a Grateful Dead concert. With truck drivers now sporting ponytails and substituting dope for

Thunderbird at dog tracks and tractor pulls, the standard
for hipness had to be properly accelerated if it was to carry
any sort of exclusionary caché at all. The homosexual style,
in and of itself, almost did the job, in that it was such an
affront to the basic inner core of your Led Zeppelin
loyalist, that even a mild hint of it (like designer jeans, or
Italian pointy–toe dancing shoes, or a beard and a crew
cut) could get you beat up in a stadium men's room almost
any night of the week. Defining the basic separation even
further was the perception shared by most of these loyalists
that to be gay was not only to be hip, but virtually the only
way to be creative. Everyone on Broadway was gay, or
surely, everyone in *A Chorus Line*, if not *The Rocky Horror
Picture Show*. Nearly everyone in Hollywood was gay.
Seventh Avenue was entirely gay. Paris, Rome, Athens, Rio,
Ibiza, New Orleans, Aspen, Santa Fe, Boise—all were
hotbeds of enlightenment, where the boundaries of the
perverse were unfettered by conventional domesticated
normalcy, where the best creative minds in the theater,
film, music, dance, fiction, fashion, and poetry mingled
with the rich and famous, wearing the best clothes, eating
the best food—and the nights were a continuous supercharged high voltage orgasm, at 140 beats per minute, at
private clubs sandwiched among the meat markets along
the waterfront, the curtained limos arriving at odd hours,
the musclebound bouncers, by day soap opera stand–ins,
greeting them at the door, and inside all of show biz, into
S&M and amylnitrate, the sixties naive trilogy of sex, dope,
and rock & roll turned inside out, and co–opted as an
exclusive franchise of the jet set and its svelte pretenders.
   Of course, this kind of social ostracism did not sit well
among the lunchpail losers, lumpy jocks, and rock &
rollers, who were among those relegated to the declassé
ranks of the bridge and tunnel brigade by the new
nightcrawler elite. Those who abstained from taking out

their hurt feelings in random acts of outright hostility—
and others who did—decided to resolve the issue by
adopting instead their own American street boy urban
working class heterosexual champion, someone who could
remind them of the dungareed verities that rock & roll
once so unarguably stood for, a guy who took no guff, wore
no makeup, and obviously liked women over men; a
superhero very much like, if not exactly like, Bruce
Springsteen! In fact, 1976 was virtually the Year of the
Springsteen, though Bruce himself didn't even put a new
record out!

As early as January, Hicksville's Billy Joel shook off his
adopted namby–pamby, touchy–feely L.A. scene, in "Say
Goodbye to Hollywood," to head back East in the hopes of
becoming the Bruce Springsteen of Long Island.
Springsteen himself had New York City as well as New
Jersey covered, spending February on the charts with
"Tenth Avenue Freeze Out." In March, Bob Seger finally
made good on 200,000 miles of legwork, in the album,
Live Bullet ("Beautiful Loser"), with his scruffy sincerity
and hoarse charisma, effectively becoming the Bruce
Springsteen of the Midwest. A few weeks later, Manfred
Mann came out with a single version of Springsteen's own
"Spirit in the Night," which hardly did as well as "The
Boys Are Back in Town," the craggy, beer–soaked anthem
from Thin Lizzy's *Jailbreak* album, released that month,
which went to number 12 in July, establishing their leader,
Phil Lynott, not only as the Irish Bruce Springsteen, but as
the metal Bruce Springsteen as well. (Manfred Mann did
considerably better with their next Springsteen offering,
"Blinded by the Light," which went to number one, the
following February). When the Ramones debut album
came out in June ("I Wanna Be Your Boyfriend"), along
with the all–girl Runaways of Joan Jett and Lita Ford
("Cherry Bomb"), followed by the Modern Lovers, with

Jonathan Richman ("Pablo Picasso," "Roadrunner"), representing a stripped–down essence of three–chord, one–syllable Springsteen–for–Kids, perhaps the man himself took notice of these various urban rock & roll jokes, deciding it was time to officially file a lawsuit against his original manager and get back to recording again, before there was no room left in the working class marketplace for his own honest underbite (although the Ramones themselves may have had an older, similarly mono–syllabic target in sight, the Beach Boys, to whom they paid quirky homage in their version of "California Sun," and the Runaways and the Modern Lovers may have had more in common with each other, as evidenced, ten years later, by a solo Joan Jett covering Jonathan Richman's "Roadrunner"). In the meantime, in L.A., while Tom Petty was gunning after both Springsteen and Dylan (by way of Roger McGuinn and the Rolling Stones ("Breakdown," "American Girl"), in August, the anti–Springsteen appeared, Warren Zevon ("Carmelita"), Jackson Browne's preppy brother–in–law–in–kind, writing of his privileged pain at least a continent and two social classes away from the bitter struggles for artistic authenticity the various Springsteens were addressing, summed up so pithily in "The Princess and the Punk," by Tin Pan Alley's own 9–5 Springsteen–in–a–cubicle, Barry Mann, in September. By November, even Jackson Browne was hoping to show his working class poetic tattoos, in songs like "The Fuse" from *The Pretender*, while Bob Seger was solidifying his honorary Springsteen runner–up status, fulfilling the Springsteen function that the Boss was unable to, with *Night Moves*, another gem of post–30 bridge and tunnel angst ("Night Moves," "Mainstreet"). Only a couple of weeks later, Patti Smith made her move to occupy the still vacant Female Bruce Springsteen slot, with her second LP, *Radio Ethiopia* (a status she would more fully lay claim to in 1978, when she went so far as to collaborate with Himself on "Because the Night").

Among the less abjectly Springsteen–based members of the dispossessed working class, much the same righteous fury was being directed at the self–contained, self–proclaimed, leading Disco edge of the music culture of 1976, resulting in an April that certainly must rank as Heavy Metal's finest month in history. While "Disco Lady" by Johnny Taylor held the top slot for the entire month, a noisy counter–revolution was roiling down below. You had the outsized comic book creature Kiss starting things off, releasing *Destroyer* (containing "Flaming Youth," "Detroit Rock City," and their first top ten hit, "Beth"). A week later, Rush's 2112 would represent a commercial breakthrough of sorts for the nasal Canadian trio of philosophic virtuousos. Robust, Zeppelin–influenced female rock got a boost the same week, with Heart's debut album, *Dreamboat Annie* ("Crazy on You," "Magic Man"), featuring Seattle's Wilson sisters, Ann and Nancy, on vocals and rhythm guitar, respectively. A week later, the aforementioned Thin Lizzy *Jailbreak* occurred, bringing the slashing guitars of Scott Gorham and Brian Robertson to these shores. That set the stage for the long–awaited Led Zeppelin release, *Presence* ("Achilles Last Stand"), a week later, which continued their penchant for upping the ante and the decadence quotient, by immediately shrieking to number one on the album charts. At the same time, on the top ten, perhaps the principal beneficiary of all this aesthetic largesse, former English pretty face, Peter Frampton, whose *Frampton Comes Alive!* was in the process of becoming one of the top–selling albums of all–time, was riding "Show Me the Way" into smash city, where the re–released rock ballad, "Dream On," by Aerosmith, was reversing its poor 1973 showing, the anguished Nazareth had just completed an amazing run with "Love Hurts," and the defiantly operatic Queen were reveling in their "Bohemain Rhapsody." A little further down, even "Shout It out Loud," by Kiss, made the Top 40.

Would it be overly crass to suggest that it was precisely this mind–numbing symphony of strutting, male revenge (and its mascara–ed Disco counterpart) that led Phil Ochs, his fragile heart bursting, to the end of his rope, in his sister's house in Queens, before the month was halfway through?

"Everyone agreed when Phil committed suicide, that an important statement had been made," Dave Van Ronk opined. "Nobody could agree on what that statement was."

Though it surely could have been something "chemical," as health professionals are so fond of diagnosing acid casualties and paranoid schizophrenics, it seemed more like Phil's classically ironic extravagant final punctuation mark, in effect highlighting his absence of affect, even on his former followers, who'd left him in his gold suit long ago for domesticated country life, and by damning inference, how little the entire folk/protest scene wound up amounting to, in the face of 1976's numbing decibels, whether wrung out of synthesizer or electric guitar, at the hockey arena or the discotheque. That along with friends and casual observers alike, even Phil could see the end coming, was documented in a conversation I had with him about his dwindling creative output only a couple of years before.

"It could be alcohol," he said of his continuing song-writer's block. "It could be the deterioration of the politics I was involved in. It could be a general deterioriation of the country. Basically, me and the country were deteriorating simultaneously, and that's probably why it stopped coming. Ever since the late sixties, what's constantly on my mind is discipline, training, get it together, clean up your act. I haven't been able to do it yet, but the impulse is as strong as ever. To my dying day, I'll always think about the next possible song."

In the Middle of the Dirt Road, where most of Phil's aging constituency had fled to safety or been banished, our foremost poets were grappling with the desire to stay relevant, with varied results. Dylan moved from championing Rubin Carter to mythologizing gangster Joey Gallo ("Joey"). Paul Simon summed up our ambivalent legacy in "Still Crazy After All These Years," and then, in a single boundless single about being single again ("50 Ways to Leave Your Lover") defined our current state of being as well. Laura Nyro's *Smile*, her first album in five years, was wistful and dreamy ("Child in a Universe"). Tough–talking Lou Reed turned sentimental ("Coney Island Baby"). The Rolling Stones were kowtowing to the Disco crowd ("Hot Stuff")—Mick Jagger was a jet set icon now, married to the walking photo–op, Bianca—while Paul McCartney, with his wife in the Wings, spent most of his righteous rage defending his latent hack proclivities ("Silly Love Songs")—the same proclivities which Carole King, after a couple of albums of glory (*Tapestry* and her prior effort with The City, *Now That Everything's Been Said*), had reverted to ("High out of Time," "Only Love Is Real"). Steely Dan's Walter Becker and Donald Fagen made a stab at being the real laureates of generational malaise, pinning the tail on the end of an era in "Kid Charlemagne" ("All the day–glo freaks who used to paint the face/they've joined the human race"). By September, Linda Ronstadt was desperate and horny ("Someone to Lay down Beside Me"), Elton John had had it with Kiki Dee ("Don't Go Breaking My Heart")—to say nothing of bisexuality—and the most exciting creative moves were coming from the tube, on "Mary Hartman, Mary Hartman" (which pro-

duced the chart single, "Baby Boy," by Mary Kay Place).
About this time, Peter Frampton was a guest at the White
House, and ex–Polaroid technician, Tom Scholz, delivered
Boston, Corporate Rock's first bedroom masterpiece
("More Than a Feeling," "Peace of Mind"). By then, even
Michael Franks was beginning to seem consequential
("Popsicle Toes"), and England Dan and John Ford Coley
worldly wise ("I'd Really Love to See You Tonight"). No
wonder Jeff Beck was turning to quasi–jazz instrumentals
(*Wired*); no wonder Joni Mitchell was heading into a
creative swandive with *Hejira*, that would alienate most of
her audience and leave her as lost as the disappeared sky
pilot of its most revealing tune, "Amelia"; no wonder the
Band was getting ready to call it quits (*The Last Waltz*)—
no wonder rock journalism was looking elsewhere for its
major stories. (It was about this time that the movie rights
for Nic Cohn's sociological treatise in *New York* magazine
on the mating habits of certain lower middle class Brooklyn natives was being bought by Robert Stigwood as a
starring vehicle for Donna Pescow and the Sweathog, John
Travolta.)

Though Donna Summer, on the strength of "Love to
Love You Baby" alone, surely reigned supreme at the
discotheque through our bisexual bicentennial year—and
was getting ready to star in a Disco film herself (*Thank God
It's Friday*, which was every bit the equal of Jo-Ann
Campbell's lone celluloid foray, *Hey, Let's Twist*, co-
starring Teddy Randazzo)—Disco's enveloping sensuality
turned the entire year into a continuous athletic orgy of
showing off and dressing up, at every turn urged along by a
beat as relentless as it was anonymous. Roxy Music defined
the terms early, in "Love Is the Drug," a lyric far more dire
than anyone was ready to listen to, even if some were
already aware of it. Elsewhere, the message was as simple
and straightforward as the numbing beat: "Love Roller

Coaster" by the Ohio Players, "You Sexy Thing" by Hot Chocolate, "Love Machine (Part One)" by the Miracles, "Disco Lady" by Johnny Taylor, "Boogie Fever" by the Sylvers, "Love Hangover" by Diana Ross, "Get up and Boogie" by Silver Convention, "More More More" by the Andrea True Connection, "You Should Be Dancing" by the Bee Gees (presaging their full Disco conversion on the *Saturday Night Fever* soundtrack a year later), "Shake Your Booty" by K.C. and Sunshine Band, "Cherchez La Femme" by Dr. Buzzard's Original Savannah Band, and "Play that Funky Music" by Wild Cherry.

The year culminated with Rod Stewart's ceremonial sacrifice of a virgin in "Tonight's the Night (Gonna Be Alright)," the song that topped the charts the week after Jimmy Carter was elected and would remain in that supine position until the beginning of the new year, symbolizing this sexually sated, creatively spent period almost as well as Barbra Streisand's bogus, self-satisfied, rock & roll remake of *A Star Is Born*, co-starring Kris Kristofferson, which remains a signal testament to how completely some of us in the Middle of the Dirt Road had become blinded, in our recent artistic upsurge, from any sense of reality ("Watch Closely Now"). As if to further highlight how infirm and unworthy and amoral and oblivious were the citizens of post-Watergate Woodstock nation, it was left to England—which had once sent us the joyous, burbling Beatles, to help us past our time of communal sobbing, and immediately thereafter, their version of our own Chicago blues, to reconnect us with our primal pain—where the star at that moment being borne most brightly was represented atop the British charts by the single, "Anarchy in the U.K.," by the feared and loathsome and hostile Sex Pistols, ready to stick their daggers right down our middle class complacency until it hurt.

Immediately surrounding the Pistols' several explosions

of eloquently obnoxious anger, a new order of working class blues came sifting out of England, merging with our own slightly more Springsteenian romanticized variety ("Blinded by the Light," by Manfred Mann), to form the eventual basis of a voice against encroaching Disco ennui, at once more assertive than Middle of the Dirt Road ("Margaritaville" by Jimmy Buffett), more literate and dangerous than Corporate Rock ("Cold as Ice" by Foreigner); as an outcast music, surely more relevant than pop nostalgia, and certainly more rebellious than Heavy Metal (Led Zeppelin was a multinational cartel, packing 76,000 heads into Cobo Hall in Detroit). During the first six months of 1977, while the soapy trials and tribulations of the old bluesy warhorse Fleetwood Mac of John and Christine McVie, and the new, folk/pop incarnation of Southern Cal's golden couple, Lindsey Buckingham and Stevie Nicks, were enthralling daytime America with their twin breakups ("Go Your Own Way," "Dreams"), and in Manhattan, the star–struck Disco era was reaching a glitteringly symbolic empty crescendo with the opening of Studio 54, Wordy Pub/Rock poets like Graham Parker ("Pouring It All Out," "Turned up Too Late") and Elvis Costello ("Less Than Zero," "Radio Sweetheart"), and crusading social reprobates like the Clash ("London's Burning," "White Riot"), were joining arms with the Sex Pistols, the Jam ("In the City"), the Slits, the Stranglers ("Get a Grip on Yourself"), the Damned ("New Rose"), the Buzzcocks ("Boredom"), Ultravox ("Dangerous Rhythm"), and Siouxsie and the Banshees in a battle not so much for space on the pop charts, but over the future of rock & roll, whose name was turning out not to be Bruce Springsteen after all, but Sid Vicious.

Like the Khmer Rouge, operating at their peak of efficiency only a few years earlier, the implicit manifesto of these post–Revolution protest rockers was nothing less than to create a rock & roll Year Zero, wiping out all vestiges of the past, with their righteous three chord attack, redefining all the terms, redressing all the grievances, restoring all the passion, and either redeeming or else erasing the sacred name of Elvis, with an Elvis of their own, who only happened to look more like Buddy Holly. In America, like the briefly famous serial killer, Son of Sam, operating out of New York City in his own sporadic heyday of vengeance on long–haired girls, a new younger class of slumming rock bands lashed out with singles and albums at an indifferent Manhattan skyline, from the Bowery—the Rio de Janiero of slums—only inches from the old Lower East Side stomping grounds of their spiritual older brothers now safely dead or into investment banking—Richard Hell and the Voidoids ("[I Belong to the] Blank Generation"), Television ("Little Johnny Jewel,"), Talking Heads ("Love Goes to a Building on Fire"), the Ramones ("Sheena Is a Punk Rocker") and Blondie ("X–Offender"). Each of these bands, speaking for many in their unnamed, uncelebrated generation, that never saw young Elvis wiggle in the flesh, were undoubtedly way past furious at being told too many times by older siblings and commentators and neighborhood winos about the splendid and glorious and creatively historic cafe society of the sixties (as well as the eggcreams at Auster's and Gem's Spa) that they'd just missed. They blasted into their own history with terse, jagged shapes and visions that were diametric miles from the yawning caution their elders were exhibiting in the Middle of the Dirt Road, that seemed more and more a passive giving way ("Just a Song Before I Go" by Crosby, Stills and Nash, "Life in the Fast Lane" by the Eagles, "Couldn't Get It Right" by the Climax Blues Band, "Wonderful World" by James Taylor, "The First Cut Is the

Deepest" by Rod Stewart written by Cat Stevens, "Home-grown" by Neil Young, "Carry on, Wayward Son" by Kansas).

Punk rebellion was also at least as many miles away, at this time, from the frenzy of the heavy metal arena, where the denizens were as united as their brothers and sisters at the discotheque, by a common sexual distraction ("Love Gun" by Kiss, "Back in the Saddle" by Aerosmith, "Some-body to Love" by Queen, "Feels Like the First Time" by Foreigner, "I'm in You" by Peter Frampton, "Barracuda" by Heart, "Foreplay/Long Time" by Boston, "Cat Scratch Fever" by Ted Nugent). Neither the disco devotees nor the metal headbangers seemed to notice much or care that New York Dolls guitarist Johnny Thunders was singing "Born to Lose," and the Sex Pistols were performing "God Save the Queen," and the Mumps, with Lance Loud (fresh from his family's five minutes of infamy on a scathing PBS documentary), were prolonging their embarrassment with "Crocodile Tears," or, certainly, that Johnny Paycheck was previewing cowpunk, with "Take This Job and Shove It." Not as long as they were getting their nightly nookie, or could band together in the simulation thereof.

This creative separation of mind and body would last until Middle America finally got a homegrown punk scene of its own, in the summer of 1977, starting near Cleveland, where it had all began, where Chrissie Hynde was born, two years before Elvis Presley changed everything (though Chrissie had already left for London to form the Pretend-ers and Rachel Sweet was another year away from *Fool Around*): Pere Ubu ("Final Solution"), the Rubber City Rebels ("Brain Job"), the Bizarros ("I Bizarro"), Devo ("Mongoloid"), the expatriate Dead Boys ("Sonic Reduc-er"), the nearby Shoes from Illinois (*Black Vinyl Shoes*). Stripped down, way out, ugly, mean, or just plain weird, it was a pie in the face of propriety, a taunt from the cheap seats at the Market Square arena in Indianapolis, say, where Elvis Presley made his last public appearance in June, before returning home to Graceland—possibly to the tune of "Rock & Roll Never Forgets" by Bob Seger, undoubtedly epitomizing "Sex and Drugs and Rock & Roll" by Ian Dury—to die a scant two months later.

Though aging legions of pre–boom adults and original rock & roll consumers, wide in the girth, grey in the ducktail, would make the trek to Memphis in the aftermath of the King's (supposed) passing, to shed their alligator tears for the end of their youth, their era, even as the funeral cortege made its way up Main Street, younger rock critics were touting newly–minted songs like "2–4–6–8– Motorway," by the first openly gay punk, Tom Robinson, and "Turn Blue," by the seminal Stooge of punk, Iggy Pop on the comeback trail, as having, in their raging abandon, as much in common with the original intent of neolithic Elvis, as the bloated, superfluous product being thrown just then onto the marketplace by Crosby, Stills and Nash, Yes, Styx, Rod Stewart, Bonnie Raitt, and Neil Young had with what America had allowed him for almost twenty years to remain.

However, where Elvis had been a pompadoured affirmation of the American melting pot Dream of ultimate assimilation, from his country and blues and rhythm and blues, pop and operatic roots, concocting a wild and salty rock & roll recipe that would be as tasty in Las Vegas as it was in Memphis, punk was primarily a negative music of wrath and pimples, played by a set of loud/fast rules that were an almost literal repudiation of such American idealistic verities. They came; they saw; they puked. And yet, if most of the music had more to do with a strictly personal response to the abject condition of adolescence (especially in swinging London), than rock & roll veracity, tradition, or the somewhat overrated notion of rebellion (Buddy

Holly was a nerd, after all, Roy Orbison a dweeb, Jerry Lee Lewis a simp, Gene Vincent a gimp, Ricky Nelson a wimp, Paul Anka a shrimp), it did offer a generational symmetry that was impossible even for a Middle of the Dirt Road dweller, comfortably listening to Linda Ronstadt and her emotional sob–sister and brother, Karla Bonoff and James Taylor, respectively, to deny.

When the storm troops of rock & roll's future did at last present for our inspection, if not approval, their own Elvis's *My Aim Is True* ("Alison"), Costello's stunning precocious verbosity may have been responsible for setting off one of the great three month periods of the post–Elvis era, in which the kind of crosscultural epiphany of the popular arts as peak emotional experience that first AM radio and then, more routinely, FM radio, was once known for, and with pride and all due modesty had sworn forever to uphold, lit up our Christmas shopping season with product from all manner of purveyors of the zeitgeist.

There was the heroically melancholy Steely Dan ("Deacon Blues") and the congenitally nervous Talking Heads' probable ode to David Berkowitz ("Psycho Killer") from their debut album. Towering supermodel Grace Jones was unleashing "I Need a Man" at Studio 54, while Grandmaster Flash and the Furious Five, further uptown, were presaging the future of Disco, by merging the ghetto dj's lost art of rapping (Jocko, Roscoe, etc.) with the equally lost art of sampling ("Flying Saucer" by Buchanon and Goodman). Randy Newman achieved new heights of satire in the vastly misunderstood "Short People," which raced to number two in the country, although it offended small–minded people everywhere. But the Sex Pistols weren't kidding on *Never Mind the Bollocks, Here's the Sex Pistols* ("Pretty Vacant"). Patently and intentionally and often musically abusive, they offended nearly everyone who had the opportunity to hear them, an experience which was, however, thankfully limited to the customs officials who wouldn't let them into the country, the record company executives who kept signing them to contracts and then throwing them off their label, and the jaded rock critics who deemed their album as among the best (or at any rate, most significant) ever made, a designation all the more noble for the album's failure to go any higher than 112 on the album charts.

A good deal more successful, if critically overlooked at the time, was the maiden effort by one Marvin Lee Aday, a rotund slab of humanity out of the Detroit road company of *Hair!* or *Grease* or maybe the Lions, who, under the nom de plume of Meat Loaf, gave us in *Bat out of Hell* a double–Springsteen dose of teen (and divorced adult in the throes of second adolescence) makeout drama called "Paradise by the Dashboard Light," about as schmaltzy and overstated as a daytime soap, with Ellen Foley as his female accomplice, and an anxious metaphorical soliloquy by Phil Rizzuto that has to rank up there with Elvis Presley nearly quoting Shakespeare in "Are You Lonesome Tonight?" Adventurous radio programmers might have had a few laughs (before getting fired) by seguing from this epic straight into Dolly Parton's country/pop crossover, "Here You Come Again," wherein buxom Dolly competently crooned what should have been, but wasn't, the theme for her forthcoming starring appearance in the movie version of the musical, *Best Little Whorehouse in Texas.*

Programmed by the same marketing types that persisted in cancelling tremendous TV shows like "The Great American Dream Machine," "The Law," "Colucci's Department," " Fernwood Tonight," and "Rudi Kazooti," the radio of the day offered little space or sympathy for the concerns of punk. By now playlist–dominated, profit–motivated, and totally–calculated, the airwaves of FM radio were reserved for the well–tested, well–worn

sounds of our ensconsed musical majority, proven axe–
mavens like Eric Clapton ("Lay Down Sally"), staunch
Middle of the Dirt Road advocates like the Eagles ("Hotel
California"), and dead southern rockers like Lynyrd
Skynryd (the posthumous "What's Your Name" was their
biggest hit since "Sweet Home Alabama")—although all
of them must have known that by then the guitar had been
once again neutered on the radio and on the charts as an
instrument of social turmoil and change and reduced to
mere accompanying prop, the modern age accordian for
those who clung to it for security. The drum machine and
synthesizer were pointing toward the sonic dancehall
future ("I Feel Love" by Donna Summer, "Dance, Dance,
Dance" by Chic) and away from the arena (*Alive II* by Kiss,
Draw the Line by Aerosmith, came out, both bereft of hit
singles; Led Zeppelin, beset by further tragedy with the
recent death of Robert Plant's son, hadn't had an album
out since 1976, or been in the Top 40 since 1975). A piano
man could make more of a mark, provided he played
ballads (from *The Stranger*, Billy Joel's "Just the Way You
Are," went to number three; the much more apt and potent
"Only the Good Die Young," spent half as much time on
the charts, and failed to reach the Top 20, though it did
draw exhilarating admonitions from the Catholic Church).
Not that you'd expect anything from *Young and Loud and
Snotty* by the Dead Boys, to be suitable, or bearable, but
even the now beloved (for their comic genius, rather than
political potential) Ramones inexplicably achieved no better than a pitiful Top 60 status for their anthemic "Rocka-
way Beach," which was nonetheless a huge leap over their
only other previous chart single, "Sheena Is a Punk
Rocker."

By year's end, with John Travolta opening in *Saturday
Night Fever*, establishing relentless Disco firmly in the grip
and the grasp of the polyester leisure suit and gold–

chained masses of middle America, and Elvis Costello, subbing on television for the banned Sex Pistols, singing the anti–radio "Radio Radio," before a decidedly different audience on *Saturday Night Live*—apparently carrying through on his pledge to "bite the hand that feeds me," by performing the tune over the objections of the show's producer, who would never let him eat lunch in the NBC commissary again—a nifty intra–generational musical rift was forming, hip versus square again, in which the devout members of the baby boom, forced to choose between punk posturing and fat–cat cavorting, nominally chose punk, if only as a reaction to the fact that Elvis's reviled "radio radio" was perfectly content at the time to have itself represented, week after week after week (ten in all), by Debby Boone's feeble cover of the immortal Kacey Cisyk's "You Light up My Life," rendering the number one position even more irrelevant than usual—as if that were possible in the same year "Undercover Angel," by Alan O'Day, "Da Doo Ron Ron," by Shaun Cassidy, and two Leo Sayer tunes ("You Make Me Feel Like Dancing" and "When I Need You") reached that vaunted peak, while Dean Friedman's quirky "Ariel" failed to even make the Top 25, and gems like "Echoes of Love" by the Doobie Brothers, "Slow Dancing" by Jules Shear's Band, the Funky Kings, "Solsbury Hill" by Peter Gabriel, "The Only One" by Geils, Van Morrison's epic "Moondance," "Closer to the Heart" by Rush, and the now semi-legendary "Calling Occupants of Interplanetary Craft" by the alleged Beatle impersonators, Klaatu, only climbed as high as numbers 66, 61, 68, 83, 92, 76, and 62, respectively..

As if to call our choice into immediate question, however, just a few months out of Elvis Presley's final year, consider the homage/desecration of Sex Pistol Sid Vicious's cover of Presley's cover of Frank Sinatra's interpretation of Paul Anka's self–glorifying evergreen, "My

Way"—which marked the King's second posthumous appearance on the charts of 1977. The Vicious version failed
to chart here, but would be released again on an LP (*The
Biggest Blow*), re-released in a live version (*Sid Sings*), sung
in a film (*The Great Rock & Roll Swindle*) and packaged
again in a retrospective album (*Sid Vicious Heritage*),
giving it, in its sheer unwillingness to die a natural death, a
weird legitimacy beyond most of the other hundred odd
versions of the Anka lyric. The Sex Pistols, themselves, on
the other hand, would last less than three weeks into
January, 1978, before splitting up, their American tour
ending in a Sid Vicious overdose that had very few in the
baby boom rooting for the doctors. Sid pulled through, but
more as a warning symbol of punk's degeneracy (in a genre
littered with degenerate warning symbols) than its contribution to the literature of the post–Elvis era; in his wake,
the arbiters of taste decided, only the groups that promised
to clean up their acts would be allowed to continue their
quests for a post–Elvishood of uncountable riches.

By the end of 1978, punk as a genre would have its first
certifiable crossover breakthroughs (sometimes under the
confounding rubric of New Wave, a less extreme affecta-
tion, the liberal arm of radical punk), with Blondie, the
second coming of Reparata and the Delrons, led by the
former cocktail waitress and potential bowling alley perox-
ide pinup girl, Debbie Harry, who had a head for low brow
sarcasm and a bod for sin ("Hanging on the Telephone,"
"Fade Away and Radiate," and punk's first Disco crossover, "Heart of Glass," which would Frug to the top of the
pop charts in 1979). The Talking Heads' main head case,
David Byrne, emerged as an exemplary male sex symbol
for the stunned seventies; unlike his two–dimensional
comic strip counterpart, his source of attraction was,
fittingly, his head, and the various mutant viral strains of
whimsy and anxiety raging therein, on *More Songs About*

Buildings and Food (containing the soul crossover "Take Me to the River," which, too, was a hit in 1979). Beating the Talking Heads second album to the charts by about a month, the sunglassed Ric Ocasek led the Cars to significant "New Wave" success, although this Bostonian pop crossover ("Just What I Needed," "Best Friend's Girl") shared with Byrne little more than a similar anorexic warble and bent lyrical bent; they were punks in label only (on their designer jeans). The majesterial Police, confirmed in 1979 as well, gained our attention in mid–1978, with the regal demeanor of their leonine leader, Sting, and his whitebread reggae crossover tribute to "Roxanne," a fallen woman who couldn't get up. In 1978, Elvis Costello cemented his critical crossover reputation as the nearest thing to Dylan Thomas since Van Morrison gave up the booze for the holy ghost, exposing in *This Year's Model* an anti–American ("Crawling to the USA"), anti–New York ("New Amsterdam") bias that certainly endeared him to the liberal guilty conscience of media–America, if no one else.

Stranded on the other side of the ocean, unable to cross over, even in the midst of all this liberal chest beating, were artsy groups destined to remain obscure, thus legendary on their old blocks, producing songs few without short–wave radios ever got to hear, and fewer still to appreciate, but which carried the same sort of in–crowd snobbery as the inevitable eight foreign films on the average movie critics yearly top ten list: Howard DeVoto's new group, Magazine ("Shot by Both Sides"), his old group, the Buzzcocks ("Ever Fallen in Love"), XTC ("This Is Pop"), the Mekons ("Never Been in a Riot"), X–Ray Specs ("The Day the World Turned Dayglo"). Limping in their tracks came Ian Dury ("Sweet Gene Vincent"), a hobbled alehouse gnome straight out of Dickens, accompanied, somewhat warily, by the equally old–world evoking trollop, Kate Bush, a luscious hermitic wench, straight out of Emily Bronte by way of Pink Floyd ("Wuthering Heights"). Not to be outfoxed, punk rock girls as variously stark and problematic as Lydia Lunch, with Teenage Jesus and the Jerks ("Orphans"), Lene Lovich ("I Think We're Alone Now"), Siouxsie and the Banshees ("Hong Kong Garden"), and the Slits ("So Tough") were also out there filling up the firmament with an unembroidered deviance that was finally too much for the once renowned "punk poetess," Patti Smith, who crossed over into Bruce Springsteen's urban badlands in June, with "Because the Night," attempting to forge a link between the thinking and the feeling parts of the working class culture that were not as yet lobotomized by the thump of disco or the clank of heavy metal.

In both of those supremely self–contained worlds, the thump went on nearly unabated but not entirely unaware of the pebbles being tossed by the unregenerate primitives outside the iron gates. Thanks to the Bee Gees and the soundtrack for *Saturday Night Fever*, the Gibb family held the number one spot for 22 weeks, including an astounding 14 in a row, with "Stayin' Alive" and "Night Fever" sandwiching younger sib, Andy's "(Love Is) Thicker Than Water." After a lull of a mere six weeks, Andy was back with "Shadow Dancing" for another seven! But the Gibbs were not the only family making noise during the same period of time. While the Village People were camping it up (or else being deadly serious) with "Macho Man," the Van Halen family of drummer Alex and his guitar virtuoso brother, Edward, were striking out in favor of the uncostumed real thing in *Van Halen* ("You Really Got Me," "Running with the Devil"), a band whose awesome guitar pyrotechnics would be offset (as well as set off) by the raunchy banter of lead singer and apparent aspiring game show host, David Lee Roth. Elsewhere, the Rolling

Stones were still wearing a little too much mascara for the
benefit of the ringside tables at Studio 54 in *Some Girls*
("Miss You," "Shattered"), but nobody berated Ace
Frehley for his garish whiteface getup even as a temporary
solo refugee from Kiss ("New York Groove"). While a new
breed of maniac metal was rearing its ugly rear in England,
in the persons of Judas Priest (*Stained Glass*) and Austra-
lia's AC/DC (*Powerage*), the original punks of rock, the
Who, were contemplating their mortality in *Who Are You*
("Who Are You," "Music Must Change"), only to experience it a week after the album came out in September,
when drummer Keith Moon died of an overdose.

Even behind the roped off velvet barriers of the Disco,
the glamour may have been fading a bit. Representing
more of a threat than pop saturation and sheer hedonistic
satiety ever could—offering a Soul alternative to Disco's
Motownization—Funk emanated more from the street
than the nightclubs of the chic ("Ffun" by Con Funk Shun,
"You and I" by Rick James, "Serpentine Fire" by Earth,
Wind and Fire). If George Clinton was its dominating
Spector (masterminding, in one way or another, the
anthemic "One Nation under a Groove" by Funkadelic,
"Disco to Go" by Brides of Funkenstein, Parliament's
Motor Booty Affair and Booty's Rubber Band's teenybop
Player of the Year, Prince was its semi–hermaphrodidic,
biracial, bisexual, bicoastal, Dylanesque anti–Christ
("Soft & Wet"), performing the admirable, if scarifying,
feat of making Donna Summer and her "Last Dance" seem
matronly—altogether too funky for a white boy to fathom.
Still, by the end of the year, a man as macho as Rod Stewart
would succumb to the Disco lure in *Blondes Have More Fun*
("Do Ya Think I'm Sexy?") and the ultra–rhythmic Chic
would have one of the biggest selling singles of all–time,
"Le Freak."

Against this foreboding backdrop, the return of Bruce

Springsteen in the working class ripped dungareed flesh ("Prove It All Night," "Adam Raised a Cain"), along with his clone chorus of 1978, must be viewed with a certain urgency. But if Springsteen was slightly overwrought, as if he knew it was up to him to re–inherit the future of rock & roll right there and then, his clones weren't faring any better. The honorary Springsteen pro–tem, Bob Seger ("Hollywood Nights") had lost much of his old neighborhood credibility by moving from the Midwest to the West. Recent rear–guard action from the Springsteen of Key West, Jimmy Buffett ("Cheeseburger in Paradise") was far too slight to be meaningful. Jackson Browne was simply drained ("Running on Empty"); Tom Petty was experiencing heavy changes ("Breakdown"). The aforementioned double–Springsteen, Meat Loaf (consistently referred to in The *New York Times* as "Mr. Loaf"), finally released his backseat saga, "Paradise by the Dashboard Light," as an eight–minute single, while the Springsteen of the Lower Depths, Tom Waits, reached a crescendo of guttersnipe ecstacy in "Romeo Is Bleeding" and "Christmas Card from a Hooker in Minneapolis." Billy Joel established his hold on Springsteen's New York turf with his ersatz tough guy celebration of 52nd Street ("Big Shot"). Meanwhile, the anti–Springsteen of the West, the natty, name–dropping Warren Zevon ("Werewolves of London") had acquired a challenger of sorts in the anti–Springsteen of the Midwest, the lionclothed arena hound, Ted Nugent ("Yank Me, Crank Me"). With every available Springsteen permutation currently occupied, peachfuzz Mississippi newcomer Steve Forbert ("You Cannot Win If You Do Not Play") seemed more than a bit retro in his quest to be "the next Bob Dylan," easily the first such next Dylan since Loudon Wainwright, who also turned up in 1978, surprisingly alive and well and unashamedly attuned to the zeitgeist ("Watch Me Rock, I'm over Thirty"). Neil Young, whom

Wainwright had supplanted as the next Dylan way back in 1970, seemed to be drifting in the other direction, but not unpleasantly, in the folkie *Comes a Time* ("Lotta Love," "Four Strong Winds").

Alternatively, the original Dylan, who had in fact come perilously close to supplanting himself earlier in the decade with *Blood on the Tracks* and *Desire*, albums that seemed to evoke his frantic heyday but may have evoked even clearer nothing more than the wishful thinking of his lost battalion of Woodstock mountaineers stranded halfway up the trail without their guide, was at his impenetrable best/worst in *Street Legal*, beginning a descent into the hellfire and brimstone of triviality that would all but remove him from his recently regained post as generational point of reference, as well as temporarily casting into doubt not only his prior legacy, but the entire sensibility of those who saw his words as garments as fine as any yet woven into the fabric of the culture, when all along he could have been just standing there as naked as "even the President of the United States." Add this to his 1978 movie, the interminable *Renaldo and Clara*, and you have a Dylan self–portrait that rivals his incomprehensible novel, *Tarantula*. Fit works, all three, for the files of A.J. Webberman, if not the dungheap of pop civilization.

They would be joined there, by the end of the year, by the inevitable Sid Vicious, the once and no future future of rock & roll. While punk and new wave were on the brink of moving past the Golden into a Tinfoil Age, with dicey works by the Ramones ("I Wanna be Sedated"), the Clash ("Stay Free"), even the coneheaded Devo ("Satisfaction"), and the promise of the Pretenders ("Stop Your Sobbing") and the Cure ("Killing an Arab") on the horizon, Sid was spiraling into a self–willed oblivion totally His Way. In October, his companion, Nancy Spungen, was found dead of stab wounds in the Chelsea Hotel, with Sid charged with her murder. In little more than three months, Sid would be dead as well: as dead as Nancy, as dead as Elvis, as dead as tormented Phil Ochs, as dead as rowdy Keith Moon, and all five of them as dead as the lost character played by Bruce Dern, walking into the sea at the end of the movie *Coming Home*—and all six of them as dead as sad Tim Buckley, whose mournful and fateful and haunting and tragic "Once I Was" played behind Dern on the soundtrack.

Eight

This Bird Has Flown

(1979–1982)

Talk about your intimations of mortality.

Not enough that Elvis went down at 42 (same fated age as Alan Freed, John Coltrane, and Lenny Bruce); not enough to witness Bruce Dern walking into the sea and taking half a generation and Tim Buckley with him, but what about the rest of us, finding ourselves approaching a middle class middle age, surprised and a little chagrined, reacting to time and changes with embarrassing verisimilitude: Dylan at 39, being born again, Lennon, the following year, at 40, starting over?

Preoccupied by youth and beauty and survival ("Do Ya Think I'm Sexy" by Rod Stewart, spent February at number one, followed by three weeks of Gloria Gaynor's "I Will Survive"), the aging principals of this solitary, ego–dominated, angst-ridden, lovelorn period, taking our cues from Hugh Prestwood's "Hard Times for Lovers," Peter Allen's "Don't Cry Out Loud," and Neil Young's "Lotta Love," withstood one psychotic moodswing after another.

If we weren't particularly broken up by—or even aware of—Sid Vicious fulfilling his death wish in February, and

Elvis Costello's career again taking it on the chin in a hotel bar in Ohio in March, when Bonnie Bramlett slugged him for insulting the likes of Ray Charles and James Brown, or the Clash on their first American tour, opening up their first set in New York with a pseudo anti–American tune, "I'm So Bored with the USA," hitting us closer to the Middle of the Dirt Road, was Tom Petty, filing for bankruptcy in May, and Little Feat's patron saint, Lowell George, dying of a heart attack at 34 in June, and Chuck Berry being hauled away for tax evasion in July. In between these signal events, we waiting in a melancholy funk, contemplating Blondie's droll ode to non–commitment, "Heart of Glass," flirting briefly with the rejuvenation of "Chuck E's in Love" by the neo–beat Rickie Lee Jones, the implied indomitability of the mellow "Sultans of Swing" by Dire Straits, the world–weary triumph of Suzi Quatro in "Stumblin' In," her duet with Chris Norman, and the abject exploitation of the Blues Brothers revival of "Rubber Biscuit." When, a couple of weeks into May, Eric Clapton married Layla—George Harrison's ex, Patti—with George in attendance, we didn't know whether to cry, cheer, or throw the bums in the navy with the Village People

By September, however, spurred, perhaps, by punk impudence, disco ennui, an activist legacy left in Grant Park, the plight of the hostages in Iran, the plight of the Sandinistas in Nicaragua, the plight of the remaining mammals on Three Mile Island, or, if none of the above, then surely "Cruel to be Kind" by Nick Lowe, "Girls Talk" by Dave Edmunds, or the historic stateside crossover of Pink Lady ("Kiss in the Dark"), if not an abject aversion to growing older—or up—this way, at last we boys and girls of the baby boom summer got back with the liberal program of our heyday, by attending an old fashioned rally against the bomb in Battery Park, New York. For sheer nostalgia, this was a pretty good pick–me–up (though it was no match for movies like *Rock & Roll High School, Hair!*, and *The Kids Are Alright*, or even the eventual album to commemorate the event, *No Nukes*— "Before the Deluge" by Jackson Browne, "We Almost Lost Detroit" by Gil Scott–Heron; Bruce Springsteen's rousing, "Good Golly Miss Molly/Devil with the Blue Dress On" medley, which was absolutely the essence of anti–nuclear testing; slightly more politically correct, if less sonically arresting, was John Hall's "Power," by the conglomerate of James Taylor, Carly Simon, and the Doobie Brothers). Even more politically correct, Linda Ronstadt stayed home with her new squeeze, California's leading liberal, Jerry Brown; undoubtedly their crowded social calendar included double dates with the Eagles' Don Henley. Ronstadt and the Eagles sang at a Brown fund–raiser in December, only two short months after suffering like most of us through the ungodly spectacle of Bob Dylan unveiling his Christianity on "Saturday Night Live," singing "Gotta Serve Somebody"—probably at the same moment that former porn star, Wendy O. Williams, taking up where Andrea True never came near, was out somewhere busting up a television set onstage with the Plasmatics, topless save for strategic pasties.

Thus, while the party on the right suggested a kind of gnarled recidivism at play ("Forever in Blue Jeans" by Neil Diamond, "Old Time Rock & Roll" by Bob Seger, "Rock & Roll Fantasy" by Bad Company, "Juke Box Hero" by Foreigner, "Dance the Night Away" by Van Halen, "Up on the Roof" by James Taylor, "Long Live Rock" by the Who) summed up by Chic's "Good Times," the party out of bounds revealed an edgy younger generation severely out of touch with the baby boom program (the Circle Jerk's "Nervous Breakdown," the Dead Kennedys' "California Uber Alles," "Highway to Hell" by AC/DC, "Gangsters" by the Specials, the Talking Heads' "Life During War-time", the Brains' "Money Changes Everything," and the Buggles' "Video Killed the Radio Star").

And so, the leading edge of the baby boom, having totally lost its edge, stumbled down the Middle of the Dirt Road into 1980, a shambles of mixed emotions, re-evaluations, mad reversals—just like the last time a Demo-crat ran for re-election! Typifying the schizoid tilt of our priorities, within the first three months of the year, a couple of our most devout bohemians had signed their names on that dreaded piece of paper called a marriage license, one month Lou Reed and Sylvia, the next Patti Smith and Fred. Then there was mainstream Linda Ronstadt singing radical Elvis Costello on *Mad Love* ("Alison," "Girls Talk") one minute, and Elizabethan Gilbert & Sullivan (*The Pirates of Penzance*) in Central Park the next. You had lofty anti-materialist George Harrison writing his autobiography (*I Me Mine*) and then trying to sell copies for $125 a pop. Paul Simon, fresh from his bit part success in Woody Allen's *Annie Hall*, revealed how far his reach exceeded his grasp (if not his clout), by writing, directing, and starring in *One Trick Pony* (salvaging from the debacle only the magnificent ode to his rock & roll beginnings, "Late in the Evening"). Like do-wop sinners diving into tuxes in the 1950s, rockers were lulled in 1980 into believing that the movies offered an artistic (or at least adult) legitimacy that was no longer the implied province of their original craft. Meanwhile, no one in the movie biz was complaining if a superstar rocker brought his audi-ence, en masse, into the Loew's State to safely navigate a chancy film across the bottom line, even if it meant casting Neil Diamond as Sir Lawrence Olivier's son in *The Jazz Singer*, or attempting to mutilate the memory of Marilyn with Debbie Harry in *Roadie* or Janis with Bette Midler in *The Rose*.

If Jimmy Carter was listening to the radio in 1980, as he relentlessly assured his rebel constituency he was, he should have been able to pick up on all the gloomy portents of his ultimate loss to California's leading reactionary, Ronald Reagan, at the end of the year, particularly if he was at all aware of what was happening to the precise country and Middle of the Dirt Road coalition that had elected him in 1976 (if not to the country itself). Peaking at number 33 on the morning of November 1, 1980, Anne Murray's "Could I Have This Dance," from the movie *Urban Cowboy*, would still be humming through the brains of a suddenly cowboy crazed nation, two–stepping to the polls in ten gallon Stetsons and $400 snakeskin boots, following John Travolta's lead from the dancefloors of Brooklyn to the mechanical bull at Mickey Gilley's nightclub in Houston, Texas, in the grip of a post–disco western fever that was the total antithesis of the macho southern rock deliverance that Carter had ridden to victory on only four years before. Where was Carter's southern rock now? In his own once pivotal native Georgia, the best they had to offer was a southern rock parody, the B–52's ("Rock Lobster," "Private Idaho") not only with inane lyrics, but with their very personas, and lopsided, peroxided bouffant hairdos, they were an affront to the proud beer–swilling Dixie tradition. Worse yet was Pylon's "Cool Dub," actually a reggae–influenced tune. Much in the way they'd once brought us back our own Chicago blues, the latest invasion of English musicians, like the Specials ("Too Much Too Young"), UB40 ("Tyler"), the Police ("Message in a Bottle"), the English Beat ("Rough Rider"), and the Clash ("Train in Vain"), were transporting reggae like contraband, sapping our rekindled activist energy with its insidious beat, political lyrics, and lenient attitude toward marijuana. In the same towns where Carter youth could have been getting out the vote, reggae was unsettling the liberal agenda with a killing disdain for any kind of law and order. (Tell me it was mere coincidence, when, as reported in the rock press, No–Nukes Carly and dreadlocked Marley collapsed within four days of each other in Pittsburgh in October).

In place of Lynyrd Skynyrd's hard–boogieying southern man was the ersatz fern bar country music of Brooklyn's Eddie Rabbitt ("Driving My Life Away"), the Lower East Side's octagenarian George Burns ("I Wish I Was Eighteen Again"), and Lake Tahoe's Kenny Rogers ("Coward of the County," "Love the World Away," "Lady," plus "Don't Fall in Love with a Dreamer," with the Bonnie Tyler soundalike, Kim Carnes). And yet, as Ronald Reagan's oily hairdo bobbed up and down in shopping malls and truckstops all across the nation through 1980, spouting similar anachronisms, what had to be even more appalling to the diminishing Carter loyalists, was that country music hadn't had such a renaissance on the pop charts since Dylan's foray into Nashville brought both Nixon and Elvis to the White House in 1969!

Dolly Parton ("Starting over Again"), taking up where Debbie Harry left off, parlayed her huge visibility into a stilted acting career, alongside noted liberal icons Jane Fonda and Lily Tomlin in the movie *9 to 5*. Former hippie, Charlie Daniels, sounded like a commercial for Chevy trucks ("In America"). No less a once–godly Eric Clapton was living on "Tulsa Time." From *Urban Cowboy*, Johnny Lee's dime–popping jukebox stupor of self-obsession ("Looking for Love"), was nothing compared to Willie Nelson's glorification of these bogus pioneers of the latest New Frontier: Reagan Country ("My Heroes Have Always Been Cowboys" and "On the Road Again"). More conclusive proof of this massive geographical shift in generational thinking was offered when Wayne Newton crashed the top 40 with "Years," his first hit in eight years; in the Reagan

Era, Wayne would be bigger than Elvis in Las Vegas, and nearly as paunchy.

In the elitist East, where you might have thought this kind of backwoods sloganeering wouldn't play to a street smart citizenry, many otherwise right–thinking left–wingers in the Middle of the Dirt Road were at that point backing away from all committed relationships, responsibilities, or political movements, preferring to exist in a mutual Pago Pago of the spirit, emotionally one foot out the door, capable of following anyone who remotely suggested the possibility of escape ("Escape" by Rupert Holmes was the number one song when the year began, "Cruisin'" was Smokey Robinson's comeback breakthrough, "Three Times in Love" was the retrogressive return vehicle for Tommy James, and ZZ Top was hidden behind "Cheap Sunglasses"), no matter how lame, halt, or musically infirm that person might have been. How else do you explain the medium and the message of Christopher Cross ("Ride Like the Wind" and "Sailing") or Neil Sedaka's unaccountably trenchant duet with his daughter, Dara, "Should've Never Let You Go")? Rita Coolidge expressed the inexpressible the best in "I'd Rather Leave While I'm in Love." J. Geils gave this particular midlife malaise its anthem ("Love Stinks").

Unlike the warring factions of 1968, taking their grievances to the streets in a bloody public forum that resulted in our worst nightmares coming to pass, in 1980, surviving Sixties veterans, souls having long since been psychedelicized, libidos anesthetized, willful spirits psychoanalyzed, were too damn wrapped up in getting out of things (relationships, apartments, debt), to prevent what would be the last Democratic era from stumbling abruptly to an end right before our eyes. Certainly, there were deals being consummated nightly with the Shah of Iran; they could have been loading the boats with guns bound for

Nicaragua in broad daylight; but nowhere in rock & roll was there anywhere near an appropriate response to be found. We were too busy turning prim, cherubic Olivia Newton-John ("Magic") into the second coming of Debbie Reynolds.

Anyone looking to our songwriting icons or to the songs themselves to lead us from these moral doldrums back to our righteous equilibrium would have to strain for meaning among the year's remaining etudes. Bob Dylan, having been reduced (elevated) to shouting (preaching) from hills much higher and more remote than any Woodstock had to offer, was nevertheless the closest to the mark ("When You Gonna Wake Up?"). Linda Ronstadt was too horny for power to think straight ("How Do I Make You?"). The usually smug and unflappable Eagles could offer no patented wisdom ("I Can't Tell You Why"). Even among the year's various Springsteen sympathizers, anguish and apathy, if not outright anomie, reigned ("Against the Wind" by Bob Seger, "Refugee" by Tom Petty, "San Diego Serenade" by Tom Waits; in "It's Still Rock & Roll to Me" Billy Joel embarrassed himself by trying to fend off the mid–life willies in a leather jacket and too-tight pants; in "Hungry Heart," Springsteen himself went out for a pack of Luckies in Newark, New Jersey and wound up somewhere West of Selena, Kansas).

Sensing an ageless need for their down–to–earth yet spiritual counsel not felt since 1968, the Rolling Stones summoned us into their den of iniquity, but "Emotional Rescue" failed to meet the challenge. In answer, instead, we turned to the insufferably perfect Kenny Loggins, with his suntanned beard and windblown sideburns, sensitive eyelashes, in a retort that would have done the Eagles proud: "I'm Alright." If that wasn't reassuring enough, Burt Reynolds hit the charts with "Let's Do Something Cheap and Superficial." Clearly, if this was the best we had to offer to define our mission in life, we deserved to lose what was left of our pathetic power base.

Humbled, demeaned, nearly empty, our baby boom legacy hanging by a thread, we even went back, if half–heartedly, to that old standby store of black music for some sacred notions we could borrow or steal. But, outside of the disco, we were virtually stumped by Prince's voluminous sexuality ("I Wanna Be Your Lover," "When You Were Mine"), Michael Jackson's precarious psychological state ("Off the Wall"). Elsewhere, it was reggae, si—among those who remembered championing it in college, like soccer—and rap, no—although breakthrough break-dance tracks like "Rapper's Delight" by the Sugarhill Gang and "The Breaks" by Kurtis Blow were gradually moving Downtown from the Bronx, like Dion's Fordham Baldies, getting ready to set a match to our stupor.

At the heavy metal arena as well, a decade of decibels was taking its mortal toll. In February, AC/DC's Bon Scott died at 34. The once proud, hard–rocking Aerosmith were definitely evincing signs of early senility, not only in deciding to cover the Shangri–Las" schmaltzy "Remember (Walking in the Sand)," but in doing so only four months after Louise Goffin (scion of Carole and Gerry) had bombed with the same tune. And Pink Floyd was (perhaps) unwittingly providing Reagan with his keenest sound bite yet ("We don't need no education") in "Another Brick in the Wall." By September, Led Zeppelin's John Bonham would be dead as well at 32, and, soon after, so would Led Zeppelin. Only Ted Nugent fearlessly kept pace with his image ("Wango Tango").

And where was punk anger in all of this, the younger generation of spiky–haired nihilists on either side of the Atlantic? Complaining, as usual ("I Don't Like Mondays" by the Boomtown Rats) or mourning ("People Who Died" by Jim Carroll) or preening ("Brass in Pocket [I'm Special]"

by the Pretenders) or worse ("Dancing with Myself" by
Generation X).

But then, aroused from a deep slumber of advanced
domesticity, his system flushed by years of primal scream-
ing, his wife's avant–garde relevance second only to that of
Yma Sumac or Edith Bunker, and his former partners'
careers safely heading in the toilet (Paul was busted,
George was in court, Ringo was auditioning for Saturday
morning cartoon shows), John Lennon, in "(Just Like)
Starting Over," forgave us for our sins, and then went out
to do the shopping. Less than a month later, Ronald
Reagan ushered in a Republican world. Two weeks after
that, while Nancy was still packing Ronnie's silk night-
shirts for their trip East, Don Henley was arrested for
possession of drugs and contributing to the delinquency of
a sixteen–year–old girl.

For the few stunned believers who remained stranded in
the Middle of the Dirt Road, there was psychosis in the air,
as the dreary inevitability of repression loomed, laden with
predictions of slashed funding for the Arts, and the drying
up of the underground well, in favor of heaping money on
the military for the revivified and rekindled Cold War with
the commies. Here was the final humiliation, a grandfather
figure come to reprimand us, and dispense cruel and
unusual punishment for the sins of our idealistic youth
going down on our Permanent Records. No one and
nothing was safe. The climate was even colder than 1968,
when the sheer numerical togetherness of rule–breakers
was a buffer against mass prosecution. We were younger
then, limber, imperturbable; within a month of Nixon's
squeaker, 100,000 were partying in Hallendale, at the
Miami Pop Festival. But twelve years had passed, and one
by one, former hippies, waking to find themselves over
thirty, could no longer even trust themselves. Somebody
would have to take the blame for this, pay for it, take the

fall, become the martyr: a public figure, controversial yet
non–violent, like Martin Luther King or Mahatma Ghandi,
who stood for everything we'd once believed in and
managed to let slip away, like Bobby Kennedy, leaving us
forever to wonder if it was all the same pack of lies, or if
anything could have been different—who cautioned us
that "The Dream Is Over," even as he laid it out in
"Imagine." With an illegal Saturday Night Special, a
25-year-old Beatle fan, as in fanatic, enacting his own
demented version of "Happiness Is a Warm Gun," ended
John Lennon's abortive return to public life after a couple
of blissful months, in front of the heavily guarded fortress
of the Dakota apartments, with astonishing, point blank
ease (in concert in nearby Hartford, Bruce Springsteen was
singing "Point Blank" when he heard the devastating
news). The rest of us went back to watching Monday Night
Football, albeit with the sound off and an FM radio tuned
to a rock & roll station. For a few weeks, FM achieved a
morbid rapport with its constituency it hadn't at all
approached or even sought for years, uniting a generation
in its sorrow and irrelevance in a sad cascade of Lennon
tunes, and Beatle tunes, to get us past a senseless tragedy,
just as in their minted prime of 1964, these tunes served
much the same dreary purpose. By Christmas, the unbearably ironic "(Just Like) Starting Over" ascended to number
one, where it would remain for five weeks, until Blondie's
"The Tide Is High" washed it away.

Talk about your intimations of mortality.

Despite Yoko's implicit promise to carry on Lennon's
good works, and the mayor's promise to name a piece of
New York's Central Park "Strawberry Fields" in his honor,
most baby boom rock fans, grappling with the thirtysomething litany of night moves, career moves, biologi
cal and cosmic clocks, or the various implosions of the nuclear family, took Lennon's death much harder than

Presley's (he'd been effectively dead for a long time), even harder than John Kennedy's (we weren't teenagers anymore, weren't at the beginning of the road)—that death rattle sounded more and more like a heartbeat, diminishing. Within a blink, Tim Hardin was dead at 39, Mike Bloomfield at 39, Canned Heat's Bob Hite at 36, Bob Marley at 36, and Harry Chapin at 39. Eric Clapton was in a hospital for bleeding ulcers, Jerry Lee Lewis was in a hospital with a hole in his stomach. Bob Dylan turned 40 to the tune of "Lenny Bruce" and "Every Grain of Sand." Jodie Foster–obsessed John Hinckley Jr. was on the loose, armed with illegal weapons; near the end of a Simon & Garfunkel free concert in New York's Central Park in September, within walking distance from the spot where the gunshot that killed John Lennon still echoed, someone vaulted the stage and hurtled toward Paul, nearly brushing his arm during the song "The Late Great Johnny Ace"—in fact, a tribute to Lennon—before security hustled him off the hustings ("Paul, I have to talk to you," he's reported to have said).

Of course, this is not to imply that 1981 was a total loss for all sectors of the music marketplace, that any of this had to do with Ronald Reagan's master plan of turning the entire USA into a California theme park police state vision of the pop forties. That would be wrong. For instance, Christopher Cross, a former roadie for Fleetwood Mac, had a great year, sweeping the Grammy Awards in February, with the lifeless "Sailing" winning Song and Record of the year. He'd be back at the top of the charts in October, with the title song from *Arthur*, a movie that celebrated the indolence of the filthy rich ("The Best That You Can Do"). Lumbering REO Speedwagon made good on years of American workmanlike (that is to say, mediocre) product, hitting number one in March with "Keep on Loving You." Country music continued its glide to generational prominence, with Dolly Parton ("9 to 5") and Eddie Rabbitt ("I Love a Rainy Night") leading the way. On their rightwing haunches would come Delbert McClinton ("Giving It up for Your Love"), Juice Newton ("Angel of the Morning"), Dottie West and Kenny Rogers ("What Are We Doing in Love"), the Oak Ridge Boys ("Elvira"), Kenny Rogers solo ("I Don't Need You"), Ronnie Milsap ("There's No Getting over Me"), Alabama ("Feels So Right"), more Juice Newton ("Queen of Hearts"), more Eddie Rabbitt ("Step by Step"), and more Kenny Rogers ("Share Your Love with Me").

If this kind of mewling self–satisfaction was par for the (restricted) golf course of country music, more disturbing was that even some of the usual suspects you could once count on for more than just a song and dance, were producing stuff that was just as parched and enervating. Steely Dan offered ample evidence in "Hey Nineteen" that they decided to break up one of our most progressive hopes against the coming dullness, simply because they were no longer able to get it up for teenage girls. Bruce Springsteen, working alone in a room with a four–track tape recorder on the forthcoming dolorous epic, *Nebraska*, took some needed time off in the sun to re-discover his Jersey youth in the person of Gary U.S. Bonds ("Hey Little Girl")—yet the spectre of a twenty year gap between hit singles (circa "Quarter to Three") must have driven the Boss back to his moldy room in tears of rage. Similar tears of lost youth were hidden in Dan Fogelberg's "Same Old Lang Syne," of lost love, in James Taylor and J.D. Souther's "Her Town Too," of lost time, in Tom Petty's "The Waiting," of lost life, in AC/DC's "Back in Black," written for Bon Scott. Of course, the memory of John Lennon couldn't have been too far from anyone's consciousness for most of the year—with John's own parting "Woman" and "Watching the Wheels," and Yoko's "Walking on Thin

Ice," and George's almost wistful "All Those Years Ago," and Paul's nearly tearful "Here Today."

And yet, deep in the faltering underground, where jaundiced hipsters still spun sides for their jaded molls, acolytes, and sycophants, there were some tunes being heard in various stages of development, played before packed rooms of up to thirty–five rabid fans a night: rococco rockabilly ("White Girls" by X), resplendant revisionism ("Gloria" by U2), suburban garage guitar ("Radio Free Europe" by R.E.M., "Ask for Jill" by the Dbs, "I Hate Music" by the Replacements), disemboweled manic thrash, by Black Flag, and Hüsker Dü, unrepentant vinyl spleen ("Moral Majority" by the Dead Kennedys). In England, as well, there were songs of social significance being written, that would fail to cross the Atlantic as hits: ("To Hell with Poverty" by Gang of Four, "Ghost Town" by the Specials, "Doors to My Heart" by the English Beat, "One in Ten" by UB40, "Clubland" by Elvis Costello, "Something About England" by the Clash)—in favor of the emotionless, synth-based "Don't You Want Me" by the Human League, destined to become a smash in 1982. Brave beyond measure in the encroaching atmosphere of 1984 three years too soon, or festering sores on the butt of melody, the existence of these songs, at least to their insistent slam dancing coteries—in which you'd be hard pressed to find anyone born before 1950 who wasn't there on assignment for some journal of Low Culture—would be the only evidence of throbbing life left in the endangered species called rock & roll, something vital and necessary to cling to in the face of the massive turn to commerciality that was preparing to debut on August first.

Out of the prevailing psychic economics of oversupply being an excuse to fabricate a non–existent demand, more than having anything to do with stretching the boundaries of an artform, or providing a real service to an audience in

need, the advent of Music Television (MTV), undoubtedly
had its roots in the baby boom filmschool explosion of the
Seventies, wherein places like New York University and
San Francisco State (and probably some other institutions
in between) produced such a crush of aspiring Scorceses in
bush jackets and khaki slacks, lugging ten tons of equip-
ment in search of 2.6 million dollars of funding, to produce
their own *Hard Day's Night*, *Head*, or *Easy Rider*, that the
rampaging spillover of failed, frustrated, stymied genius
without adequate portfolio, just naturally resulted, with
the gradual tapering of high ideals into fast–buck deals
over the short haul of the real world syllabus, in the
proliferation, if not the preponderance, if not the overnight omnipresence, of corporate-financed, musically oriented short subjects, aka Rock Videos—the natural
outgrowth of the ego monster we created with *Roadie*,
Xanadu, *Fame*, *The Jazz Singer*, et al.

Although it gave us, in its first few months of stumbling
infancy, pleasures as curious and various as "Girls on
Film" by Duran Duran, the giddy veejay Martha Quinn,
and David Byrne's quintessentially neurotic performance
in the Talking Heads' "Once in a Lifetime," MTV did
relatively little at the outset to advance either rock & roll
or the virtually dormant artform of video (pioneered by
visionaries like Nam June Pak, Ernie Kovacs, and Captain
Video). Instead, these early three-minute vignettes were
abject, undisguised (and obscenely expensive) commercials for the albums from which the single, or video, was
extracted, empty of historic or visual significance beyond
the benighted return to cultural prominence of the lip–
synch (a network television series was eventually spawned
that catered to the enormous new interest in this deserved-
ly moribund deceptive stunt first foisted upon us by Dick
Clark on "American Bandstand"), and the momentary
thrill of seeing a heretofore favorite performer thrust into

the humiliating role of rivaling the acting talent of a Neil Diamond, Debbie Harry, Kris Kristofferson, Dolly Parton, or Olivia Newton–John, in a high school production of what might have been an otherwise meaningful song. A triumph of form over substance, of financial might over scruffy indigence, the Rock Video was the perfect symbol of the Reagan Era, in which the rich would get richer and the non–conformist would be sacrificed on the altar of the bottom line. Though it did at least provide a lot of work for failed filmmakers, non–union actors, grips, technicians, script girls, and the occasional photogenic rock star, after its August first debut to the tune of "Video Killed the Radio Star," Music Television would be more than the new FM radio for a new (white) generation: it would be Big Brother, standarizing not only what would and could become popular, but, with its indelible repetition of video images, stuffing, as if with plugged nickels, our collective memory banks as well.

It was bad enough that a TV star, of the soap opera variety, Rick Springfield, spent the first fortnight of the MTV–Era at the top of the charts, with "Jessie's Girl," but, following it, for the next nine unendurable weeks, was the utterly mundane Diana Ross/Lionel Richie title tune from the movie *Endless Love*, completing the musical destruction of the engrossing Scott Spencer novel that was begun with the casting of Brooke Shields in the role of Jade in the movie. If this was the taste level to which popular culture had descended—with Blondie going disco ("Backfired") and Elvis Costello going country (*Almost Blue*), heavy metal getting soft in the head ("Who's Crying Now" by Journey"), country music getting fat in the belly ("All My Rowdy Friends Have Settled Down" by Hank Williams Jr.), and rap getting booed off the stages of the Clash tour—then perhaps the TV Generation's ultimate perversion of rock & roll was merely an apt commentary on our advanced creative stasis!

Certainly, by the end of the year, whatever our initial qualms may have been, the rock & roll pioneers of the baby boom had dramatically come to terms with MTV—with none other than the aging disco dandy, Rod Stewart, emerging as a kindly hip uncle figure in "Young Turks," narrating a heartwarming mini–series about a much younger couple (was that Rachel Sweet in the female lead? The girl was another Annie Golden!) starting off in life from a funky two room flat with Rod's sexy blessings. Taking sex a bit further, but only for those for whom a squat thrust was erotic, Olivia Newton–John went from failed Debbie Reynolds, to second–rate Jane Fonda, in "Physical," which spent the last ten weeks of the year at number one, qualifying it as not only the biggest hit of the year—and the decade (bigger even than the equally whiter than white "You Light up My Life," by Debby Boone)—but the biggest hit since Guy Mitchell's "Singing the Blues," in 1956—when Eisenhower was in office and Ronald Reagan was still a spry kid in his fifties, running the actor's union! And if you think that was a coincidence, then also consider that Reagan's first year in office just happened to result in the lowest amount of songs hitting the Top 100 than any year in rock & roll history since . . . 1955—down nearly 20 percent from the year before and down 90 percent from the generation's creative heyday of 1966, when some 743 songs made the charts. Now, maybe there was a petroleum shortage, and a whopping national recession on the way, but then again it was still a fearsome glimpse at what rock & roll fans could expect for the remainder of the decade if baby boom energy was removed from the songmaking and receiving process.

Things didn't improve much in this regard in 1982,

which was the next worst year in rock & roll history since 1955 for total records on the charts. But, MTV was ensconsed in our Ultimate Living Rooms now, so we seemed to care about it less. Like it was our second shot at eternal youth, with no draft lottery to spoil our late thirties as it did our late teens and early twenties, or else, under-employed, or out of work, living through the closest thing to the Great Depression since Martin & Lewis split up, we had nothing better to do but watch in fascination as MTV served as a catalyst for a fullscale Tapehead Invasion, based around the Rock Video. Nearly the cultural twin of The Cult of Youth, except for the absence of Jackie Kennedy and her pillbox hat, the Video Revolution even resulted in the reincarnation of the familiar 45th site of the Peppermint Lounge, erstwhile home of the Twist, where state–of–the–art videos were shown from state–of–the–art TV screens, interspersed with vintage TV clips and Felix the Cat cartoons (shades of the Joshua Light Show!). Although it would be several years before saner heads would plunder the vast nostalgia vaults for entire baby boom TV networks, and the prices of VCRs would come down enough to allow the man on the street to watch feature films previously the exclusive domain of the filthy rich and traveling rock bands on the road, MTV had no lack of round–the–clock programming for the short–attention–span masses.

As opposed to the raised fist salute of your basic rock & roll utopian, communal, Woodstockian, we–want–the–world–and–we–want–it–now arena posture, MTV, being an indoor sport, designed for watching in spurts, between trips to the fridge for a Heineken, promoted more of a passive, sedentary, solitary, fragmented experience. Three times removed from the music, by artifice, by lip–synch, and by the staunchly conservative nature—and tiny speakers—of the television set itself (where Elvis's pelvis has yet to be seen, except on PBS), MTV's call to inaction was nevertheless a welcome relief to the feedback and flashback-scarred youth of the Sixties, many of whom were by now parents of nascent rock & rollers themselves. If momentarily perturbed by rock video's portrayal of women in cages and in chains and in varying stages of undress in biker bars, it took only enough time to click the remote control around the expanded cable menu of channels, for many of us to form a great and unifying rationalization that would all but ensure MTV's eventual takeover.

Because we saw ourselves as the Media Superstars the media had seen us as growing up—the first generation to be certifiably hipper than our kids—if the Revolution was going to be televized after all, who better to be in control of the cameras? Big Brother was us! Besides, if wartime images of the Vietnam wounded on the nightly TV news of the Sixties had turned following generations into politically apathetic, avaricious businessmen, Young Republicans, then what would a little cleavage do to the MTV generation—turn them into virginal show music fans! Not everyone was similarly farsighted in this matter; in fact, significant numbers of parents proved to be not only less hip than their kids, but far stricter than their (admittedly notoriously permissive) parents. Seeing on television for the first time what was actually going on below Elvis's waist—and in his dreams—sent them into such a delirium of protest you'd have thought they were back in college petitioning for coed dorms.

Of course, the ensuing call for censorship was the best publicity MTV (and its sole mode of programming, the Rock Video) ever could have had, replete with echoes of rock & roll's penchant, from Elvis to Elvis, for evoking the ire of midland bluebloods fearing for the moral fabric of our youth. Thus, like nothing else on television, MTV became a cause, like *Hustler* magazine, that warranted protection not for its product, but on principle. Outside of the principle, however, and the ire, as misplaced—if predictable—as it was, MTV was still a long way from rock & roll. For one thing, it had no black roots. Neither, for that matter, did television, unless you wanted to count the "Amos & Andy Show," but MTV was never about television—certainly never about video, per se—as much as it was about the record charts, controlling them, reinventing them for demographic purposes, under which premise the absense of black faces could be otherwise disguised as astute programming.

For another thing, while early rock & roll existed primarily in the mind (you could go years before figuring out what Del Shannon actually said in the chorus of "Runaway," and not diminish the power of the tune), the memories shaded by the passage of time, on MTV, even if you couldn't understand the words, or what the hell the actions meant, you could nevertheless easily see what was going on, and seeing, if it didn't make things any more believable, did significantly demystify what was on the screen, reducing it to what it was, and nothing more. The more literal the translation, the less the song had a chance of winning over the right side of the brain. Conversely, the more surreal the video, the less the song seemed to matter at all. In 1982, the first full calendar year of the Video Age, it was made abundantly clear that MTV—and by inference the record labels and their khaki cadre of filmmaker conscripts—would operate on both sides of the debate, with the singer, the song, the arrangement (to say nothing of the segue) bowing down before the starmaking power of the Camera, the resultant rock video eventually to become indistinguishable from the commercials that separated them, which seemed more and more like songs themselves: the product as product as product.

Because we were too tired or apathetic to change the

channel—there was nothing on except "Hill Street Blues" —we were happy to give MTV an extended benefit of the doubt, if only for our not quite squashed wishful thinking that its actual hidden agenda was to glorify our baby boom heritage, with a 24–hour montage of our heroic past, and a celebration of our continuing influence, the aging of rock into its most appropriate mid–life livingroom format, with baby boomers at the helm, calling the tune and the shots. In this way it fulfilled a fantasy even larger than the old one from the sixties in which all hippies moved to someplace like Montana and then seceded from the Union.

Nostalgic for girl–groups? We've got 'em, as precocious and adorable as they come ("We Got the Beat" by the Go–Gos), or, alternatively, as tawdry as the skirts in the old neighborhood ("I Love Rock & Roll" by Joan Jett). When the Go–Gos came back in August riding surfboards in "Vacation," cheeky and cherubic as Connie Stevens in *Where the Boys Are,* you knew there were droll and maybe even revisionist minds at work. We had the Stones, right before our eyes, just sitting on a stoop like regular city guys, in "Waiting on a Friend." We had Bowie as well, starting off the year demolishing buildings in "Under Pressure." Lots of high tech hardware behind that one. Even Carole King made a video of a rare concert performance in New York ("One to One").

Like veteran ballplayers at the advent of free agency, cashing in on the hard years of nickel and dime obscurity, or radio comedians reinventing themselves on television, or boat people washing ashore on mythic Coney Island before they closed the Parachute Jump, or none of those things, lots of mouldering record stars profited from losing their souls to the Video Age, not least among them, Rod Stewart, who had apparently been doing videos as far back as 1978's "Hot Legs," which surfaced in all its sexist glory, in form and substance not exactly a quantum leap from 1982's "Tonight I'm Yours," and Steve Miller, who finally started earning back a portion of his 1966 advance, wisely deciding to refrain from appearing in his subsequent number one tune, "Abracadabra." J. Geils went so far in his conversion to adopt the inside parlance of the burgeoning milieu in "Freeze Frame," following their even more abject pandering in "Centerfold," which prophetically played on the predilections of an aging demographic that would soon usher into prominence the grand concept of the Video Playmate. Even the revelation, brought startlingly home in that first year of videos, that the long–haired rockers in outsized teeny arena bands like Asia ("Heat of the Moment"), Toto ("Rosanna"), Scorpions ("No One Like You"), Loverboy ("Working for the Weekend") and Fleetwood Mac ("Hold Me") were in all probability older than everyone else in their concert audience, was not enough to stem the juggernaut.

Although moved primarily by financial necessity, certain bands emerged in the Video Age as more suited to the form than others, discovering sometime after the fact, a flair for this kind of extemporaneous mugging, not unakin to what the Beatles might have felt when viewing the rushes for *A Hard Day's Night* (though most videos were scripted and budgeted if not directly influenced more on the order of the self–conscious, megabuck follow–up, *Help!*). Surely the Cars, in "Since You're Gone," were the antic equal of the Monkees in *Head!* Stevie Nicks found an image for herself, wrapped in swirling scarves and seafoam in "Edge of Seventeen (Just Like the White–Winged Dove)" and "Gypsy," with performances that far surpassed Donna Summer in *Thank God It's Friday* and the ineffable Pia Zadora in "I'm in Love Again," but stopped just short of the Waitresses in "I Know What Boys Like." By these standards, Billy Idol, in "Hot in the City," and

Tommy Tutone, the band, in "867-5309—Jenny," compared favorably to Elvis Presley in twenty–nine of his thirty–seven movies. Billy Joel affected a young Woody Guthrie—or was it a tall Mickey Rooney—in *The Grapes of Wrath*, in the populist "Allentown," while John Cougar went after both James Dean and John Travolta, with the middle–American semi-tough routine in "Hurts So Good." Slighty artsier of intent, were the post–punk British bands, like the Human League ("Don't You Want Me"), Soft Cell ("Tainted Love"), the Cure ("Killing an Arab"), and A Flock of Seagulls ("I Ran"), who'd all no doubt just seen *Last Year at Marienbad* at the same Fleet Street cinema on the same rainy weekend. Finally, even the notoriously pure in heart Bruce Springsteen issued a video from his spare and unrelenting *Nebraska* album, the appropriately austere, b&w "Atlantic City"—a film noir mise–en–scene not unlike its cinematic double, starring Burt Lancaster and Susan Sarandon, directed by Louis Malle—in which the Boss, like Dylan at Woodstock, is present only in his significant absence.

If it was a statement he was trying to make with his non–presence in "Atlantic City," something to merge with the lyrics of this common man lament for what the hard times were doing to us all, it might have been to point up the irony of record companies having the big bucks to lavish on videos, when fewer and fewer singles were making the charts, supposedly because we were in a recession. He might have gone on to speculate, as the mass murderer Charlie Starkweather almost certainly must have, as he was being strapped into the chair in "Nebraska," that we were using what little money we had to encourage the narrowing of our choices down to what we could see—and what we could see was invariably even less than what we got on television, where everything was not only bigger than life (the problems, the solutions, the sets), but also smaller than life (squashed, confined, repressed into a jellomold of prototypical manufactured existence). No room on MTV for irregular fellows like the Angry Samoans ("They Saved Hitler's Cock"), Richard Hell ("Staring in Her Eyes"), Green on Red ("Aspirin"), Hüsker Dü ("Obnoxious"), the Replacements ("Dope Smokin' Moron"), Elvis Costello ("The Long Honeymoon"), Marshall Crenshaw ("Cynical Girl"), Richard Thompson ("Wall of Death"), Heaven 17 ("We Live So Fast"), the Minutemen (*What Makes a Man Start Fires*), or (of all people) Charlie Daniels ("Still in Saigon," the song equivalent of the movie, *Coming Home*).

On the other hand, the Boss could have just been too busy with domestic chores, serving as best man for two of his blood buddies of the Asbury turf, at Southside Johnny's nuptials in August, at Miami Steve's wingding in December.

Neither was MTV interested in irregular females, if they weren't in cages: Laurie Anderson ("O Superman"), Kate Bush ("The Dreaming"), Ferron ("Up a Misty Mountain"), Nanci Griffith ("Working in Corners"), the Waitresses ("No Guilt"), Moon Unit Zappa ("Valley Girl"), Joni Mitchell ("You Dream Flat Tires"), Josie Cotton ("Johnny Are You Queer?"); it even missed the best high note of Linda Ronstadt's career in "The Moon's a Harsh Mistress."

And certainly, MTV had no use in its squeaky clean Reaganesque worldview for blacks—as did rock radio in general. The sixteen and a half tunes that made the Top 100 of 1982 were the lowest total since . . . 1956, shattering the record of seventeen, previously held by the next lowest year, 1981. Somewhere beyond the camera and the radio, in malevolent shadowy Clevelands of the inner ear—the third eye of the third world—hip–hop and rap bespoke the end of Harmony, even as above the ground, Stevie Wonder's collaboration with Paul McCartney on

"Ebony and Ivory" seemed so much token post–Spector, post-hippie, lip–synch lip service—topping the charts just in time for Peace Week, starring Stevie and the usual casting call for aging hippies: James Taylor, Linda Ronstadt, Jackson Browne, Bruce Springsteen, Joan Baez, Bob Dylan, and Bonnie (isn't it too bad about her lapsed career) Raitt. Buried in 1982 was "The Message" by Grandmaster Flash ("Don't push me/I'm close to the edge"), "Apache" by the Sugarhill Gang, "Planet Rock" by Afrika Bambaataa, and other tunes that no white man, on his own time, could have had the wisdom, the courage, or the ears to pick up on.

Much later in the year, a new beginning for MTV could be glimpsed in Michael Jackson's *Thriller*, and its hardly veiled plea for rock acceptance (Eddie Van Halen on guitar on "Beat It") and, in passing, world unity. Matched against this tune was Michael's evil twin, Prince ("1999"). Eventually, the two would provide a battle of mortal mirror images as weighty and primal as the ones in the past that pitted Elvis and Pat Boone, the Rolling Stones and the Beatles—one which MTV would reluctantly have to tune in.

If 1982 was a year of baby boom regression from game if dwindling hipsters to couch potato chips off the old block, it was summed up admirably, if undoubtedly inadvertently, by the virtual avatars of sloth, Crosby, Stills and Nash, in "Wasted on the Way," a discursive ramble about those of us who "got what they deserved," while the rest of us sat there transfixed. It was a chilly year, even from the couch; in March, while Barbra Streisand sang "Memory," from *Cats*, alone in the moonlight, withered, ancient, expecting to fly, John Belushi died of a drug overdose at 33, Randy Rhoads, heavy metal's latest white guitar hope, died in a plane crash at 26, David Crosby was arrested in Los Angeles for possession of guns and drugs and driving under the influence of cocaine, and the Doobie Brothers broke up. We stared straight ahead, zoning out on "Key Largo" with Bertie Higgins in April, Charlene's revivified psycho babble, "I've Never Been to Me" in May, and Willie Nelson's heart–wrenching "Always on My Mind" in June. When Lester Bangs died of a heart attack at 33, he took with him the ghost of Rock Journalism as a higher calling —everyone else out there practicing it was either trying to become a rock star, discover a rock star, write the bio of a rock star, or sell out big to Hollywood with a screenplay about a rock star. By the end of the summer, WABC in New York, the dullest of the Top 40 stations of the 1950s and 1960s, but a cultural artifact nonetheless, would switch from oldies to an all-talk format, effectively ending an era in New York City radio, and joining Murray the K, the erstwhile "5th Beatle," up in rock & roll heaven (or, actually, in some limbo just outside its pearly gates, from which locale Murray had been broadcasting without a station since his demise in February, by now undoubtedly having scammed and schemed and doubletalked his way into the first exclusive posthumous chat with John Lennon).

In case anyone was entertaining a notion of getting off the couch more often, before the year was over, David Blue, Greenwich Village chum of Dylan, Ochs, and Eric Andersen, would die while jogging at the age of 41. In case anyone was thinking of taking Marvin Gaye's "Sexual Healing" literally, there were the first reported cases of AIDS, coming over on the same boat that brought us Donna Summer. While the Clash was pondering "Should I Stay or Should I Go" and Robert Plant was effectively "Burning Down One Side," we took in the Who's final concert from Toronto on pay–per–view cable, and satisfied our lustful and/or aerobic urges watching Patty Smyth tear up the scenery in the low budget romp, "Goodbye to

You" by Scandal, and lithe Toni Basil in a cheerleader outfit, mime her way through "Mickey," unaware of the monumental impact this breakdancing choreographer would have upon the remainder of the 1980s, as would be heard on what was left of the sexless, sterile, staccato stations of rock & roll radio.

Somewhere in the stricken wilds of Maryland, Spiro Agnew must have been smiling.

Nine

Middle of the Dirt Road

(1983–1986)

"Where have all the hippies gone?" the legendary poet, Fug, and Brooklyn College graduate Tuli Kupferberg, reflected one afternoon circa 1980, during an interview. "Some of them are still on the Lower East Side," he said. "You see a lot of kids with long hair—some of them are not kids. And you don't just see them on the Lower East Side. If you travel a little you'll find there are outbacks where they don't realize the 1960s have ended. But the vast majority are more or less out there in Middle America, and when push comes to shove, either in their private life or in some sort of political crisis, it's not going to be too easy to predict how they'll react. They may not have adjusted that well. They may not have bought all the crap that's been handed to them. I see that whenever I meet someone who has on a three–piece suit and tells me he used to be a Fugs fan. It doesn't just happen once, and I'm sure it doesn't only happen to me. There's that little twinkle in his eyes. He still remembers the great times. He wonders if he's done the right thing."

Slowly being depleted by then of our generational mandate, our once–vocal minority, our collective muscle, our dogmatic militance, our righteous imperatives, our most fervent role models, and with no imminent direction home, all such former Fugs fans, repatriated Woodstock nationalists, now huddled for comfort in the Middle of the Dirt Road, would be doing considerable battle with that statement during the warmongering, Big Chill year of 1983, and in the arid Reagan years that followed, each believing in its hopeful prophecy according to his (and in some cases her) need for emotional Geritol and psychic spinach as the go–go eighties got up and went buy–buy–buy.

Aside from the infirmities of age, and an insidious but apparently inevitable domestication process that threatened to remove not only rebellion but music itself from among our top ten priorities, further mitigating the prospect of our resuming the quest for moral greatness we'd abandoned on Sugar Mountain, the year's aforementioned Hollywood version of the greying of the baby boom, *The Big Chill,* insisted on propagating as if it were an essential part of our universal past, the relatively harmless sounds of our AM–radio Motown youth, when the races were united in a struggle against a common them (who only years later turned out to be us). As the first white guy of the year to exploit this potentially debilitating fixation, Phil Collins ("You Can't Hurry Love") was immediately hoisted into a Middle of the Dirt Road primacy that would carry him through the remainder of the decade and past it, solely on the basis of his balding, Columboesque, pug–ugly, self–effacing manner, the Everyman opposite of the dandy Rod Stewart, which would shortly come to a scrutiny far more thorough and widespread than the nascent MTV could provide, on the nuevo detective show as rock video, *Miami Vice.*

The trifecta of Motown, MTV, and baby boom nostalgia made a big winner out of Michael Jackson as well during the same period. With his pristine image as lead singer of Motown's favorite sons, the Jackson 5, now pasted into a generation's scrapbook as if it were our own baby pictures, the possessor of Motown's most amazing feet performed the rather amazing feat of breaking down MTV's color bar with his undeniably contemporary yet timeless moves. Michael's Moonwalk, adapted from the psychedelic era's black light prison break strobe effect, was a modern day backpedal; the groin grope was the kind of primal reassurance we could as a gender and a generation under siege certainly appreciate. Whether elegantly fending off the advances of both the Sharks and the Jets in "Beat It," or playing out his Orson Welles actor–writer–director fantasies in his own home horror–movie, "Thriller," or swearing his impotence to "Billie Jean," Michael, becoming more and more sexually identical to his kid sister, Janet ("Young Love")—who was only a year or two away from usurping him—virtually defined the mood of this burgeoning baby medium, MTV, whose unprecedented penetration accounted for the *Thriller* album selling more copies than any before it in recorded history, in its inverted way providing suburban moms and dads and kids alike an indelible image of Gene Kelly reborn as Johnny Mathis.

Hardly had we time to figure out if this was an affront to or an affirmation of our fondest baby boom makeout memories, than Prince, still dogging Michael's dodgy tracks, whipped out three steamy singles during a five month period ("Little Red Corvette," "1999," and "Delirious," before going off to make his own vanity production, *Purple Rain*), thereby topping Michael at his own amateur auteur game (recalling the great standoffs of the past, from Kelly and Astaire to Chubby and Hank) and all but driving the last of the early baby boom stragglers, having now turned thirty, into the clutches of Jane Fonda's advanced aerobics tapes to keep apace.

Responding with our last gasps to the year's disco imperative, as noted by Irene Cara ("Flashdance . . . What a Feeling"), Taco ("Puttin' on the Ritz"), Kool and the Gang ("Let's Go Dancin'"), David Bowie ("Let's Dance"), and the Kinks ("Come Dancing"), many of our leading advocates in the Middle of the Dirt Road, after nearly a decade of dancing, preferred to eschew the bump and grind for the more esoteric pleasures of indulging our famous bile. Billy Joel was bent on single–handledly reviving our sacred, if currently moribund, protest tradition ("Allentown," "Goodnight Saigon")—especially now that Jackson Browne was preoccupied with a sociological study of his high school graduating class ("Lawyers in Love"). Of course, there was always Crosby, Stills, Nash & Young, making sure the government's macho forays into Lebanon and Grenada would not go unobserved ("War Games"). Out of tiny Athens, Georgia, R.E.M.'s "Radio Free Europe" was a whisper in the dead of night, possibly having as much to do with our new warlike destiny as it did the coming of solidarity in Poland, at the same time as its jangly freshness reminded us of rebel R&B breaching the static on the AM dial of the 1950s—even though it sounded more like "Do You Believe in Magic," seeping out of the basement of the Albert Hotel in 1964. U2, as well ("New Year's Day"), showed great promise as the one arena band capable of rousing Tuli's slumbering giant of an electorate into its full latent potential.

But before we could be so mobilized, there would be plenty of excuses bandied about by this once over–zealous over–30 generation. Eric Clapton begged off with a malady we could all identify with ("I've Got a Rock & Roll Heart"). Todd Rundgren had something better to do ("Bang the Drum All Day"). Donald Fagen was lost in nostalgic reverie ("New Frontier"), as was Bob Seger ("Old Time Rock & Roll"), and Bette Midler singing Marshall

Crenshaw's rockabilly redux ("Favorite Waste of Time"). Carly Simon's best moments of 1983 came in romanticizing her New England young adulthood ("Menemsha"). But none of them was as unwilling to become a part of the time and the solution as Linda Ronstadt, who left her generation of songwriters completely, for a stroll through the chestnut fields of yesteryear ("What's New?"). Chrissie Hynde, still getting over the death of her lead guitarist, James Honeyman Scott, had bills to pay ("Back on the Chain Gang"). Elvis Costello had his Motown–informed literary mission to fulfill ("Everyday I Write the Book"). Hall & Oates's wife wouldn't let them out of the house at night ("Family Man"). Paul Simon was unable get out of bed ("Allergies")—his doomed romance with Carrie Fisher (daughter of archetypal Debbie Reynolds herself) was too draining for a quintessential divorced fifties rock & roll guy to spring back from like she was just another Annette Funicello he met running on the beach. Paul would soon have to leave the country, to clear his head. (Back on the same beach, we found Dennis Wilson, the only Beach Boy who knew how to surf, inexplicably drowned at age 39). Only Elton John among us was able to say "I'm Still Standing."

Perhaps no one had a better reason for an extended honeymoon from righteous fervor than the aforementioned ex–boxer (and probably ex–boxboy) Billy Joel, whose legendary letch for the super–model, Christie Brinkley, resulted not only in the froggie kissing the princess for a change, but in an entire album's worth of courting songs worthy of an Elizabethan squire or a Broadway show ("Tell Her About It," "Uptown Girl," "An Innocent Man"), evoking Billy's Long Island fifties, the world's Long Island fifties, circa 1962, when good girls appeared prim and virginal on the cover of *Seventeen* magazine, singing do–wop, and men wore men's clothes. In Billy's successful quest, the battle between the sexes the men of the baby boom fifties had long since despaired of winning was a clear–cut triumph to which we could all raise a hearty toast— even if none among us could either identify with it or fathom it.

This victory of aging baby boom sexuality was so improbable and short–lived, however, as to be of indecipherable influence on the contemporary pop charts as viewed over MTV, where the image of Ray Davies' "Lola" come to life as the cross–dressing Boy George O'Dowd, lead singer of Culture Club ("Do You Really Want to Hurt Me"), seemed more the uneasy norm, in tune with the Michael Jackson–inspired sexual confusion of the day. Epitomized by the year–ending stentorian tandem of David Bowie's "Modern Love" and Pat Benatar's "Love Is a Battlefield," the new Mating Game, for whoever had the stomach to watch it, was being vividly depicted for the younger folk by role models as gender inspecific and disparate as the crewcut Annie Lennox of the Eurythmics ("Sweet Dreams [Are Made of This]"), the crewcut Billy Idol ("White Wedding"), and the precariously coiffed Mike Score in A Flock of Seagulls ("I Ran"). ABC's Martin Fry ("The Look of Love (Part One)"), Spandau Ballet's Tony Hadley ("True"), and the dubious duo of George Michael and Andrew Ridgeley in Wham ("Bad Boys"), all evoked dapper Brian Ferry in his effete prime. As if delivering a final body blow to what was left of the traditional macho fantasy, you had the compulsive Sting, of the Police ("Every Breath You Take," "King of Pain"), the foppish Adam Ant ("Goody Two Shoes"), and the GQ coverboys, Duran Duran, who minced through their international playboy act ("Hungry Like the Wolf," "Rio"), less the second coming of Sean Connery than the resurrection of suntanned George Hamilton.

In defiance to what any older citizen would have rightly

proclaimed as the coming moral and sexual anarchy, there was only Patty Smyth's completely unfettered ingenue in("Goodbye to You," "Love's Got a Line on You"); more in synch with the unsavory program was the loinclothed all–female Total Coelo ("I Eat Cannibals") and Brooklyn's jaded Cyndi Lauper ("Girls Just Want to Have Fun," "She Bop," and the guilt–inducing "Money Changes Everything"), none of these being the kind of girls you'd want to share your last pint of muscatel with on a blind date. For instance, the clearest idea of the "fun" Cyndi had in mind could be gleaned from a close listening to her cover of the Prince tune, "When You Were Mine," with its most compelling image, the boyfriend's lover "sleeping in between the two of us" (so much more potent for its obviously never having been made into a video), being even more significant—in the Freudian slip view of pop history—for Lauper's own gender confusion of the lover in question in successive verses: "I know you've been seeing another girl"/"I know you've been seeing another guy."

Elsewhere, the message in the criminally licentious portrayal of Bow Wow Wow's jailbait front girl Annabelle Lins ("Do You Wanna Hold Me") was all too apparent, probably what Brian Setzer and the Stray Cats were talking about in "Sexy and 17" (and definitely what the Police had been warning us about in 1981 in "Don't Stand So Close to Me," to which ditzy Stevie Nicks offered in 1983 the conclusive answer song, "Stand Back"). Responding as only a red–blooded male wished he could, Def Leppard's stylized misogyny ("Photograph," "Foolin'"), in this context, spoke as many volumes to younger men, as the return of a Slade tune to the top of the charts ("Cum on Feel the Noize," by Quiet Riot), said to those old enough to have been thwarted in their attempts to do the horizontal bop to the tune of Slade's previous landmark anthem, "Mama,

We're All Crazee Now," which debuted back in another halycon year of sexual uncertainty, 1976 (and which would return, in a Quiet Riot rendition, in 1984).

Among the saner reactions to the year's disquieting drift, Thomas Dolby's affair with a computer ("She Blinded Me with Science") and Peter Gabriel's lobotomized "Shock the Monkey" stand out for their naked honesty. ZZ Top's "Sharp Dressed Man" was a near breakthrough of irrepressible normalcy. But as an ultimate snide response to the various sexual and stylistic attempts by the younger generation to baffle and ruffle their elders, and to undermine and undo the edifice of pop culture we'd bequeathed them (if only they were smart enough to appreciate it), the entire period would produce no better reverse anthem than Randy Newman's profoundly obnoxious "My Life Is Good," in which the droll Rand offered his services as superstar role model to no less a lofty figure than the Boss, Mr. Bruce Springsteen, himself.

By the end of 1985, I am convinced Bruce would have gladly taken him up on it.

Within that timespan, during which he would eventually be perceived by his former devout legion of scruffy fans—which contained 95 percent of the rock critics in America—as the cause for all the evil in the world, Springsteen would be married and Ronald Reagan would be re-elected president, perverting Springsteen's own hymn to a soldier in a body bag, "Born in the USA," for his devious use as patriotic sound bite. Bright as a toothpaste commercial, Springsteen would make several hideous videos during this same 1984–1985 spread, appearing in them this time, in his brand new Joe Piscopo body and Calvin jeans, including the surreal but spiffy "Dancing in the Dark," directed by Brian DePalma. Buoyed by his sudden aquiescent accessibility, MTV, itself in the throes of desperately trying to attract a hip audience to go with its

captive horde of Twinkie junkies, in using Springsteen as
the perfect foil for its upscale agenda, quickly turned him
into a white Michael Jackson, rendering whatever sexual
integrity his marriage to a celluloid starlet hadn't already
robbed him of—which, in the eyes of his street–bred early
followers, was practically all of it—as tamely moot as that
of the whimpering chorus boy of "Thriller," "Beat It," and
"Billie Jean," while repaying him in the riches we bestow
upon only the safest of sex objects.

Of course, even staunch baby boom apologists had to
have been suffering severe psychic qualms since awakening
at the outset of our Orwellian year to the grizzly spectacle
of Bob Dylan pandering to the unrelenting eye of the MTV
cameras, crooning to a cleaning lady in "Sweetheart Like
You." Closer to addressing our unwillingness to give up the
ghost of a truly relevant and redeeming generational
statement were Jump N' the Saddle, in their eulogy to the
highly–influential Three Stooges ("The Curly Shuffle"),
which was not only an heroic approximation of the Chevy
Chasian pratfall from grace we'd all experienced, but
undoubtedly the force behind the epic return to the charts
of Aerosmith's Three Stooges–inspired chant, "Walk This
Way," a scant two years later, as revived by rap's best rock
group, Run–DMC ("Rock Box"), with assistance by the
originals—leading, a scant year after that, to Aerosmith's
own Three–Stoogian return to the hard rock heart of a
generation after a decade of drying out.

Then Jackson Browne released "For a Rocker" paired
with Huey Lewis's rousing football cheer ("The Heart of
Rock & Roll"), in which he invoked the sacred name of
Cleveland (future site of the as–yet unbuilt Rock & Roll
Hall of Fame)—assuring us, by inference, of our continu-
ing role as rock models to a younger, if dubious, citizenry.
But at that telling point, we lost Chrissie Hynde, who
stripped away her dour, no frills, down to earth shoes

veneer, to reveal her need for traditional security, in
"Middle of the Road," admitting to her age and motherhood ("got a kid, I'm 33")—five months later she'd be
married, but not to Kinky Ray Davies, the kid's father. At
least Bette Midler was capable of giving as good as she got
from Mick Jagger at a steamy nightclub in "Beast of
Burden," with a chance fling a good deal more satisfying,
one hoped, than Laurie Anderson's cryptic encounter with
William Burroughs in "Sharkey's Day" and "Sharkey's
Night" (to say nothing of Bette's own brief, and literally
forgettable, encounter with Geraldo Rivera).

It is nevertheless quite possible that a still single
Springsteen drearily concluded, about this time, that aside
from snagging himself a supermodel like Christie, or the
daughter of an original dreamgirl like Debbie Reynolds,
the best he had to look forward to for female companionship was someone in the giggly image of the Go–Gos,
whether it was devout wrestling fan Cyndi Lauper ("Time
After Time"), the airheaded Bananarama ("Cruel Summer"), the multiple personalities of Tracy Ullman ("They
Don't Know") or the chubby Go–Gos themselves ("Head
over Heels"). The nasal Canadian folksinger Ferron might
have been a Bruce soulmate ("Snowing in Brooklyn"), but
he never answered her letters. Even so unabashedly natural and unashamedly camera friendly a naif as Patty Smyth
quickly succumbed to the kind of strident overstatement
that would have turned the Boss off, while making only Pat
Benatar proud, in "The Warrior." Hitting the nail on the
head about the pitfalls of modern romance for Bruce, as
well as anyone in the over–30 generation still out there in
the cold was Tina Turner, finally sans abusive Ike, in the
feminist anthem, "What's Love Got to Do with It."

Adding to his woes about then, not only had a pockmarked Springsteen of Canada arisen in the person of
Bryan Adams (1983's "Cuts Like a Knife"), but there was

the even more disquieting notion of a sulking celluloid Springsteen, as seen in the cult film (*Eddie and the Cruisers*); its signature Springsteenian tune, "On the Dark Side," by the abject John Cafferty and the Beaver Brown band coming back to haunt Bruce on the heels of his (and not coincidentally, the film's) 1984 resurgence. His empire shaky, his image cloned beyond calculation, is it any wonder then that Springsteen, an admitted fan of Prince, who would never in his life be able to dance like him, or command the kind of harem alluded to in Sheila E.'s "The Glamourous Life," approached his signal eight–night Homestand at the Meadowlands gig in September of 1984 in despair of ever exhibiting the romantic state of mind best exemplified by Prince's then–current "Let's Go Crazy"? Celebrating his thirty–fifth birthday by dancing with his mother on the stage in front of 20,000 people, like a proud bar–mitzvah boy who could do no wrong, in his black bar–mitzvah t–shirt, brand new hard body courtesy of a local body shop, it was impossible not to see in his eyes the sad protagonist of his own "My Home Town," this average working class baby boom guy showing his son around the doomed borders of the old neighborhood. Except, in the heartbreaking emptiness after his traditional two–hour encore, once the well–wishers had filed out, their mouths filled with potato chips, he had no son, no child at all, no wife, no prospects.

If it was at this point that the fates conspired to allow an outsider to insinuate himself into rock & roll history, or, more particularly, Bruce Springsteen's personal history— which, for the remainder of the period would be virtually one and the same—for the first time since the notable fiasco at the Bottom Line in 1974, it was certainly not of my own volition that I wound up in the middle of such a monumentally messy situation. Had I been operating entirely as a free agent, I might have righteously clung to the

high road, like Dick Cavett or David Frost, reminiscing
with the subject about the scuffling days when the New
York Times compared him to Allen Ginsberg and El Topo
in the same article, and we laughed about it over burgers at
the CBS commissary with CBS picking up the tab. I'd have
stuck to safe terrain, anecdotes, and memories of Paul's
Mall in Boston and Max's in New York, the Hojo's on I–95
at three in the morning, where we embraced like veterans
of the Spanish Civil War, the bowling alley at Madison
Square Garden at four in the morning, where I broke past
security on alley one to share another grand reunion. Our
several conversations, filled with innuendo and non–
sequitur, and usually taking place way after midnight, in
the bowels of one cavernous hall or another, conspired to
defy easy categorization, if not coherence. And that was
the way it was supposed to be.

But, this was 1984, and I was in the pitiless grasp of a
major career move myself, not quite as major, of course, as
the career move that precipitated the assignment upon
which my own career move hinged, but major enough—in
an era of career moves for a segment of baby boom adults
finally facing up to the bleak necessity of stringing several
of these moves together into a sort of chain of financial
cause and effect—to have resulted in the kind of gossip–
inspiring inquiry that was implicit in the successful execu-
tion of a five–part feature for America's daily.

"What about marriage and family?" I quote from the
transcript of that fateful tete–á–tete.

"You don't rule it out," he replied, tersely.

"Have you been close at all?"

"To marriage? No," he ruminated sincerely. "Generally, music has been the center of my life for a long time," he
went on. "But I think you can have those things too. I don't
think I can't because of my business. I think people tend to
use the conditions of their job to avoid certain things. If it's

the right moment, the right person, the right relationship . . . maybe you change the way you do the job. You have to have it in perspective. I've been with my sister and her kids, where certain feelings match the intensity that I get onstage. It's a different type of experience. It's not something I want to miss out on."

Although the article would not be published for a couple of weeks, during which time the tape of the interview was never out of my sight, except for the brief period when it was being transcribed by a bonded emissary from Price Waterhouse, it is by now a matter of sordid public record that before the end of that selfsame eight night stint, maybe even the next night, for all I know, someone, not me, would bring around the actress, Julianne Phillips, to one of these meet–and–greet affairs, where Springsteen, suddenly staring thirty–five in the face, with no son, no daughter, no wife, would fall, like Eddie for Debbie, like Eddie for Valerie, like Billy Joel for Christie (like Bob Seger for the bimbo in "Hollywood Nights")— like his own bosom no–retreat no–surrender cronies Miami and Southside, for whom he'd served so solidly and so well the year before as best man—like a sack of mashed potatoes at the feet of a pineapple princess.

Compounded by his nearly successful attempt to lindy on "Dancing in the Dark," Springsteen's perceived double buying–in to the idea that the system works was not, however, accepted as just another Eddie and Valerie/Billy and Christie every– underdog–has–his–day celebration of the American Dream. Rather, it was as if this regular short–sleeved city saint in an arena of teased–haired sinners, in claiming his gossip column accoutrements, had soiled the very ozone with his lust, in the process becoming no better than a pitiful landed yuppie, leaving his sacred soul as downpayment in the John Cougar Mellencamp suburban development of "Pink Houses."

In that selfsame arena, Eddie V. wasn't hurt at all by his own human failings viz the opposite sexes: succumbing to the Hollywood enticements of Valerie Bertinelli, or consorting with Michael Jackson on "Beat It." In fact, just a little over a year after that famous example of his freebie noodling hit the top of the charts in 1983, his own opus, "Jump," occupied the same vaunted number one position, leading headbangers of the world to reunite behind similar guitar boy's club statements like "Bringing on the Heartbreak" by Def Leppard, "Round and Round" by Ratt, "Bang Your Head (Metal Health)" by Quiet Riot. Then there was the revival of Slade itself, made possible in part by a grant from Quiet Riot (and in another part by the fictionalized documentary of their life, *Spinal Tap*), with the irresistible "Run Runaway." The Scorpions accounted for the uplifting "Rock You Like a Hurricane," Night Ranger the zenophobic "(You Can Still) Rock in America," and Sammy Hagar the irrepressible "I Can't Drive 55." Louder still, the queen's original bat–man, John "Ozzy" Osbourne, came up with "Bark at the Moon." While the various members of Kiss were still in their locker rooms fervently scrubbing off their outmoded makeup in order to capitalize on the revivifying return of grunge to the mainstream ("Heaven's on Fire"), and all the teenybop riches that implied, Mötley Crüe were applying the mascara to "Looks That Kill," a particularly ironic commentary, considering the fact that their lead singer, Vince Neil, would by year's end be the drunk behind the wheel in an accident that killed another passenger in the car. But of such misadventures were legends (and careers) made.

Still, don't you think it had to be Valerie whispering in Ed's other ear like the various other Yokos of rock history, like Buddy's Marie Elena, like Mick's Bianca, like Brian Wilson's Elliot Landy, when neither "I'll Wait" nor "Panama," nor the estimably rocking "Hot for Teacher," sufficiently capitalized on the mega–success of "Jump," the words that only a stagewife had the savvy as well as the guts to utter: "You're better than that other bum! Get rid of him! But, before you do, take out the garbage." By the end of 1984, David Lee Roth's head would be in a Glad bag, replaced by the compulsive speedster, Sammy Hagar, well on its way toward becoming so much biodegradable mulch.

Similarly, Springsteen's long–sought rapproachment with the forces of age and commerce, his attempted lindy with glitz, was seen by his bloated, left–leaning, two left–footed minions, as entirely the product of his overweening if pitiably human desire to satisfy the careerist ego of his Hollywood squeeze. Whether this is being too hard on poor Julianne or too soft on Springsteen, during the next year and a half, the *Born in the USA* album would lindy him into album sales surpassing the Johnny Mathis level, and approaching Michael Jackson, and the rest of us into a virtual furor of do–good guilt, as a generation in the Middle of the Dirt Road at last arose, nearly as one, for the first time since 1976 or so, when people still watched "Saturday Night Live," to claim its share of the radio.

Echoing Lou Reed's 1965–1966 naive wonder at the phenomenon of there being "A lot of us," aging hippies (there are no other kind) of the baby boom middle class stepped awed into a similar 1984–1985 realization. Coming up on twenty years later, hitting that mythical singles–bar dividing line between thirtysomething and fortyish, we stepped outside the safety of our isolated suburban enclaves to ponder some irreducible questions about our worth, our impact, our mission in the post–Elvis, post–Twist, post–Bohemian, post–Beatles, post–Vietnam, post–hippie, post–disco, post–punk, post–rock & roll world, only to discover that indeed, and as usual, there were "a lot of us" former Fugs fans, weathering the same dilemmas, burdened with as much post–rock & roll torpor, malaise, agita, and psychic baggage, strangers in a strange, Republican land, simultaneously casting our dimes into a jukebox that suddenly spoke for our concerns (although when a Fugs album did come out, in 1985, entitled *Refuse to Be Burnt Out*, none of us even knew of its existence).

This is not to say we were immediately at our best. Laura Nyro, awash in single motherhood ("To a Child") and a newfound gushy commitment to all things earthy, female, and primordial, was merely sappy in *Mother's Spiritual*. And the best you could say about the Everly Brothers long–awaited reunion could be summed up in Don's tune "Asleep." Yet there were a lot of wasted urban squatters, their memories of rebellion still clinging to crawlspace in their guts, as if it were a rent–controlled apartment in Manhattan, who found solace in replaying the new/old Velvet Underground boxed set, the old/new Lou Reed recapitulation to matrimony, or Gil Scott–Heron at his most intelligible ("Re–Ron") or Tom Waits at his least ("Gin Soaked Boy"). For those with the capacity to get beyond the psychic lower back pain of emotional risk, suddenly there was R.E.M. making the charts again with "South Central Rain," the all–girl Bangles transmogrifying the Beatles with the optimism of "Live," written by the Paul McCartney clone, Emmitt Rhodes, and the nostalgia of their own "Going down to Liverpool," their harmonies as effervescent as first love, at sixteen, thirty–three, or forty–five. Rank and File breathed folk/rock on "Long Gone Dead"; Suzanne Vega sighed Sylvia Plathian introspective art/folk on "Marlene on the Wall"; Rickie Lee Jones swooned ersatz beatnik jazz on "The Real End"; and U2 inhaled the fire of protest on "Pride (In the Name of Love)."

As invigorating and ecologically correct as this return to the Middle of the Dirt Road was, it was unfortunately not enough to offset a third generation disco/protest movement, which was at that moment fomenting in the mosh pits of suburbia. Inspired by Black Flag, Black Sabbath, the Angry Samoans, and further down the faulty California coast, by the Minutemen's tearjerking "History Lesson, Pt. II," if not by Ronald Reagan's reactionary agenda, recalcitrant teenage boys nudged and bumped and brutalized each other like partipants in a rugby scrum, rather than be reduced to asking any girl of their own age to dance to the speedcore boogie of thrash that was born in Lars Ulrich's garage ("Seek and Destroy," by Metallica). In Prince's Funkytown, Minneapolis, the ragged Replacements ("Sixteen Blue") and the blunt Hüsker Dü ("Turn on the News") spoke with similar eloquence to the concerns of the assembled throttled teens in search of a lost cause.

In New York, as well, where the forgotten–if–not–gone Donna Summer herself may have been lost to aspiring divadom, the recurrent drive for ritualized physical expression through the indoor sport of dancing was also moving toward another generational epiphany, provided by New York's School of Performing Artsy champion, Irene Cara ("Breakdance"). It was plucky Irene who ushered in a mini–trend of breakdance movies within the larger trend of big–screen dance movie musicals like *Flashdance* (as opposed to the small screen dance movie–musicals called "rock videos"—also called "Pepsi commercials"). Thus we had *Beat Street* and *Breakin'* (from which the Top 100 received "Breakin'—There's No Stopping Us" by Ollie and Jerry, and "Beat Street Breakdown" by Grandmaster Melle Mel), their signature steps emanating from Michael Jackson's pioneering Moonwalk. As polished and professionalized by June Taylor TV types like Toni Basil and the up and coming Paula Abdul, this newest dance sensation would come to its fruition in the modernized urban grunts and growls of rap, encapsulating a night rhythm of the street called hip–hop, that would dominate the remainder of the decade—and the minds of white converts like the Beastie Boys ("Party's Getting Rough")—to say nothing of boom boxes till the end of time.

But no nasal gypsy or staggering rapper could so much as hold a roman candle to the undulating keester of the year's most favorite chorus girl. Squiggling her way in ankle length capris through "Holiday," "Borderline," and "Lucky Star," Detroit's (She's no Lady) Madonna Ciccone proved herself throughout the year as every bit the Blonde Bombshell Jo–Ann Campbell never was, more cycle slut than Ronnie Spector in her adenoidal prime, with a penchant for self–dramatizing that left the late Mary Weiss of the Shangri–Las crawling in the dust. Easily out–chanteusing Debbie Harry, leagues more calculating than Stevie Nicks, far brassier than Pat Benatar, street–tougher than Chrissie Hynde, kitchier than Cyndi Lauper at her kookiest, or even Streisand in her schmaltzy Third Avenue period, this Mother of all Donnas could have passed for just another pseudo–deep working girl in tights, pumps, and a pop–up brassiere, but was actually more deviously cheesecake than a thousand scrungy pinups in a thousand leering poolhalls from here to 1962. Aggressively epitomizing the terrible tease of the fifties, from the woman on top vantage point of the eighties, Madonna's swooning "Like a Virgin" was not only the year's top song, but would become the most popular song of the rest of the decade, ringing in 1985 with a prophetic message that was as tantalizing as it was improbable.

As usual, those of us in the Middle of the Dirt Road had too high a purpose in mind to pay much attention to anything that smacked of disco. Equally ennobled by the former Boomtown Rat Bob Geldof's year–ending quest for knighthood ("Do They Know It's Christmas?") and Bruce Springsteen's penchant for opening soup kitchens at each stop along his Herculean 1985 tour route, we took enor-

mous chauvinistic joy in finally seeing the dream of Jim
Morrison's "We want the world and we want it now"
realized by Lionel Richie and a cast of every pop star
who'd ever been (or hoped to be) nominated for a Grammy
("We Are the World"), followed by a series of similarly
ostentatious and nationally (and sometimes international-
ly) televized gatherings in support of farmers, world peace,
Greenpeace, and AIDS research and against apartheid.
Mimicking the patriotic spirit (and album cover) of Springsteen's *Born in the USA*, a red, white, and blue reunion was
once again suggested, between the civil–warring halves of
the male baby boom generation, wherein redneck longhairs driving trucks and short–haired former hippie inside
–trading stock brokers could symbolically embrace in the
soiled coveralls of John Cougar Mellencamp.

This prompted some of our most revered artists to
respond in kind with new generational imperatives.
Loudon Wainwright fended off all inquiries as to his
personal relevance in "How Old Are You." John Fogerty,
with his miraculous faculties intact, made a gallant comeback in "Centerfield," and while he was at it, got back at
the man he accused of stealing all his legendary copyrights, in "Zanz Can't Dance," the tale of a pickpocketing
pig (which would cost him the next few years in lawsuits).
England's legendary odd couple, Rod Stewart and Jeff
Beck, shook hands for a remake of the Impressions' stirring
"People Get Ready," but their tour lasted only about ten
minutes (or not enough time for Jeff to get famous again).
Springsteen himself, after finally tying the knot with his
showbiz cutie in Oregon, saw his evocation of his high
school "Glory Days" continue his hitmaking string as if he
were another Spectorian Prince. Yet, while he had certainly accomplished this trek toward mass acclaim with all the
relentless determination and due haste of a nine–legged
centipede pushing a molehill up a mountain with his nose,

his core legion of self–appointed image regulators could only see in this unexpected culmination, the seeds of his downfall, as well as, no doubt, their own. And, sure enough, less than a week after the wedding, as if to confirm their most paranoid fears, while Bruce was temporarily removed from the picture, perhaps squeezing in a honeymoon between sell–out dates in Pittsburgh and Albuquerque, some government wives, fresh out of fundraisers, decided to form a knitting and nit–picking club called the Parents Music Resource Center, ostensibly to prevent any more unsuspecting teens from committing suicide to Ozzy Osbourne records, but more likely in reality a frantic attempt to wrest their share of publicity out of the hands of Washington bimbos like Elizabeth Ray and Rita Jenrette.

In 1985, they needn't have bothered. Baby boomers had control of the pop machine once again, and were determined to raise the literacy level of the multitudes, using words of at least five letters apiece. Considering how few of us were still falling asleep to Top 40 radio at the age of thirtysomething/fortyish, and running out to the store to buy the latest singles, to which we did the latest dances and lip–synched at our parties, before stacking them neatly away in a vinyl laminated carrying case, we had to take tremendous hormonal pride in how many current hits adhered so closely to our much–mutilated but still standing baby boom rock & roll agenda. You had proudly balding Mark Knopfler defining post–hippie enmity toward the glossy world of MTV, if not the aquisitive yuppie spirit endorsed by the Reagan eighties ("Money for Nothing"). At the same time, there was Phil Collins virtually defining his aging audience's baffled but implacable demeanor ("Easy Lover," "One More Night," "Sussudio," "Don't Lose My Number"). Both Pete Townshend and his former front man in the Who, Roger Daltrey, issued commanding performances of Pete's moving anti–war tune, "After the Fire." Canada's leading pacifist, Bruce Cockburn, had a sudden change of heart ("If I Had a Rocket Launcher"). From East L.A., Los Lobos was the essence of down at the heels, down on the stoop philosophy ("Will the Wolf Survive?"). The Talking Heads made their quirky peace with parenthood ("Stay up Late"). Even creaky "Saturday Night Live" was by no means quite dead as a cultural determinant, giving us a quintessential baby boom city kid after our own hearts in Billy Crystal, who told us what we all needed to hear, in "You Look Mahvelous."

Several of our vainest cohorts took his tongue–in–cheek message literally. There was Robert Plant taming down his mating squeal into something almost bearable, in "Rockin' at Midnight," as if he realized his audience saw him more as Tom Jones now than either Carl Perkins or George Michael. Which was not quite the same thing as the solo Mick Jagger ("Just Another Night"), slowly turning more and more into Don Knotts. What about Foreigner, attempting to live down their former womanizing ways, in "I Want to Know What Love Is," with a gospel choir in the background just to lend their confession credibility? Even Don Henley, who had sunk to his lowest point upon the last Republican landslide, achieved something near a mournful epiphany in "The Boys of Summer"—though a careful reading of the song may lead one to the stunned conclusion that it was written about the same crazed Lolita who'd been the cause of all his troubles in the first place (she'd be almost twenty by now). More determined than either of them to avoid the crippling self–knowledge that had all but destroyed us as a gender, as a generation, certainly as a force in the singles bars, the newly solo David Lee Roth turned "California Girls" and "Just a Gigolo" into his personal go–go statement of the I'm–Ok–You're–Not–Eighties.

Betraying our weakness for generational pandering, the ghosts of Jackie Wilson and Marvin Gaye were summoned forth as if they were Abraham, Martin, and John, by the Commodores ("Nightshift"). A scant six months later, playing further on our sympathies, Chrissie Hynde and the reggae group UB40, updated Sonny & Cher's nasal anthem, "I Got You Babe," as if it were a cherished part of their collective pasts. Virtually the next morning, you could have switched on your television to the heartwarming spectacle of David Bowie and Mick Jagger together, "Dancing in the Streets." By the end of the year, we could hardly contain our salty tears, when the Jefferson Starship, with the gravelly voice of Grace Slick still stuck there somewhere in the mix, bade us into one last grand communal pile, in "We Built This City." A much more ominous example of this kind of uninspected nostalgia was proferred by Bryan Adams, in "Summer of '69," which got as far as number five on the charts, masquerading as one of us, a Woodstock vet, baby boom rock & roller, when, if anyone had their calculators handy next to the remote control, they could have figured out that Adams couldn't have been twenty–three or twenty–two or even eighteen in that bloody crossroads of a year (he was only supposed to be twenty–two or twenty–three now). If so, he'd lived through it—if at all—to the tune of Tommy James and the Shondels' "Crystal Blue Persuasion," or the Archies' "Sugar Sugar," as a virtual toddler; had only number–dropped it onto our emotional turntables because he had the cunning to see how many of us were still living frozen in that moment sixteen years before and the memory of our unique mandate, vainly struggling to move beyond it into the future, like the remains of the Democratic party.

Closer to our fondest outlaw fantasies of that long lost witching year of 1969 was the former Eagle, Glenn Frey, in another episode of *Miami Vice*—based on his tune "Smuggler's Blues." This tale appealed so much to our thwarted monkey–suited dreams of freedom being just another word for nothing left to lose, that the producers opened the next season of the show with Glenn Frey redux, in "You Belong to the City," not as satisfying as theater, but a higher charting item. Others old enough to remember our bloody apex in Chicago, and not too embarrassed to admit it, were gathered around fabulous, vault–looting career retrospectives of Bob Dylan ("Percy's Song," "I'll Keep It with Mine," plus the most revealing interview Dylan ever gave, to former boy–wonder–rock writer–turned–grownup–teenage–movie–magnate Cameron Crowe, in the accompanying booket), and the Velvet Underground ("Lisa Says"), or the doom–ridden breakthrough Tom Waits epic *Raindogs* ("Union Square"). There were even young guys in this club, younger than Bryan Adams in 1969, whose wrenching cries echoed deep in the sagging gut of white American soul: from the Replacements in the North ("Swinging Party") to R.E.M. in the South ("Cuyahoga") to gin–soaked Danny & Dusty in the West ("Miracle Mile") to John Hiatt in the Midwest ("She Said the Same Things to Me") to the Hooters in the East ("Where Do the Children Go").

Having not only gained the world, but become the world, the bread–earners of the world, the new fatcat establishment of the world, the surviving men in the Middle of the Dirt Road were not entirely home free, however; many who despaired of making Madonna feel like a virgin again came to appreciate the new English Lord Byron of depression, the single–named Morrissey ("How Soon Is Now"). Others, like Richard Thompson, were reduced to the wretched snivelings of the newly–divorced ("She Twists the Knife Again"), while his ex–wife was coming on strong and decisive ("Can't Stop the Girl").

Typically, while the voices of the men howled and squalled in turmoil (Billy Squier's near career–ending video romp "All Night Long;" Freddie Mercury's harrowingly prophetic "Love Kills"), the women continued progressing toward a communal strength that was not necessarily exclusionary, yet was symbolized by Aretha Franklin's pairing with Annie Lennox in the eminently practical under the circumstances, "Sisters Are Doing It for Themselves." In the meantime, Kate Bush achieved new heights of sexual athleticism ("Running up That Hill"). The Roches were nothing if not accommodating ("Love to See You," "Love Radiates Around"). If Madonna's "Material Girl," was almost too blatantly pragmatic, she was certainly a more imposing presence than Cyndi Lauper ("The Goonies 'R Good Enough"), who had by then begun to align herself with no less a pillar of the male breed than Peewee Herman ("Theme for Peewee's Playhouse")—years before the man would himself become a public example of Lauper's own "She Bop," in a movie theater in Tampa (while Madonna would go on to make a fortune doing the same thing for a lavish coffee table dirty photo book).

Out on the rough streets of R&B, where the image of women had been taking a beating for decades, "Roxanne Roxanne" by UTFO, was a far cry from a pushover, and in "I Wonder If I Take You Home," by Lisa Lisa and Cult Jam, you could almost hear another Ronnie Bennett coming around again, two decades younger, and a hundred years wiser. Cultured Whitney Houston, on the other hand, was high above the fray, in "You Give Good Love" and "Saving All My Love for You." Far more cunning and cool was Sade, in "Smooth Operator."

As creatively abundant and hopeful as the period might have been for those of us in the Middle of the Dirt Road, during a fourteen day span around the dawning of 1986, things took a decided turn for the worse, when four men, representing four distinct eras, reached, in one way or another, the end of their personal roads: the underground's last best hope, Dennis Boon of the Minutemen, flaming out in a car crash; nostalgia's eternal teenager, Ricky Nelson, going down in a private plane; folk/rock apologist, David Crosby, heading off to prison; and heavy metal's most soulful poet, Phil Lynott, succumbing to heart disease at 34. Not too long thereafter, the country at large took a hard one in the gut, when the space shuttle carrying the world's first teacher/astronaut, Christa McAuliffe, exploded on television, killing everyone aboard. Only rock & roll, we mumbled in a haze; life and life only.

The immediate rock & roll response was pretty much a blur of patriotic damage control: "R.O.C.K. in the USA," by John Cougar Mellencamp "For America" by Jackson Browne, an anti–drug song, "American Storm" by Bob Seger, "Hands Across America" by the Voices of America, "Living in America" by James Brown, "Calling America" by ELO, "Voice of America's Sons" by John Cafferty— culminating in the opening of Dollywood in July.

Obscured for the moment, was the sudden prevalence of rampant sexual revisionism, made all the more poignant by the safe sex backdrop of America's further realization of the AIDS epidemic, as symbolized by "That's What Friends Are For" by Dionne Warwick, to benefit AIDS research. You had "Sex as a Weapon" by Pat Benatar, "What Have You Done for Me Lately" by Janet Jackson, "Addicted to Love" by Robert Palmer, "Typical Male" by Tina Turner, "Sorry Somehow" by Hüsker Dü, "Modern Woman" by Billy Joel, "Sledgehammer" by Peter Gabriel, "If She Knew What She Wants" by the Bangles, and "You Give Love a Bad Name" by Bon Jovi.

That this nascent heyday of yuppie splendor, with our

children having become Republicans, like Alex Keaton on "Family Ties," had resulted in an AIDS–inspired sexual caution was a source to many in the baby boom generation of grave ambivalence about the free love ethos we'd left as perhaps our signal rock & roll legacy. Although it was, in a certain existential sense, both intellectually symmetrical and poetically just that teenagers of the 1980s also be faced with the same life and death choices we'd come of age to in the days of LSD and the draft lottery in the 1960s and early 1970s, what was so bad, many of us, parents now, pondered, about the fear of sex, and a return to the kind of dread and condoms we had to grow up with in the fifties, when not only mom and pop, the police, and the government, but VD lurked behind every backseat encounter? To ensure these stunted adolescents a stunted adolescence of their own, we presented them Billy Vera's heartbreaking "At This Moment," rescued from a long dead 1982 album, and used as a backdrop for Alex's TV romance (which was also Michael J. Fox's real life romance), on not one, but two different episodes of "Family Ties," until the arduous rise of this retro, sax–honking, white R&B, prom night slow dance epic up the charts of 1986, week by week to number one in January, 1987, came to represent a mythic reaffirmation our most basic "Father Knows Best" fantasies of generational continuity in the face of the Beastie Boys' "(You Gotta) Fight for Your Right (to Party)" (even if one of them was the son of the playwright Israel Horovitz). Which meant that if, as in generations past, our revolution against the norm was going to slowly turn into a soggy, sodden, weekly ritual of tilting brews along with Norm on "Cheers" anyway, we might as well let our sons and daughters join us in that degenerative process, as long as they did so to the tune of the Genesis' beer commercial, "Tonight Tonight Tonight."

From every quarter in 1986, tradition threatened to

reign in the momentum of our special mandate for continued hipness beyond the age of forty. Barbra Streisand
returned to Broadway ("Somewhere"). Twisted Sister returned to Long Island ("Leader of the Pack"). John Cougar
Mellencamp returned to the farm ("Rain on the Scare-
crow"). David Byrne returned to his analyst's couch
("Once in a Lifetime"). Jermaine Stewart returned to the
morality of the fifties ("We Don't Have to Take Our
Clothes Off"). The Bangles returned to the harmonies of
the sixties ("Manic Monday"). Tom Scholz's Boston deliv-
ered a record owed since the seventies, before their label
asked them to return the money ("Amanda"). The Art of
Noise returned Duane Eddy to the recording studio
("Theme from Peter Gunn"). Eddie Money returned
Ronnie Bennett to the microphone ("Take Me Home
Tonight"). Little Richard returned to his primal roots
("Great Gosh a–Mighty"). Paul Simon returned to Little
Richard's primal roots ("You Can Call Me Al"). Nick Lowe
returned to the altar ("I Knew the Bride When She Used to
Rock & Roll"). Huey Lewis returned to the old values
("Hip to be Square"). The Rolling Stones returned to
bedrock ("One Hit [to the Body]"). Eddie Van Halen
returned to the piano he played as a little boy ("Dreams").
Southside Johnny returned to Tin Pan Alley ("Walk Away,
Renee"). Ben E. King returned to the Brill Building
("Stand by Me"). The Monkees returned ("That Was Then,
This Is Now," "Daydream Believer"), as did the Beach
Boys ("Rock & Roll to the Rescue," "California
Dreamin'"), as well as three renegades from the Jefferson
Airplane/Starship, Kantner, Balin, and Cassidy ("It's Not
You, It's Not Me"), as well as Bonnie Raitt with yet another
album, *Nine Lives,* ("No Way to Treat a Lady")—but
nobody cared. Several prime generational voices returned
in creaky vehicles, offering little inspiration: "Shelter Me"
by Joe Cocker, "Let Me down Easy" by Roger Daltrey,

"Stranglehold" by Paul McCartney, "Heartache All over
the World" by Elton John, "All I Need Is a Miracle" by
Mike & the Mechanics, "So Far Away" by Dire Straits, and
"I Want to Make the World Turn Around" by Steve Miller.
Whitney Houston returned "The Greatest Love of All,"
the theme from a 1982 movie about Muhammed Ali, to the
charts of 1986, but its stay at number one outlived its funky
co–author, Linda Creed (who died of cancer at 37).

When Aerosmith returned with Run DMC ("Walk This
Way"), it was mostly a new generation which took notice
that the threatening beat box message of rap was getting
ready to advance beyond the Jersey Turnpike into the
living rooms of Heartland America. Older folk, baby
boomers, and their green followers, who still believed in
the Middle of the Dirt Road commitment to revelation
through rock & roll, disdained the street justice of rap for
the comforting social programs implicit in "The Way It Is"
by Bruce Hornsby and the Range. Awash in psychedelic
Watergate flashbacks over Iran/Contra, we cleaved to the
worldly spirituality of Van Morrison ("In the Garden"),
Neil Young's fading heroics ("Hippie Dream"), Sting's
munificence ("Russians"), Anita Baker's class ("Sweet
Love"), R.E.M.'s earnest questing drone ("Fall on Me"),
David & David's bigtown cynicism ("Welcome to the
Boomtown"), Firetown's smalltown truth ("Rain on You"),
Timbuk–3's acoustic wisdom ("The Future's So Bright I
Gotta Wear Shades"), the earnest bluster of the new,
history–of–Springsteen set ("War," "Thunder Road").

Compared to the crass, seemingly intentional lowering
of the common denominator proceeding apace in all other
pop contexts, from rap to wrestling, from horror movies to
heavy metal, these were the lonely triumphs of our sophisticated sensibility, oases of reasoned discourse in a world
where Madonna's strident "Live to Tell" and "Papa Don't
Preach," were regarded as veritable pinnacles of contem-

porary anomie. As unnerving as the self–appointment of
this self–annointed self–promoter as generational
spokesmodel should have been, we still didn't pay her
coffee klatch opinions much heed, regarding her puff
pieces as posturing, closer to PMS than the PMRC. But, by
doing so, we wound up allowing the previously immaterial
girl to cross the line, ever so adroitly, from actress to
activist, from performer to participant in the moral agenda
of the marketplace, a lapse for which we (or at least Pepsi
Cola, and soon thereafter, the Time–Warner medialopolis)
would soon pay dearly.

Ten

What Forty Looks Like

(1987–1990)

In the realms of country music, where a teenage constituency hasn't existed since 1846, it's fairly standard issue for a Willie Nelson, or his kindred brother–out–law, Waylon Jennings, or almost any of their Stetsoned brethren, to manfully declaim sentiments on the order of "(Made It to Forty) I'm Still Wearing Jeans," to emphasize and romanticize their ability to withstand the compunctions of grown–up conformity. Those of the former Alternate Culture, who had come to regard country music as the nearest thing to Klan singalongs (and who would rate Neil Diamond's "Forever in Blue Jeans" as the nearest thing to living death), but were still in fervent search of a defining credo in 1987, as many in our target baby boom demographic began to approach and pass that millstone four–oh milestone separating youthful pomp from adult circumstance in the face of the continuing Reaganization of America, were more than happy to settle for the miraculous top ten breakthrough of the Grateful Dead to provide the required sacred sustenance ("Touch of Grey"), with Jerry Garcia's escape from the lip of the chasm—to eventually become an AA sponsor—becoming a mirror image of our pride, indomitability, and resilience (forgetting for the moment the Dead's grassroots organizational powers that would put the liberal party to shame).

Bouyed by the Dead's survival instincts, we took heart in certain other early signs of the unraveling of the conservative mandate: the teary Ken and Barbie doll downfall of Jim and Tammy Faye Bakker, the public lynching of super patriot Ollie North, the new prison–striped collar of stock traitor Ivan Boesky—so soon after Black Friday II— culminating in the encouraging conversion of no less a paragon of nouveau yuppie values than Michael J. Fox (The *Secret of My Success,* featuring "The Secret of My Success" by Night Ranger), into a working class rocker in *Light of Day* (from which came "Light of Day," ostensibly by Michael J. and Joan Jett, as the Barbusters). These seemingly random events may have caused us all to finally open up, as a wily, still unpredictable mass audience, to Paul Simon's verbally resplendent bas–relief of the modern age, "The Boy in the Bubble"—although the tune's chart run lapsed some 87 notches below Madonna's quintessentially irrelevant "Who's That Girl" (and six notches below Paul's own ineffable primal journey, "Graceland").

Soulfully bolstered, we managed to lift our empty glasses when Richard Thompson and his legendary Fairport Convention cronies advised us all to "Meet on the Ledge," a rousing call to emotional solidarity in spite of the massive wrinkles in our master plan to conquer the world, or at least, the radio airwaves. Leonard Cohen, having already been through an Arab–Israeli war, was one of the first to volunteer to lead our return to power, in "First We Take Manhattan." He was joined by Miami Steve Van Zant, just back from Sun City, and on the heroic "Trail of Broken Treaties." Loudon Wainwright, evolving into a modern Mose Allison, by way of e. e. cummings, proffered his usual sage counsel against getting anyone's hopes up too high, in "Hard Day on the Planet" and "The Back Nine." Robbie Robertson's return to recording was made all the more poignant in "Fallen Angel," a eulogy for his former Band–mate, Richard Manuel, but a credo for the rest of us (" . . . it's not for nothing . . . "). Indeed, all over the radios of 1987, there were sympathetic young turks unwilling to let us retreat from our self–proclaimed destiny. You had XTC invoking the deity ("Dear God"), Skid Roper and Mojo Nixon invoking the King ("Elvis Is Everywhere"), Robert Cray invoking Watergate ("Smoking Gun"), Billy Bragg invoking the ghost of Phil Ochs ("A New England"), U2 stoking our guilt ("Without or Without You"), Danny Wilson evoking Steely Dan ("Mary's Prayer"), and R.E.M. not only evoking the Byrds, but limning the dimensions of what hung in the balance, in "It's the End of the World as We Know It (and I Feel Fine)."

Despite this, most of us were either unable or unwilling to sufficiently get it up at forty for another go–round with the pop cultural fates. As aging, balding, beaten down husbands and brothers of the bride who used to rock & roll, we hadn't really been the same since Springsteen left us for his Mansion on the Hill: cloistered, remote, blinded in his artistic eye by the magnitude of his 1984–1985 social and musical successes, "doing the job in a different way," his fall into the worst of fat–cat Republican bliss must have meant that we, as individuals and as a generation, would have to be content to measure our chances for redeeming social significance against Bob Seger threatening to become Frankie Laine ("Shakedown"), Heart threatening to become the Andrews Sisters ("Alone"), Led Zeppelin threatening to become the sound of yet another generation ("Here I Go Again," by Whitesnake), and the Starship threatening to go on forever, albeit sans Jefferson, sans Airplane ("Nothing's Gonna Stop Us Now").

But when Bruce finally issued his initial papers from

those lofty premises, it was possible to hear, listening for the first time to "One Step Up," in a parking lot in front of a 7–Eleven, not only the future of Middle of the Dirt Road (the future of rock & roll was now R.E.M.), but a glimmer of dischord on the set of the Hollywood Newlyweds. Just like when he went out for that fateful pack of cigarettes in "Hungry Heart" in 1980, the lyrics to "One Step Up," together with the scarifying images of "Tunnel of Love," the Elvis Costelloian incisiveness of "Brilliant Disguise," and his "Growing Up" redux tribute–to–but–nothing– like the Four Seasons "Walk Like a Man," offered a fairly harrowing generational midlife portrait of a regular guy married to the wrong girl, still with no son, no daughter, to tool around with in the pickup on a visit to the old hometown, turning up the sound just a little bit when that John Hiatt wistful masterpiece about growing up at forty, called "Learning to Love You," came on the radio (assuming it was played on the radio at all in 1987, which it probably wasn't). But it was obviously a deep despair that brought him—and us—to that country music bar in a town three red stoplights from home, re–entering adolescence no longer in search of Maria Muldaur anymore— who would only remind us of our advancing age—but instead of a twenty–year–old in the image of Maria, in whose wholesome googly eyes we could see ourselves as we might have been.

Seemingly for just such fantasy purposes was Natalie Merchant, of 10,000 Maniacs, invented, whose lilting lisp and awkward proto–Stevie Nicks moves brought us face to face with the ghost of our glorious beatnik past ("Hey Jack Kerouac," "Verdi Cries"). Then there was Patty Smyth, reminding us of former life escapades out on the D train, in Tom Waits' "Downtown Train" (from the 1986 movie, *Down by Law*). Sad–eyed Suzanne Vega prowled the lower depths of Maria's Washington Square in "Gypsy," and charted the downward progress of the old neighborhood since we'd left town for the suburbs or the exurbs or the mansion on the hill in "Luka." Transplanted Texas bohemian dreamer Nanci Griffith ("Trouble in the Fields," "Beacon Street"), emerged from obscurity about this time, fairly begging us to dust off that secret novel we'd abandoned in 1975, so that we could read it to shy, mysterious Kate Bush, who'd always be there to comfort us as she did Peter Gabriel ("Don't Give Up"), when it was rejected.

Unsettled, morose, in the grip of desperate fantasies ("Back in the High Life Again" by Stevie Winwood), some of us were actually goaded to leave the confines of our comfortable couches of middle age, arriving at the disco in the leather jackets of our twenties, to attempt to do the latest hot cha cha on the arm of Gloria Estefan ("Rhythm Is Gonna Get You") or Lisa Lisa Velez ("Head to Toe," "Lost in Emotion"), stately Whitney Houston ("I Wanna Dance with Somebody Who Loves Me"), or statuesque Anita Baker ("Caught up in the Rapture"), only to be confronted with such unseemly visions as raunchy Samantha Fox, the second coming of Andrea True ("Touch Me [I Want Your Body])", post–feminist precursor, Julie Brown ("The Homecoming Queen's Got a Gun"), jailbait Debbie Gibson ("Only in My Dreams"), the teasing Janet Jackson ("Control," "Let's Wait Awhile"), erratic Cyndi Lauper ("Change of Heart"), impatient Jody Watley ("Looking for a New Love"), hagged out Debbie Harry ("French Kissin'"), and the inevitable, loud Madonna ("Causing a Commotion"). This new urban dancefloor, it turned out, was still in the grip of the one remaining true alternate culture extant, the now–depleted gay constituency, led by the Pet Shop Boys ("It's a Sin"), New Order ("True Faith"), and Depeche Mode ("Strangelove"). It was a place where the willful deviance of Prince ("If I Was Your Girlfriend," "I Could Never Take the Place of Your Man"), competed with the streetwise caution of Kool Moe Dee ("Go See the Doctor") and the Fat Boys ("Protect Yourself/ My Nuts")—where the strange changes embraced by the Cure ("Why Can't I Be You"), could make pretty boy George Michael's entreaty of "I Want Your Sex," seem just as likely a call for the operating tables of Sweden as for the bed of the model in the video. No wonder we found ourselves suddenly identifying with the words of the recently dried out hard rock hitters of the seventies, Aerosmith, in "Dude (Looks Like a Lady)."

In fact, like Bruce's belated take on modern romance after all the fantasies were stripped away, this new nether nightworld we'd invaded was hardly the welcoming place we'd imagined it to be, now that the mantle of the underground had been passed from the baby boom back to the outcast, declassé, Black, Latin, and teenage communities, from which rap arose, like jazz, like blues, like rhythm and blues, like rock & roll before it. As a group, these warring factions were united in at least one common purpose, to mark us as universally passé—if by no other means than through the use of explicit language that would render George Carlin's seven dirty words, if not Andrew Dice Clay's entire contribution to Western Civilization, as laughably trivial as the stunted vocabulary of the average thirteen year old boy ("We Want Some Pussy" by 2 Live Crew).

So we hastily retreated to the safety of our backyards, where we got to wear our jeans only on the weekend, making do with the small triumphs of our surviving rock–inspired Middle of the Dirt Road repertoire of inside jokes, like that three week stretch in November, when a pair of long–buried Ritchie Cordell–authored Tommy James tunes succeeded each other on the top of the charts, in new renditions by such vaunted younger generational beacons as sexy Tiffany ("I Think We're Alone Now," a lyric whose liberating message had similar reverberations twenty years later for parents of kids as for the kids themselves), and the truculent Billy Idol ("Mony Mony"). Playing further on our unquenchable appetite for crino-lines, middie blouses, and itsy–bitsy bikinis, we fell victim to the Beach Boys crooning "Let's Go to Heaven in My Car," from the movie *Police Academy IV*, and teaming up with the Fat Boys on "Wipe Out," from the movie *Disorderlies*, and Los Lobos reviving the legendary fifties' B–side, "La Bamba," in the Richie Valens biopic of the same name, and Peewee Herman giving us the immortal "Surfin' Bird," from the Frankie and Annette reunion movie, *Back to the Beach*, and the Bangles simonizing Simon & Garfunkel's "Hazy Shade of Winter," in the movie *Less Than Zero*, from which bloodthirsty Slayer also dusted off the epic "In a Gadda Da Vida." For a generation whose children would soon identify Michaelangelo and Leonardo only as turtles, and Howard Kaylan and Mark Volman as disc–jockeys, we were given the original Turtles "Happy Together," as cameoed in *Making Mr. Right*. Almost equally heartwarming was the Dustin Hoffman and Warren Beatty duo of Chuck and Lyle on the immortal "Little Darlin,'" from *Ishtar* (easily Hoffman's best perfor-mance as a songwriter since *Who Is Harry Kellerman . . . and Why Is He Saying Those Terrible Things About Me?*). Culminating a nostalgia–drenched rock & roll movie-song year, what could have been more appropriate than Righteous Brother Bill Medley and Smothers Brothers Sister Jennifer Warnes celebrating our universal girlgroup sixties with "(I've Had) The Time of My Life," from the unconscionably retrogressive *Dirty Dancing?*

Not surprisingly, by the time Bruce's "One Step Up" was played out on the radio, peaking at number 13 in April of 1988, the rest of his sentimental constituency had taken two giant steps back down, away from anything near revelation and continued creative growth and toward the comfortable rose–colored myopia we'd been foresworn as a generation to avoid like the pin–striped suits and fedoras of our parents, as epitomized by Bobby McFerrin's contagiously mindless "Don't Worry, Be Happy," from the movie *Cocktail*, whose infantile motto would become through the rest of his farewell tour, Ronald Reagan's virtual happyface signature on the blank check of America he would hand over to George Bush. Further blunting our momentum at this crucial time, we once again gave in to our notorious preference for wallowing in a rarified generational glorification not unakin to what our younger siblings and progeny were weathering daily under the processed glow of MTV—this time on our very own grown up baby boom video music television channel, called VH–1.

On the air since 1985, VH–1 exploded into a demographic fruition around 1988, just in time to spin us into another stupor of self–recognition. Beyond the "Hullabaloo" and "Shindig" re–runs (and the once a year obligatory *Reggae Sunsplash*), through the magic of kinescopic minutiae, and the glut of current airspace to fill, we were everywhere faced with faces from the past, both younger than yesterday, and older than ourselves. We marveled at how fit George Harrison looked in "Got My Mind Set on You." Elton John gave us not only a new wig and beauty mark, but the ghost of Marilyn Monroe, in "Candle in the Wind." For a moment, had we not known better, we would have sworn that was David Johannsen, of the born too soon New York Dolls, winking at us behind a toast in "Hot Hot Hot," under the monicker of Buster Poindexter. The Pet Shop Boys revived Dusty Springfield in "What Have I Done to Deserve This." Sting was nearly overcome with breathless irony ("Be Still My Beating Heart"). George Harrison came back to further play on our infamous sympathies ("When We Was Fab"). At this point, even Michael Bolton's blatant career move (reviving Otis Redding's teardrenched "Dock of the Bay," to reflect his own more tendentious journey), touched a naked nerve. We were still fab, weren't we, still annointed with the blood of the Kennedys—still massive, unpredictable, *right*?

"Sure, this generation changed things," Paul Simon, the oldest living boy in New York (second in the world to Dick Clark), blithely suggested to me in an interview that appeared in *Playboy*. "That baby boom population blip will always continue to be the thing responsible for change, until they don't have money to buy things anymore. I don't think we were as conformist as other generations," he mused, "but I think we were just as materialistic. Selling out is a tradition in this country. Abbie Hoffman turned himself in to promote a book."

Though every generation invariably contends that things were so much better in the old days, when they were young, that the body of work produced back then, the sound they got stuck on and stuck with in their awakening prime, is still more sophisticated, adventurous, and relevant than any of the garbage these new kids have yet been able to come up with, it's a particular baby boom conceit that this generation succeeded, for a time, in raising the level of discourse in almost all of the arts, especially rock & roll, to match our Ivy League pretensions, the hippest, smartest, richest, artsiest mass market imaginable. As the principals in this cosmic conundrum, at least a few of us remained determined through 1988, to spar with our implied commitment, spurred on by James Taylor's plea to his somnambulant audience to awaken and remember everything, in "Never Die Young" and the even more explicit "Baby Boom Baby." But it was the Beached Boy, Brian Wilson, who more pungently reminded us of what we'd lost ("Love and Mercy"). Donald Fagen, one half of Steely Dan, came out of the semi–retirement he'd been in since 1982, only to fast–forward himself completely past this strange tense present, in "Century's End," from the movie *Bright Lights, Big City*. By then, hearing Tiffany doing for the Beatles ("I Saw Him Standing There") what she did for Tommy James a year before, wasn't half so heartening. We much preferred to get fetal with our mellow crooners of yesteryear, like Brian Ferry ("Kiss and Tell"), the Pet Shop Boys reviving Willie Nelson and Elvis Presley ("Always on My Mind"), Boz Scaggs ("Heart of Mine"), Hall & Oates ("Everything Your Heart Desires"), Robert Plant ("Tall Cool One"), Jonathan Richman ("Gail Loves Me"), REO Speedwagon ("Roll with It"), the Moody Blues ("I Know You're out There Somewhere"), and Louie Armstrong ("What a Wonderful World"), revived from 1968—when few, if any, of us old enough to know better, believed such propaganda—to adorn the soundtrack of the curiously ebullient *Good Morning, Vietnam*. Though we could definitely empathize with everything that had gone wrong since then, no longer did we have any idea about how to fix it. Except for Michael Jackson, who stared deeply at "Man in the Mirror"—and decided to fire his plastic surgeon.

One of those selfsame lost and presumed dead or hopelessly bourgeoise voices from the 1960s next took a crack at jolting us from our massive cold sweat of 1988: Mrs. Fred Smith of Detroit, poetizing as only she could, like a wicked witch of the Midwest, where not even the local little theatre group could have probably stomached her unswerving liberal turpitude, to say nothing of her Eau de Shangri–Las stench of rock & roll truth, chiding us with the Plastic Onoesque "People Have the Power," before pointing the eerie moving finger directly at us in "Paths That Cross." There on that crossroads of youth and age, rebellion and resignation, Patti ran into ageless Leonard Cohen ("Tower of Song") and Joni Mitchell, in Indian drag ("Lakota," "The Tea Leaf Prophecy") and the newly-toned Cher ("We All Sleep Alone"), and wracked and ancient Little Feat, who got back together for the Lowell George in us all ("Hanging on to the Good Times"). Youngsters like Tracy Chapman ("Fast Car," "Talkin' Bout a Revolution"), Nanci Griffith ("Gulf Coast Highway"), Lyle Lovett ("L.A. County"), Timbuk-3 ("Eden Alley"), the Christians ("Ideal World,"), They Might be Giants ("Ana Ng"), the Talking Heads ("Nothing but Flowers"), and 10,000 Maniacs ("Like the Weather"), joined them, trilling their numbing chants directly into our inner ear, urging us to reassert ourselves, make our numbers count.

Inching forward, we only got so far as the TV tube, where Rod Stewart cavorted through "Forever Young," once every fifteen minutes over VH-1. In fact, we knew we were forever getting older all the time, more and more fragile, could go at any second, like Roy Orbison in the humpbacked Traveling Wilburys ("Handle with Care"), who left us shivering on a high note at the end of the year, in our rockingchairs, listening to whale sounds, zithers, bagpipes, Old Age music more befitting our softened sensibilities ("Orinoco Flow" by Enya). Sure we had dreams of revisiting our essential Orbisonian essence with one last aching "Oooby Dooby" into the void, of actually making that statement, twenty years in the process, setting out onto the open highway of self ("Cheyenne" by the Del Lords, "White Buffalo" by Rod MacDonald). But few of us made it past the local bar on the corner, where we let the professional amateur athletes at the summer Olympic games do our dreaming ("One Moment in Time" by Whitney Houston), while we proceeded to overindulge in the grape ("Red Red Wine," by UB40), wax bitter about cruel fate ("I Want You to Hurt Like I Do" by Randy

Newman), and drown in regrets ("I Blinked Once" by Steve Forbert), multiplied by your basic liberal guilt over James Brown having to go to jail for Willie Horton's sins ("Prison Blue" by Jimmy Page).

In the light of these and other ingrained infirmities, about the best the best creative minds of the generation could come up with at that point was to revive "The Twist" by Chubby Checker (and the Fat Boys) and send it into the top forty for the fourth time in twenty years. But this time it failed to ignite a baby boom charge either toward the ballot box or the cover of the barely breathing *Life* magazine. So, as Reagan's man George swept through the electoral college like Red Grange cutting calculus, we drew no consolation from our feat of hoisting to the top of the more and more alien pop charts, with the last remaining vestige of our collective strength, the only band around that was older than the Wilburys, older than the Grateful Dead—older than us—the beloved Beach Boys ("Kokomo"). If these somewhat soiled, ignoble, generational icons were leading us onward toward the end of the decade, even though their former guiding light had a loose bulb, who among us could claim in our advancing years anything closer to a slim perfection? A product of the baby boom, as much as rock & roll—and vice–versa—we limped with them through a "post baby boom–era" mid–life crisis, trusting no one under thirty or over fifty, our dreams of glory lost to adding machines and washing machines, and control of the remote to our kids, their lithe digits honed by Nintendo. That these kids failed to fathom our legendary hipness, reverting to generational stereotypes ("Parents Just Don't Understand" by DJ Jazzy Jeff and the Fresh Prince), only made their salient points about tortuous city life ("Welcome to the Jungle" by Guns N' Roses), the bleak mantra of existence ("Birth, School, Work, Death" by the Godfathers), the unpleasant realities of social intercourse

("No Condom, No Sex" by BWP), suicidal teens ("Someplace Better Than This" by Steve Wynn), depressed teens ("In My Darkest Hour" by Megadeth), and pregnant teens ("Thanks for My Child" by Cheryl Pepsii Riley), that much harder for us to accommodate into our own understandably wounded funk.

When Roy Orbison reached "The End of the Line" in the Wilburys, and died on the charts of 1989 with "You Got It," it hit all of us of a certain age just a bit higher than the gut. Karla Bonoff was not necessarily thinking of him when she wrote "Goodbye My Friend." But we sang it for him anyway. Eric Andersen was thinking of other spirits in the night, when he sent us a tape from his new home, Sweden, with the epic "Ghosts upon the Road," recalling every Kerouac behind a harmonica out of the green 1960s; a couple of years later he'd finally get to release his lost classic, "Time Run Like a Freight Train." Just a bit further down the line, Lou Reed was on his motorcycle, bearing the ghost of Andy Warhol on his shoulders, reuniting with former Velvet partner John Cale to debut a memorial song–cycle ("Hello It's Me") that would come out in album form in 1990, as the magically mournful *Songs for Drella*. Mike Rutherford was trying to come to terms with a father figure himself about this time, this time being about time for us all ("The Living Years").

The thought that we might disappear from the charts of time entirely without ever again establishing our mark upon a year, an era, the way we did routinely through our teens and twenties and thirties was undoubtedly what drove a lot of now concert–phobic folks to witness the Rolling Stones tour of 1989, to be among the singalong throngs at Shea Stadium, and elsewhere, challenging the chill, as well as our burgeoning potato–based legacy— even if we had to pay for the tickets. While younger cats and critics derided them as dinosaurs, and the Stones themselves flaunted their "Mixed Emotions," we huddled in our end zone seats as one, deliriously cheering as if Mick and Keith and Co. were the reincarnation of the '69 Mets. The same imperative caused us to also pay our personal tribute to Paul McCartney, as he showed off "My Brave Face," in another massive tour, performing Beatle songs for the first time in over twenty years; performing them audibly for the first time ever! Next we nominated Cher— to go against Madonna as our own philosopher queen in residence—who showed us another side entirely in the all–but revealing video of "If I Could Turn Back Time." Laura Nyro did not look nearly as daringly fit in her own return to divadom ("Broken Rainbow"), but her voice was still haunting. Unfortunately, Carole King, inexplicably stepping out from behind the keyboards to don an electric guitar, in "City Streets," was as embarrassing as any fortysomething matron trying to play charades at her daughter's sweet sixteen (but could have made a neat opening act for Dion, who did a better job of airing out our dungareed fantasies in "King of the New York Streets"). Instead of submitting to his lower instincts, as he had when Ronald Reagan started us all down this steep artistic incline called the 1980s, Don Henley dredged from the pit of his soul two tunes that equalled his earlier in the decade high point of "The Boys of Summer." With "The End of the Innocence," in 1989 and "The Heart of the Matter," in 1990, he virtually defined Middle of the Dirt Road ambivalence and angst. Billy Joel contributed his Master's thesis on contemporary history in our baby boom defense ("We Didn't Start the Fire"). If Leo Kottke was drolly acquiescent in the woebegone "Jack Gets Up," and Tom Petty perhaps a bit too strident in "I Won't Back Down," Neil Young was not only timely, but timeless, in his pre–Jimmy Connors at the U.S Open performance of "Rockin' in the Free World."

With Neil all the way back, as bedraggled and recalcitrant and uncalcified and unrepentant at forty as he was at
twenty, the notion of yet another generational resurgence,
twenty more years rocking in a world of our own, suddenly
wasn't just an outrageous beer commercial between Super
Bowl Sunday and March Madness. Surely, it was a testament to our unfathomable continued hipness as consumers
—leading the Who to join the Beatles and the Stones on
the road again, and the members of Aerosmith to find their
lost virility in a public conveyance ("Love in An Eleva-
tor"). Even Randy Newman was coping a little better with
his divorce ("I Love to See You Smile," written for the
movie *Parenthood*). Elvis Costello had found in "Veroni-
ca," a girl worthy of his wit (and his collaborator, Paul
McCartney, had found a partner worthy of John Lennon).
The B–52's sounded as if they'd never left the funny farm
("Love Shack"). U2 brought B.B. King back to the charts
("When Love Comes to Town"). Bette Midler, fresh from
dropping sixty pounds in *Ruthless People*, reminded us of
the days when she was known for her exemplary taste in
songs and songwriters, uncovering the recent country
chestnut, "Wind Beneath My Wings," in her new film,
Beaches. The songwriting team of Alan Menken and Howard Ashman (who'd previously summed up our guttural
fifties in "Suddenly Seymour," from the musical *Little
Shop of Horrors*), emboldened us all in our efforts to
embrace the recurrent fantasy of our collective destiny, in
the ebullient "Kiss the Girl," from *The Little Mermaid*.

It was indeed such a dreamfield of good faith, that our
own dateless Queen of the Hop, Bonnie Raitt, was allowed
to take yet another stab at showing us What Forty Looks
Like in the Middle of the Dirt Road (courtesy of a tune
from our favorite baby boom songwriting son, John Hiatt,
"Thing Called Love"), from the ironically–entitled album,
Nick of Time. Yet, when Hiatt himself chose to confront us

as a force for social unrest at the newly relevant, renovated Newport Folk Festival of 1989, under the auspices of politically correct ice–cream magnates, Ben and Jerry, his poignant "Through Your Hands," flew right over the heads of the assembled rebels, lounging in their yachts in the Newport marina. No middle class revolutions would spring from these premises where once Dylan sang "Playboys and Playgirls" and Ochs sang "The Ballad of Medgar Evars," and the youth of the world titled at every windmill of conformity, a mere . . . 26 years before. But did that mean we were ready to go silent into that last late Longine's Symphonette in the Sky, handing over our sacred mission as well as our Top 40 to philistines who had never even witnessed Elvis in his prime, Dylan, the Stones, and the Beatles in their prime, the Kennedys in their prime? Perhaps, as Stan Ridgway postulated in his majestic "Mission in Life," we were, like R.E.M., just getting ready to add more power to our eventual generational response ("Stand"), as if, reminded of our role as prognosticators, if not instigators, of everything righteously left–wing in the world, by who else but Bob Dylan ("Political World"), we had gained some essential inspiration from the crumbling of the Berlin Wall, and the subsequent cold–war commie dominoes tumbling in Eastern Europe.

Certainly, kindred tunes by novelist Larry McMurtry's acerbic son James ("I'm Not from Here"), the Indigo Girls ("Closer to Fine"), Nanci Griffith ("It's a Hard Life Wherever You Go"), the Replacements ("Talent Show"), Peter Case ("Traveling Light"), the Washington Squares ("Pride of Man"), Michelle Shocked ("Anchorage"), Pierce Pettis ("Legacy"), Camper Van Beethoven ("When I Win the Lottery"), Frank Christian ("Three Flights Up"), Kate Bush ("This Woman's Work"), and even Edie Brickell & New Bohemians ("What I Am"), suggested that those who followed us down the path of bohemia may not have entirely let the buildings collapse, the streets degenerate, the eggcreams at the corner candystore turn to foam.

However, by the waning days of the decade, it was clear that the eternally repressive forces of radio had once again succeeded in fractionalizing the undaunted prominence of our vision, our experience, our exalted buying power into a bewildering array of mini–market boutique formats, Middle of the Dirt Road being swamped by others like Adult Contemporary ("Vision of Love" by Mariah Carey, "How Am I Supposed to Live Without You" by Michael Bolton), Lite Rock ("Black Velvet" by Alannah Miles, "Another Day in Paradise" by Phil Collins), Alternative Rock ("Enjoy the Silence" by Depeche Mode, "So Hard" by the Pet Shop Boys), ersatz "basketball" jazz ("Silhouette" by Kenny G.)—along with tuxedo–clad Golden Oldies for the Elvis sighters in the crowd, and Classic Rock for the remaining beer–drinking former metal diehard hordes. This calculated melange all but assured the nervous establishment that music would never again approach the terrifying unity it once possessed, when a generation as one could get behind the energizing power of a particular song—leaving the way open for film to regain its edge as the superior popular art form. Which wasn't as bad as the fact that even TV commercials had by then begun to acquire the hip caché of Major Statement, with no separation between the Church of art and the State of commerce, a particularly odious message, made even more intolerable by its being delivered by the dread Madonna, whose 1989 hit tune, "Like a Prayer," also doubled as a Pepsi commercial—definitely a marriage made in Hell— enabling this Warholier–than–thou Baby Jane to extend her fifteen minutes of fame for another hundred thousand minutes or so.

Parents now, our main concern, however, was no longer about making love or art or revolution, but with our kids, and how to prevent them from doing any of those things. And Madonna wasn't the only one out to pervert our Middle of the Dirt Road program. From messages as divergent as the anti–war bluster of second–generation flower children, Metallica ("One"), and the morning–after nausea of Skid Row ("Youth Gone Wild"), the literate militance of Public Enemy ("Fight the Power"), the off–color breakthrough of black heavy metalists, Living Color ("Cult of Personality"), the earnest recovery anthems of Stevie Ray Vaughan ("Wall of Denial") and Mötley Crüe ("Dr. Feelgood"), the tortured artistic souls of Queensrÿche ("I Don't Believe in Love"), and the Cure ("Disintegration"), and Tone Loc's one–man urban renewal ("Wild Thing"), it was becoming apparent that the rifts widening between the races, the ages, the sexes, the classes, the dreams of the future and the realities of the dispossessed, were bringing to the awakening decade, a shivering signal moment of American unease.

Engrossed in a pleasant brown cocoon of bedroom reveries, access to which required a commitment no more strenuous than a nightly visit to HBO or VH–1, it was understandable, if not especially admirable, that most of us were more preoccupied just then with the ministrations of George Bush in his playroom of the White House and the manipulations of the money men in the boardrooms of the nation's Savings & Loans, than with our children downstairs in the game rooms of hip hop culture. Besides, whenever we tuned in the radio to eavesdrop on their secret coded language, to which our own well–established hipness gave us instant access, we were pretty much reassured to discover that nothing of substance had really changed since the days when we were twelve (Elvis), thirteen (Annette Funicello), fourteen (Connie Stevens), or fifteen (Chubby Checker). The kids still preferred dance to revolution, their own Annette a feisty cherub with laugh-

ing feet named Paula Abdul ("Forever Your Girl,"
"Straight Up," "Cold Hearted"), former protege of Janet
Jackson ("Miss You Much"). Like us at thirteen (Fats
Domino), fourteen (the Drifters), fifteen (Curtis Lee), they
took their lessons in life and love from somewhat assimi-
lated black performers, like Young MC ("Bust a Move"),
Tone Loc ("Funky Cold Medina"), 2 Live Crew ("Me So
Horny"), Bobby Brown ("My Prerogative," "On Our
Own," "Roni"), DJ Jazzy Jeff & the Fresh Prince ("I Think
I Can Beat Mike Tyson") and white performers who
attempted to be as black as, say, the Jackson 5, like the
New Kids on the Block ("Cover Girl," "Hangin' Tough,"
"You Got It (The Right Stuff)") and Simply Red ("If You
Don't Know Me By Now"). As we did at their age to the
Everly Brothers, Dion & the Belmonts, and Joey Dee & the
Starlighters, they responded to certain groups as much for
primitive sex appeal as for any profundities buried beneath
the grease, though what the songs implied seemed pro-
found enough to them at the time—("I'll Be There for
You" by Bon Jovi, "Heaven" by Warrant, "When the
Children Cry" by White Lion). Like us back then, they
could also be taken in by a slick presentation of a Brill
Building song, mistaking the fake for the authentic, in a
high–tech world where one man's Virtual Reality is
another's Grammy award ("Girl You Know It's True" and
"Baby Don't Forget My Number" by the since discredited
mimers Milli Vanilli). No, with the surviving Rod Stewart
("My Heart Can't Tell You No"), the Doobie Brothers
("The Doctor"), 38 Special ("Second Chance"), and Phil
Collins ("Two Hearts"), like so many Crosbys and Comos
and Sinatras before them, staunchly refusing to move out of
the mainstream, we could rest assured that the protest
music of the young would be driven further underground
—as the particularly observant Faith No More observed in
"Epic," ("You want the world but you can't have it")—

where such unformed, adolescent opinion has historically belonged, except in the sixties, when we were coming up (our attitude of entitlement documented in Jim Morrison's timelessly profound: "We want the world and we want it now!").

Thus, if we had not as the 1990s commenced been able to entirely remake the Top 40 into something resembling the country charts, where no song relates to anyone who isn't white and hasn't been divorced at least twice (although we did begin to accomplish this on the album charts), it couldn't be for want of trying. Didn't we, after all, see to it that Bonnie Raitt made good on twenty years of our sustained largesse, by allowing her to bankrupt the Grammys in 1990, thus paying back all of her bad debts of the seventies and eighties? Given our advancing age, mortality as a subject continued to intrigue us; the movie *Ghost* gave us two competing versions of "Unchained Melody" by the Righteous Brothers. Shel Silverstein won an Academy Award for "I'm Checking Out," which Meryl Streep sang so convincingly in the anxious film by the immortal Debbie Reynolds's prodigal daughter, Carrie, *Postcards from the Edge*. And Richard Thompson spoke to us from beyond the grave in the winsomely gruesome "Now That I Am Dead." But none of these tunes were enough to prevent a tragedy like losing Stevie Ray Vaughan in a helicopter crash, just before "Tick Tock," his long–awaited collaboration with his brother, Jimmie Lee, became his first chart single, from cutting even further to the unknowing chill of fate.

So who could really blame us if we were prone to favoring the genetic redundancy of Wilson Phillips ("Hold On"), and Nelson ("Love and Affection"), the no–Stones' riff unturned Black Crowes ("She Talks to Angels"), the sixties saturated Karl Wallinger and World Party ("Way Down Now"), the psychedelic deja vu of Deee–lite's Miss

Kier ("Groove Is in the Heart"), the deep–throated folk–rockisms of John Gorka ("Full of Life"), Ferron ("Heart of Destruction") and Christine Lavin ("Sensitive New Age Guys"), Bette Midler's throwback protest sing–a–long ("From a Distance")—even the mudslinging bad–boy gunslingers, Guns N' Roses ("Civil War"), were dead ringers for their reborn street gurus, Aerosmith ("Janie's Got a Gun"). Besides, wasn't almost anything still better than the "Hanky Panky" of Madonna, the bald–faced anti–Americanisms of Sinead O'Connor ("Nothing Compares 2 U"), or any of the other flagrant examples of how limited in scope the benefactors of our pop tradition had become ("U Can't Touch This" by MC Hammer, "Ice Ice Baby" by Vanilla Ice, "Deep Deep Trouble" by Bart Simpson)?

If, as some suggested, we had seemed to lose our basic taste for black music in this new decade, it was only because the urban landscape was now peopled by foreboding figures totally unlike your affable Coasters and Drifters and Crystals of the old neighborhood. While this music has always attempted to plumb the urban root, today's rootlessness plainly defied yesterday's urbanity. To the ghetto blast of "Banned in the USA" by 2 Live Crew, "I Left My Wallet in El Segundo" by A Tribe Called Quest, "Superfly '90" revived by Ice–T, "The Humpty Dance" by Digital Underground, "The Booming System" by L.L. Cool J, "Get a Life" by Soul II Soul, and "Elvis Is Dead" by Living Colour, the borders of Janet Jackson's "Rhythm Nation" seemed to have been gerry–mandered to exclude even those of us former White Panthers, inveterate liberals, who would be inclined to agree that Ice–T had a point ("Freedom of Speech") and Public Enemy a legitimate agenda ("Fear of a Black Planet")—if only they didn't have to get in our face about it, or move in next door.

As unreconstructed blues fans, supporters of the Arts,

NPR, and PBS, it was patently unfair to accuse us of not having a place in our hearts for choice black music, even in 1990. "The Shoop Shoop Song (It's in His Kiss)," for instance, was not only featured in the movie *Mermaids*, by Cher, but also served as the basis for the musical, *Mama, I Want to Sing*, on the life of its original singer, Doris Troy. PBS gave the black movie director, Spike Lee, prime time television space in 1990 for the Persuasions' do–wop credo, "Looking for an Echo," on his hour–long special, *Do It A Cappella*. On the soundtrack to his film, *Mo' Better Blues*, Lee supervised the creation of a classic rap tune, "A Jazz Thing" by Gangstarr, which comprised an oral history of jazz. Assuaging any vestige of leftover guilt, it was the baby boom minions who elevated childhood blues hero Robert Johnson ("If I Had Possession over Judgment Day") into sales in 1990 approaching Michael Jackson (if you factor dollars earned by the Johnson boxed set in terms of their 1920 spending power).

Indeed, the moral magnitude of our demographic buying habits had by 1990 gone beyond just black music, catapulting many rock–flavored songs into the higher priced arenas of film and theater, epitomized by the release of *The Rocky Horror Picture Show* boxed set, containing rarities such as the immortal "Planet Shmanet Janet," which was sung by Tim Curry in the movie, but never included on the soundtrack album. Unfortunately, such an atmosphere of advanced careerism virtually guaranteed the arrival of Madonna to bespoil the terrain by somehow coercing Stephen Sondheim off his Broadway pedestal to write her a few tunes for *Dick Tracy* ("More," "What Can You Lose," and "Sooner or Later [I Always Get My Man]," for which he was awarded an Oscar, presumably for his embarrassment). Randy Newman, on the other hand, achieved a generational equipoise with the lower–priced but trendy accessibility of TV; his theme for *Parent-*

hood ("I Love to See You Smile"), was still charming as the small screen lead–in for the sit–com of the same name, but not so his involvement with "Cop Rock" ("Under the Gun"), Stephen Bochco's failed attempt to fill the non–existent alphabetical, if not, musical niche between "Miami Vice" and MTV, the following season. But, in fact, it was on television where the most significant and unsettling job of presenting a music–inspired social vision to a baby boom audience of the 1990s was perpetrated not by Bochco, MTV, Oliver Stone, or Don Kirshner, but by the director David Lynch, in "Twin Peaks."

It was in the moody soundtrack to this endless TV movie, that virtually all of the clues not only to the murder of Laura Palmer but to our musical future were contained in references to the songs of one of our all–time favorite baby boom years, 1960—when a hopeful young JFK rode out of Boston so jubilant and so doomed and a Mousketeer named Annette Funicello was our reigning pineapple princess, with a dark side only a David Lynch could have portrayed so cunningly, so deliciously. Only if you were on as intimate terms with the pop charts of 1960 as was the undoubted radio slave Lynch—who certainly had to be among the few to have tuned into the Statues' 1960 version of "Blue Velvet," that predated the Bobby Vinton smash by two years—could you fully understand how the desperate destinies of the characters living in Twin Peaks, steps away from the Canadian Border, Vancouver, aging hippie playground of ponytailed men and women, who disappeared at the end of the 1960s with their homemade guns and recreational drugs (and vice versa), applied to our own current life and death struggle with our elusive mandate.

Nineteen sixty was a year of uncommon darkness in rock & roll, moody as the Fleetwoods–inspired "Twin Peaks" theme by Julee Cruise ("Falling"), hypnotic as the cool

jazz Viscounts ("Harlem Nocturne"), trembling with repressed anger ("Because They're Young" by Duane Eddy),
and laden with dreams of romantic death ("Teen Angel"
by Mark Dinning, "El Paso" by Marty Robbins, "Running
Bear" by Johnny Preston, "Clementine" by Bobby Darin,
"I Shot Mr. Lee" by the Bobbettes, "On the Beach" by
Frank Chacksfield, and, of course, the Ray Peterson classic,
"Tell *Laura* I Love Her"). But none of these tunes would
define the year as well as "The Theme from 'A Summer
Place'," from the Troy Donohue/Suzanne ("the New Debbie Reynolds") Pleshette movie, which cut to the heart of
thwarted young love, parents versus children, purity versus
corruption—with haunting strings under the guidance of
Percy Faith. In 1960 America teenage morality and good
music was defined by "The Theme from 'A Summer
Place'," a place that was safe and warm, where good girls
were afraid to wear their yellow polka dot bikinis, and
dreamed instead of puppy love with Annette's "tall" Paul
(Anka). But just as in "Twin Peaks," a rumbling guitar and
insouciant saxophone netherworld existed below the surface of every seething dream (Johnny Burnette sang
"Dreaming" in 1960), ready to explode into multicolored
fireworks of self expression (Jack Scott did "Burning
Bridges" in 1960, Harold Dorman did "Mountain of
Love," Marv Scott recorded "Move (Two!) Mountains").
Wasn't Skip & Flip's "Cherry Pie" a big hit in 1960? You
know it was. While *A Summer Place* was Hollywood's
answer to *West Side Story* (itself becoming a movie in
1960), "Twin Peaks" was nothing less than Lynch's *Northwest Side Story* version of the eternal subterranean teenage
condition run amok in honor and betrayal, sex and violence, warring tribes and establishment corruption, the
imposibility of escape—why else would he cast those two
forgotten hunks of 1960, Richard Beymer and Russ
Tamblyn, for such prominent roles in "Twin Peaks," re-

uniting them for the first time since they were matched in *West Side Story!?* Coincidence? I think not.

But, in a musical coincidence whose staggering irony even David Lynch could not have scripted, the Northwest arose in the wake of the series' cancellation as our latest white hope of a rock & roll revolution, as if in direct response to David Lynch's "Twin Peaks" vision of a nation and a generation suspended in 1960, at the edge of a New Frontier all over again—as if in answer to his urgent plea for parents and children together as one to wake up at last and smell the coffee.

Postscript

Moving to
Montana Soon
(1991–   )

As I said at the outset of this opus, it's no easy task, staying on the cutting edge, even if you're in the steady employ of the media. You have to keep changing your hairstyle, learning the latest exhausting dances, the latest secret handshakes. But it's no easier coming to grips with the ending of your era, the patronizing young turks expecting you to amble off into the sunset of all creative thought. In this regard, I think it was Johnny Carson who best summed up the ambiguous longings implicit in the baby boom generation's evolution from the Cult of Youth to the Woodstock condominium–commune awaiting us around the bend, when he was heard to mutter with uncharacteristic but appropriate bitterness on his final farewell hour after thirty years on the pop cultural throne, in response to the occasion of Jay Leno replacing bandleader Doc Severinson with jazz virtuouso Branford Marsalis, a statement that should stand as a defining credo for our entire legendary musical crusade.

"The words hip and young aren't synonomous," Johnny said, more or less under his breath, but a withering eternal truth nonetheless, that no doubt washed right over most of us as we twisted in our sheets, pausing to occasionally dab at our moist eyelids with a kleenex and wonder what the future would bring.

Actually, we were still trying to make some sense out of the comment made over a year before, also on television, by a generational spokesman supposedly much closer to our collective definition of hip, Bob Dylan, when he appeared at the 1991 Grammy Awards, no spring chicken himself at fifty, to accept his lifetime achievement award.

"It's possible," Bob droned in his signature rambling mumble, "to be so defiled in this world that your own mother and father will abandon you. And if this happens, God will always believe in your ability to mend your own ways. . . ."

As if hearing the ghost of Dylan garbologist, A.J. Webberman, howling through the bones of that remark, a reported 27 percent of those who viewed the deposed Master on the podium, spent at least the next several minutes attempting to decipher not only the personal relevance and social significance of the statement, but also how it applied to our upcoming journey through our forties, through the nineties, singularly bereft of genera-tional artistic precedents to navigate us safely past a wholesale slide toward Broadway ballads, Las Vegas schmaltz, and Golden Oldies for our continued creative nourishment.

However, if we were to merely gaze at rock & roll in the early 1990s, to see what our legacy looks like, and whether or not it has become so defiled in this world that we, its own mothers and fathers, should abandon it, we'd have to be humbled, if not convulsed, at the spectacle of the Who in front of a 135– piece orchestra, the Rolling Stones on a 75–foot movie screen, Paul McCartney conducting an oratorio, Sonny Bono elected mayor of Palm Springs, and

Country Joe & the Fish's Barry Melton trying to get himself elected to the judiciary in San Francisco. We have produced $60 coffee table books on the Beatles and Elvis Presley, and made available $50 Compact Disc retrospective boxed sets by Led Zeppelin, the Byrds, Dylan, the Clash, and Aerosmith to assure us of our historic worth. And, as if that were not enough, early in 1992, at the plush Waldorf–Astoria hotel in Manhattan, as it had for the past seven years, a self–congratulatory institution called the Rock & Roll Hall of Fame proceeded to induct several more legends, both living and dead, into their august assemblage—at $1,250 a plate. (Next year in Cleveland, they promised at the event, though as yet the actual Hall planned for that estimable city isn't even an anteroom). Nevertheless, to quote Billy Crystal—who must have been heavily paid off to cede his post on the dais as generational master of ceremonies, to some erstwhile rock critics for the occasion—all the guys there that night looked mahvelous, even in tuxedos—real rock & roll and dirt road beacons like John Fogerty, Keith Richards, Jimmy Page, Jeff Beck, Neil Young, Carlos Santana, Robbie Robertson, B.B. King, Steve Cropper, and Ernie Isley—all grooving to Dylan's "All Along the Watchtower," during the final jam, as if their best days were still ahead of them—and if them, then what about us, up here in the cheap seats?

Although we have certainly failed to bring about most of the salient benefits outlined in our rock & roll agenda to save the world, the whales, the rainforest, the ozone, and bring down the bourgeoisie—or, at least, to legalize pot—our efforts toward uniting an emasculated urban midcentury generation of men who lost—and were lost in—Vietnam, with their guilt–ridden brothers who hooted them on from the sidelines were at last partially realized in 1990–1991 with a "healing" war, complete with laser light shows, Whitney Houston's "Star Spangled

Banner," and months of victory parades to expunge forever
the dreadful aftermath of our "divisive" 1960s war. For
those still clinging to the tenets of the Alternate Culture,
whose National Anthem was sung instead by Roseanne
Barr, the early part of the decade was particularly enjoy-
able as well, laden with Gene McCarthy flashbacks in the
person of Zenmaster Jerry campaigning against pot–
smoking, draft–dodger Bill. And then Bill and Al and
Hillary and (the dreaded Madam of the PMRC) Tipper
completed their run toward the White House as a kind of
updated baby boom tag–team Bob and Carol and Ted and
Alice (or Peter, Paul and Mary and Mama Cass), defeating
forty years of the entrenched, established, Perry Como and
Rosemary Clooney sound of George and Barbara Bush, in
what was hyped as the most crucial presidential campaign
since 1968, if not 1960. It almost made you want to get out
your passport and think about moving to the once and
future hippie state of Montana soon.

In that metaphorical Montana, where Sonny Bono is
Mayor and Willie Nelson Secretary of the Treasury, James
Brown Chief of Police, and Jonathan Richman our resident
poet laureate ("1963"), Doc Severinson Bandmaster General, and Johnny Carson the all–night deejay, the radio
station of the nineties would always be attuned to the
Middle of the Dirt Road whims of the suddenly robust
baby boom constituency, the sublime sensibility of those
whom Paul Simon pointedly profiled in "Born at the Right
Time," his 1990 comment on the extents of our proprie-
tary commitment toward the notion of rock & roll having a
high end. It would have been on Radio Montana, in 1991,
for instance, that you could have cried with Richard
Thompson over the loss of his motorcycle ("1952 Vincent
Black Lightning") and Joni Mitchell on the loss of her
virginity ("Ray's Dad's Cadillac") and Robbie Robertson
on the loss of his youth ("Resurrection"). It was there in

Montana, on Frank Zappa's floss farm, where cryptic Bob
Dylan would justify his lifetime achievement award with
another major career retrospective ("Blind Willie
McTell"). It was where the once prolix Declan McManus
began to veer toward the (Lou) Costelloian side of his
nature ("The Other Side of Summer"). In this Montana
state of mind, a wounded tourist from the city could find
Steely Dan virtually reassembled ("Pretzel Logic" by the
New York Rock & Soul Ensemble), and Roger McGuinn,
high on Sugar Mountain ("King of the Hill"). James Taylor
came to the spas here to regain his vigor ("Copperline"),
and Tom Petty his whimsy ("Learning to Fly"). Lou Reed
came to mourn some fellow bohemian dreamers ("Magic
and Loss"); many other compatriots gathered here a while
later to pay homage to Queen's lead singer, Freddie
Mercury ("Bohemian Rhapsody"). At the Bonnie Raitt
Shopping Center ("Something to Talk About"), Rod Stewart demonstrated cleansers to an attentive audience of hip,
former Earth Mother housewives ("The Motown Song")
and Genesis took dancing lessons ("I Can't Dance"). At the
nine–feature Cineplex, the only movie playing was *Until
the End of the World*, temporarily fixed on the Patti and
Fred Smith incantation "It Takes Time." It was only in the
hippie state of Montana in the early 1990s that the ghost of
Elvis Presley was allowed to prowl for paparazzi to its
heart's content ("Walking in Memphis" by Marc Cohn,
"Viva Las Vegas" by ZZ Top, the entire soundtrack to
Honeymoon in Vegas); here alone that Eric Clapton could
find sanctuary after the loss of his young son ("Tears in
Heaven"). R.E.M. came here on retreat from their kiss–of–
death embrace by the establishment ("Losing My Reli-
gion") to re–read the Leonard Cohen songbook ("First We
Take Manhattan"). In the mystic waters of Lake Montana,
U2 at last glimpsed the folly of their former pompousity
("Mysterious Ways," "One"). After years stranded in the

outside world without a voice, Mike Watt resurrected the Minutemen here ("Flying the Flannel" by fIREHOSE), and Dave Thomas Pere Ubu ("Oh Catherine").

Which is not to say we didn't allow any younger folk admittance across our mythic borders into Higher Understanding. The music of Loud Sugar ("Instant Karma Coffeehouse") played in all the elevators in the mall. Tori Amos could come and sit on our lap anytime ("Winter"). In Chris Whitley ("Living with the Law"), Kirsty MacColl ("Walking down Madison"), Brenda Kahn ("Lost"), Billy Bragg ("Sexuality"), Sam Phillips ("Raised on Promises"), Bob Dylan's son–in–law, Peter Himmelman ("Woman with the Strength of 10,000 Men"), and David Wilcox ("She's Just Dancing"), we found youngsters we could invite over for a cappuccino to regale with glory stories of our bygone cultural revolution and how we planned to resurrect it. Some of them, young, gullible, malleable, who still believed in fairy tales and dinosaurs, might believe those stories, almost as much as we did, believing in their own chances to make a difference with their music, too, even after reality or old–age set in. We didn't have to remind them that, as teenagers in the 1990s, whether they resided in *Wayne's World*, or in Seattle ("Smells Like Teen Spirit" by Nirvana, "Alive" by Pearl Jam), their numbers were so insignificant as to render their messages virtually meaningless on a long–term scale—unless they had the blessings, if not the participation, of the baby boom behind them.

Neither was our Montana any kind of totally lily–white state, like our good neighbor Arizona to the south. Why, in 1991 and 1992 alone, there were tunes on our airwaves by P.M. Dawn ("Set Adrift on Memory Bliss") and Boyz II Men ("Motownphilly," "The End of the Road"), Color Me Badd ("I Adore Mi Amor"), Paula Abdul ("Blowing Kisses in the Wind,"), and the Triplets ("You Don't Have to Go

Home Tonight"), that could have come straight from the early 1960s heyday of harmony and Civil Rights, rivaling Paul Simon for do–wop and Phil Collins or Rod Stewart himself for that Motown sound. For the even more musically liberated, the punk/funk/reggae blend of Fishbone ("Sunless Saturday"), the Red Hot Chili Peppers ("Give It Away") and Primus ("Jerry Was a Race Car Driver"), probably brought some smiles from the few fans of the Specials still among us; as did the union of thrash rockers, Anthrax, with the notorious Public Enemy, on the latter's "Bring the Noise," to those who hoped it would return the favor Run DMC did for Aerosmith in 1984 with "Walk This Way." At the other end of the racial spectrum, Marky Marky & the Funky Bunch ("Good Vibrations" and "Wildside"), did at least perform the useful function of expunging Vanilla Ice from the airwaves. Encouraged, the Beastie Boys greeted 1992 with "Pass the Mic."

Trouble is, when, thirty years later, such harmonious integration still extends only to the pop charts and the ballfields, clearly you'd have to say the symmetry of the poetry of soul we'd long propounded has largely fallen on deaf ears—much as that latter day makeover saint Michael Jackson postulated through the rampant destruction and groin–groping of the outro to his prescient video for "Black and White." Bowing to his fear of being held accountable for his statements, Michael eventually toned his message down. But the message was out, nonetheless; the beast had sprung from its cage for the world to see, in films like *Boyz in the Hood* ("Growing up in the Hood" by Compton's Most Wanted), *New Jack City* ("New Jack Hustler" by Ice–T) and *Juice* ("Know the Ledge" by Eric B. and Rakim); in boom box tunes on the radio ("Gypsy Woman [She's Homeless]" by Crystal Waters, "How to Kill a Radio Consultant" by Public Enemy, "Victim of the Ghetto" by the College Boyz, "The Language of Violence" by the Disposable Heroes of Hiphopracy, "Appetite for Destruction" by NWA, culminating in the subsequently banned "Cop Killer" by Ice–T); and later all over the nightly news in stark and disquieting images of the L. A. riots, taped just blocks from where they were completing the latest episode of "The Fresh Prince of Bel Air."

These developments eerily echoed a remark Melvin Van Peebles made to me nearly twenty years before, in discussing the music of the 1960s. "Isn't it interesting with all the protest songs," he'd said, "that no black protest songs came out, or protest singers. There were two or three songs, but no real black protest singers ever rose out of that." If the hip–hop culture of the 1990s has at last taken Van Peebles up on his challenge, with blacks in fact the only poets and protesters given any credibility in today's rock & roll, they have done so with no white baby boom mentors. Our played out revolution meant nothing to these street–bred city rebels with just cause; to them we're too old, too fat, too safe, too white, too intimidated, too guilty even as we pull our kids out of schools and ourselves out of the cities to offer them much in the way of artistic salvation, no matter how many Dylan songs we've memorized or how noble our descent into their neighborhoods to take a peek at Annie's baby may once have been. Luckily, those of us who had by then escaped to Montana, the memory of our legacy reduced to sneaker commercials, were too far gone into moodily calculating how our once huge numbers could have dwindled so quickly and quietly back to the one–freak–per–block ratio of old, to even fear for our pitiful lives and property. Our ears were fixed instead on the two new Springsteen albums for further guidance: redundant and prosaic, they offered just the homey touch we needed ("Human Touch"). A marriage to the right girl who had been there all along was something even his faithful fans no longer had the heart or the stamina to deny him; at least he hadn't, as we'd once feared, turned himself into Lenny Bruce (although he did bear a chilling resemblance to him in the "Human Touch" video)—or either of those other two Albert Goldman subjects, Elvis and John Lennon, for that matter. Besides, the kids ("Pony Boy"), the middle class trophies ("57 Channels and Nothing On"), the resurgent optimism ("Better Days"), while numbingly bland as rock & roll, certainly defined the lot of the baby boom generation slouching through the Middle of the Dirt Road as good or better than anything with the word teen in the title.

And in certain essential ways it was no different from the kind of escapism through fantasy and dancing that impelled some of the other popular groups of our early 1990s years of plague and poverty, like the Divinyls ("I Touch Myself"), Cathy Dennis ("Touch Me [All Night Long]"), Prince ("Cream"), Latour ("People Are Still Having Sex"), C&C Music Factory, featuring Freedom Williams ("Gonna Make You Sweat"), and Right Said Fred ("I'm Too Sexy"), of which the undisputed role model was still Madonna, who freely indulged her penchant for living on the extremes of both, in her various musical ("Rescue Me," "Justify My Love," "Erotica") and non–musical (tell–it–all biographies, know–it–all documentary, see–it–all photo book) projects, resulting in her being rewarded for her cultural clout, as 1992 commenced, with something like 60 million bucks to indulge her grandest fantasy of all: that she could act, dance, write, sing, and play baseball like a real Major Leaguer.

Ironically, it was Bruce's eternal anti–altar image, Warren Zevon, who forced those of us remaining in the Middle of the Dirt Road into the gut–check of all–time, with the painful "Renegade." In the guise of a Civil War remembrance, Zevon spoke to the rebel in everyone of a certain age and time, living out of touch with the mainstream for the last twelve to twenty years, like residents of the dying South. Among its other messages, the tune not only acknowledged and justified and forgave and explained and even encouraged the new decade's massive, baby boom return to country music, but implied how deeply and for how long so many of us may have misunderstood Bob Dylan's much reviled *Nashville Skyline*, as an unbelievably prophetic and sadly unheeded call to just this sort of psychic bearhug with our generational other half before any dreams of the 1960s could be redeemed in the 1990s.

Allowing for the moment this mindbending conceit, it could then be seen as another momentous step toward mending the divided soul of our dungaree culture that PBS' homage to the Civil War resulted in so much work for a lot of old folkies ("Hard Times Come Again No More" by Kate and Anne McGarrigle, "Follow the Drinking Gourd" by Richie Havens), leading the following year to Garth Brooks shaking hands with Billy Joel ("Shameless"), Dwight Yoakam getting into a pile with the Grateful Dead ("Truckin'"), Tammy Wynette offering a cautious curtsy to the KLF ("Justified and Ancient"), and the Kentucky Headhunters returning us to our deepest roots ("The Ballad of Davy Crockett"); leading, a year after that, to Garth Brooks, easily country's most assimilated performer since Elvis, releasing as a single a protest song ("We Shall Be Free") that optimistic folks were comparing to "Blowin' in the Wind." Of course, as if to deflect any serious contemplation of this crucial issue, when last seen Bob Dylan himself was collaborating with Michael Bolton ("Steel Bars"), recalling his years ago dalliance with Carole Bayer Sager, and characteristically further confounding our expectations with as much impish verve as ever.

But this familiar chord had been struck once again, even

if unintentionally, and the cause this time taken up, the implications apparent for the casual Dylanographer and the inveterate chartwatcher alike, echoing prescient Lynch high on his "Twin Peaks": We're going to need all of us together, acting in concert, if we're ever going to get out of these blues alive. And in the light of the Zevonesque reading of the Dylan scripture, it can be seen that the Dirt Road embrace of Country and the Country embrace of Pop are but two of the various signs of this possible healing unification. Noted in this postscript alone has been the heroic Appomattox enacted by the aging hawks of doves of the Vietnam Era, the only slightly less monumental accord effected by headbangers and gays at the Freddie Mercury benefit, the heartwarming black and white merger of metal and rap, as epitomized by Anthrax and Public Enemy; even Springsteen's embrace of middle class middle age has to be seen as positive proof that there *is* a cure for a hungry heart. Finally, there was word of a clandestine country/rap/gospel/jazz meeting taking place just over yonder, in the form of the landmark "Tennessee," by the black group Arrested Development, matched against the even more undeniable arrival of a pronounced hick tune, "Achy Breaky Heart" by Billy Ray Cyrus to the number four position on the pop charts, just in time to welcome Arkansas' favorite son into the White House.

So in tribute to Maria Muldaur's kid, Jenny, releasing her first record in 1992, maybe the words of my second favorite psychedelic dreamgirl of the 1960s, who made a wrong turn on her way to the Monterey Pop Festival in 1967 and wound up at the Free Hippie Festival instead, who missed her exit for the Woodstock Festival in 1969, and never got to play, the former flower child Sandy Hurvitz, aka Uncle Meat, aka Essra Mohawk, when I met her in 1980, will not sound so far–fetched and idealistic and naive when they're repeated in the 1990s; will instead seem unaccountably savvy.

"When we were teenagers the world belonged to us," Essra told me. "Not that it always belongs to teenagers; it belonged to us. We're not teenagers now and it still belongs to us, because we're the majority, therefore the consumers, the market."

Ten years later, even the stragglers among us have come to terms with the fact that we're no longer the only market; but, what could be just as important, we're the marketers now. The kids still have to dance to our tune. Soon that fifty–year–old grandpa, Mick Jagger, will be claiming at sixty, "No way will I be doing this at sixty–four!" And a sixty–four–year–old Paul McCartney will be conducting the Boston Pops. By then Bruce Springsteen will be the father of a teenage girl himself, at which point he will no doubt be crooning, "Born to Stay Home," in an effort to prevent her from hopping aboard the solar–powered motorcycle of some bewhiskered Boss–Come–Lately in Town. Without a doubt we will live to see Bob Dylan replacing George Burns as a wily generational codger; Madonna replacing Johnny Carson as cultural determinant; each with a talk show, where the opening monologue will be sung. As a previously disenfranchised, disenchanted, disgruntled population blip, taking our music with us through the ages, isn't it only natural for an observer to wonder now that the left has regained some power, if and when the right song comes around, whether on the radio, or, more likely, on TV, or, even more likely, in a movie, what kind of an immense, unimaginable, maybe even mythic, consensus it might inspire, provided we haven't fallen asleep in front of "Nick at Night."

"This generation is now taking control of the world— and the world will change," Essra had crooned. "I know these people," she said, "and I'm one of them and they're all like me, and the world will be ours because we're the ones who've survived and maintained and therefore can do it and mean it."

And the walls of the rest home will shake, rattle, and roll again.

Index

DATE DUE	
MAY 1 8 1999	
MAY 1 5 2000	